Laruelle and Non-Philosophy

Critical Connections

A series of edited collections forging new connections between contemporary critical theorists and a wide range of research areas, such as critical and cultural theory, gender studies, film, literature, music, philosophy and politics.

Visit the Critical Connections website at
www.euppublishing.com/series/crcs

Laruelle and Non-Philosophy

Edited by John Mullarkey and Anthony Paul Smith

EDINBURGH
University Press

© editorial matter and organisation John Mullarkey and Anthony Paul Smith, 2012
© The chapters their several authors, 2012

Edinburgh University Press Ltd
22 George Square, Edinburgh EH8 9LF

www.euppublishing.com

Typeset in 11/13 Adobe Sabon
by Servis Filmsetting Ltd, Stockport, Cheshire, and
printed and bound in Great Britain by
CPI Group (UK) Ltd, Croydon, CR0 4YY

A CIP record for this book is available from the British Library

ISBN 978 0 7486 4535 0 (hardback)
ISBN 978 0 7486 4534 3 (paperback)
ISBN 978 0 7486 4536 7 (webready PDF)
ISBN 978 0 7486 6476 4 (epub)
ISBN 978 0 7486 6475 7 (Amazon ebook)

Contents

Introduction: The Non-Philosophical Inversion: Laruelle's Knowledge Without Domination

John Mullarkey and Anthony Paul Smith

> Due to this necessary mutation, we must first change the very concept of thought, in its relations to philosophy and to other forms of knowledge. This is an inversion that concerns a reversal of old hierarchies, but through a formulation of a new type of primacy without relationships of domination; without relations in general.[1]

François Laruelle is not the 'next big thing' in Continental philosophy. His thought does not aim to correct, reduce, or supersede that of Derrida, or Deleuze, or Badiou. That 'same old game' of importing European master-thinkers into Anglophone philosophy – each new figure superseding the previous model – is over.[2] Or rather, the next big thing could be, if we can accept the challenge, to think that there are only small things, small thoughts, everywhere and within every individual – 'quantum thoughts' or 'fractal' thinking. For, what Laruelle offers us is a new vision of philosophy as a whole that is neither the right nor wrong *representation* of reality, but is a material *part* of the Real, though one that always tries to refract the Real through itself, in a '*mixte*', 'amphiboly' or 'dyad'. Each philosophy is a mediation of the Real, though of a very strange kind to be sure. The work of non-philosophy is an experiment with what results in our knowledge from seeing philosophy in this way.

Laruelle is associated pre-eminently with this term, 'non-philosophy' or, as he has called it more recently, 'non-standard philosophy'. He describes non-philosophy as a 'science of philosophy', a science to which he has dedicated the better part of his life. Non-philosophy is not, however, an anti-philosophy. Laruelle is not heralding another 'end of philosophy', nor the kind of internal critique of philosophy common in much post-Kantian European thought. Rather, modelling non-philosophy on an analogy with non-Euclidean geometry, he proposes a broadened, pluralistic science of thought and philosophy, as well as a major reworking of philosophical concepts brought about by the introduction of new axioms. The 'non-' in non-philosophy should be taken, therefore, in terms similar to the meaning of the 'non-' in 'non-Euclidean' geometry, being part of a 'mutation' that locates philosophy as one instance in a larger set of theoretical forms. Hence, Laruelle's use of the term non-philosophy is neither a dialectical negation, nor even something contrary to philosophy. Non-Euclidean geometries do not negate Euclid's, but affirm it within a broader or amplified paradigm that also explains alternative geometries that are only *apparently* opposed to it. Likewise, non-philosophy is an abstract conception of philosophies that allows us to see them as equivalent in value.[3] It enlarges the set of things that can count as thoughtful, a set that includes extant philosophy, but also a host of what are often presently deemed (by philosophers) to be non-philosophies and non-thinking (art, technology, natural science). Consequently, Laruelle integrates extant examples of philosophy with examples of what *those same philosophies* regard as their opposite. In this democracy of thinking, all thought is equalised *when regarded as* raw-material for non-philosophy, that is, as part of the Real rather than as representations of it.

It is crucial in all of this to realise that, despite its sometimes abstract and abstracted appearance, non-philosophy is a *practical* theory; indeed, it is a performative practice – it *does* things (to philosophy and to 'Theory' generally). This practice of non-philosophy involves taking the concepts of philosophy and extracting any transcendence from them in order to review them so that they are no longer seen as representations, but re-envisioned as parts of the Real. Thought is identified with the Real; it is immanent to it – this is Laruelle's opening hypothesis or axiom. This identity, however, is real rather than logical, such that all thought, including philosophy's, is actually *caused* by the Real, though in a special form of causation – a 'determination-in-the-last-instance' that is also called 'occasional cause'. This 'last-instance' is the far-side of the axiom or hypothesis of immanence, a kind of wager.

Philosophy, in this view, becomes the material of non-philosophy rather than its object. As such, non-philosophy is *not* some form of higher-order representation of philosophy, or metaphilosophy.[4] Non-philosophy as a practice never appeals to the meta, to some kind of transcendence behind material and lived practice, and so non-philosophy is always a *use* of philosophy. On account of this apparent ventriloquism (that transforms the speech of philosophy into its own speech acts), non-philosophy will often look similar to philosophy – like simply 'more philosophy', be it Spinozist, Derridian, Deleuzian, Badiouian … This impression itself is neither false nor true but simply the product of philosophical narcissism, which cannot see anything other than itself in other forms of discourse (while being blind to itself and its mediations when purportedly gazing at the Real directly). So, for example, Laruelle's idea that thought should think of itself as immanent to the Real, rather than as a representation that transcends it, looks like something that Gilles Deleuze might say. Yet Deleuze would say it *in the name of his philosophy* – the image of thought he has in mind is as depicted in *his* (type of) explanation, with all its architectonics of virtual versus actual; organism versus BwO; war machines; rhizomes, etc. – hence his desire to explain the Real. Even though Deleuze embraces multiplicity and a variety of kinds of thought (artistic and scientific as well as philosophical), nonetheless, the highest thought, the creation of concepts, belongs to (Deleuzian) philosophy alone – *he* explains the Real: not Boulez, nor Artaud, nor Bacon (they provide the matter for the philosopher).[5] For Laruelle, however, there is no explaining the Real, because *every thought, Deleuzian or not, philosophical or not*, is as good or as bad an explanation as any other – for they are *all* (non-summative) material parts.

This emphasis on the materiality of philosophy – viewing the form and content of philosophy as matter – is not to be understood according to standard materialist approaches: the techno-scientisms of computationalism, biologism or physicalism. What Laruelle says of photography in *The Concept of Non-Photography* is no less true of philosophy *qua* matter for non-philosophy as it is of anything else. His approach is, he writes,

a materiality without materialist *thesis* since every thesis is already given in it, in its turn, as 'flat', just like any other singularity whatsoever. Far from giving back perception, history or actuality, etc., in a weakened form, photography gives for the first time a field of infinite materialities which the photographer is immediately 'plugged into'. This field remains beyond the grasp of any external (philosophical, semiological, analytic, artistic, etc.) technology.[6]

A 'field of infinite materialities' – not one or other reductive domain to which philosophy, and everything else, can be reduced (and through which thereafter, philosophy can explain everything else by proxy of it becoming a philosophy 'of physics', 'of mathematics', or 'of biology', etc.).

In all of this, Laruelle might sound Kantian (human thought cannot represent the 'thing in itself' but only in a mixture of its own constitution with the raw manifold of things in themselves). Yet non-philosophy is a more extreme position than that, because it is not just *metaphysics* that is asked to forego its supposed power to represent reality, but any philosophy that would hope to *represent* anything real, that believes that it can adequately think the Real through its own putative powers (of questioning, wonder, deduction, induction, intuition, will to power, affective encounter, sympathy, selfless attention, and so on). Laruelle's challenge concerns all self-styled philosophical thought especially, including the logic of inference – it is not the critique of a so-called metaphysics of knowing alone. Kantian transcendental deduction must be included in this line-up of methods in as much as it too believes that reality can be thought, or *inferred*, through *its own philosophical method*. Each method of philosophical thought, because it hopes to *represent* the whole *exclusively*, misses its target in part, because it is partial (just *one* method).[7] Yet this is not to say that each and every philosophy misses it entirely. The Real is indifferent to, or resists, each attempt at representing it, because every thought (philosophical or non-philosophical) is already a part of it (and how can a part be, that is, re-present, the whole?). There is something more but not mysterious in the Real – namely its resistance to being represented (as a whole). This 'more' is not a summative quantity, however, such that we might get a perfect picture of the Real were we simply to add all the extant thoughts 'of' it together. Rather, the 'of's here are precisely what bars them, what makes them 'partial' (in every sense of this term).

Philosophy needs to lose its vocation in representationalism, in the sense of its own *sufficiency*, its own power (through whatever method, new or old) to capture reality in its thought. It needs to think of itself as immanent to, a part of, the Real, rather than as a representation that transcends and thereby captures the Real.[8] But this demand should not be confused with some kind of philosophical, and so transcendent, normativity. Rather, for philosophy to think itself as immanent to the Real is merely to simplify itself, to *see* its own practices clearly without any hallucinations, including normative ones. Philosophy can choose not to do this, as it normally does, but non-philosophy simply is this shift. Ironically, though, to make this change takes very little: it certainly does not involve creating a new philosophical method; rather, it involves a change of vision, a revision of philosophy somewhat like a figure-ground shift in perception. Instead of thinking that philosophy stands out as a figure that gathers everything else around it, but also behind it, suddenly we see philosophy melt into its background. However, and here is the mutation within this analogy, no new figure emerges in its place. Rather, the background is left alone throughout; it is indifferent (and undifferentiated). Everything thinks – not just philosophy. Despite this last dis-analogy, the likeness with the figure-ground has another virtue in that it is optical, it involves a change in vision, such that individual philosophies are now seen as material parts, are revised (revisioned) to be seen as parts of the Real, or, as Laruelle puts it, a *vision-in-One*. This vision is not, however, empirical and representational (be it based on the human optical apparatus or that of some other organism): it is an *abstract* vision, though one that is asserted at the outset (an axiom) rather than being created through an act of abstraction from various particular specimens of visual perception.

We described non-philosophy above as a 'ventriloquism' of the other (one that *plays the dummy* so that it can re-enact the speech of philosophy) – this was a way of understanding what Laruelle means when he says that non-philosophy 'clones' philosophy. But perhaps a better analogy for this 'cloning' lies in the game of *charades*. There are three basic approaches to playing charades that can be compared with philosophy and non-philosophy. The first two, and most common, methods involve one player analysing the name of a film, book, play, etc., into its component parts – either words or, at a finer level of analysis, syllables. Then, those words or syllables are mimed to the other players; that is, an attempt is made to show what those individual words refer to in the world so that the players might guess the name correctly. The problem with this method is that, all too often, the player who guesses correctly does so on account of *already knowing* the relationship between the mime and the word's being mimed (frequently because he or she knows the person miming quite well, and the way that his or her mind works, that is, the associations he or she habitually makes in 'their world'). The method is circular: they have arrived at the name by miming a world *already* shared with others, not by miming the film or book or play *itself*. The second most common strategy is to take the words or syllables and convey them by analogy with other words ('sounds like') that are easier to mime, perhaps because they are biological or physical terms referring to something concrete. This would be a reductive approach, though, that only succeeds by making the verbal analogy an end in itself – miming a physical phenomenon, say, rather than a film.

Laruelle, however, takes the third, least common and most 'abstract' approach, and tries to mime the film, book, or play *in one gesture, in itself and as a whole (not via its name)*. If *philosophy* as a whole were the chosen object, then non-philosophy *mimes* philosophy in-One, that is, in One gesture, and as part of the 'Real-One'. Philosophy is not broken down into its component terms (Aristotelian wonder, Cartesian doubt, Hegelian dialectics, Heideggerian questioning, or whatever else) as though *one* of those terms could stand for the whole of philosophy. This would only work for those *who already believed* that *all* philosophy is, in essence – i.e. when good, when true, etc. – Heideggerian, or Hegelian, or some such thing. Nor is it conveyed by reducing it to *another* domain such as physics, neuroscience, or linguistics. That, again, would simply assume that this reductive domain already *is* identifiable with philosophy, a move begging the question as to what philosophy is (which was the whole point of the charade in the first place – to mime philosophy as a whole, universally). Laruelle, instead, takes the charade seriously both because he wishes to convey the identity of *all* extant philosophies equally – not just of one of its parishes to its own devotees – but also because it is a mime that respects the whole of philosophy, while at the same time (re)viewing it in a new light.

What Laruelle discovers in practising this is that the gesture (which is actually a set of 'postures' or performative 'stances') that best conveys all of philosophy equally is the one invariable structure common to all philosophies – its lowest common denominator, so to speak. And the name of this denominator is 'decision'. Each and every philosophy involves a decision (understood broadly, not merely in intellectual, voluntary, and self-conscious terms) – namely, *to explain or represent the Real in one exclusive way – its own*. It is as if the part, a philosophy, could be the whole; it is as if it, one 'school' of philosophy, was *not* already a party to an ongoing dispute as to what philosophy is but the universal victor of a now defunct quarrel.

Now, a response to this approach might be that that is just what an explanation must be – a part standing for (referring to) the whole. And it might be added that this *is* perfectly possible: after all, 'San Francisco' refers to San Francisco, even when uttered in San Francisco, i.e., when a part of it. An utterance can refer to its referent without having to *be* the referent. Yet, though most theories of reference contain presuppositions about the nature of representation that many would contest (not just Laruelle), were we to ignore them and focus solely on philosophical representation, we would still find something very peculiar in its practice: for it claims to refer to the Real in essence, with no essential omitted, and not just to another part or accidental aspect of the Real (mysterious though that ability might be too).[9] Philosophical explanation is special because it claims to reduce the Real *in every essential part completely* to itself, to one part (even when practised by physicists, neuroscientists, or psychoanalysts when they also offer us their 'theories of everything'). Of course, philosophy does not see this representation as such a reduction – it leaves its own ability to gain such a godlike view (where the whole becomes the part) as a mystery. And non-philosophical 'explanation' is special too, because it reforms what we mean by explanation as such, removing any transcendent pretensions (representationalism) it may have in philosophy or in non-philosophy: explanations are always *incomplete* because they are material parts rather than immaterial representations.

Decision, then, is the invariant structure of philosophy. To 'decide' is to cut oneself off from the Real, to represent it – *decaedere* (*de-* 'off' + *caedere* 'cut'). To represent, to cut off, to de-cide. But a part cannot actually be a part without belonging to the Real, and so it cannot represent the Real at all. The Real is indifferent to its parts. Laruelle's non-philosophy, on the other hand, takes that decisional structure of philosophies and mimes it, performs it, such that, instead of representing the Real in being cut off from it, it performs as a part of it, comes out of it (as an occasional cause, at least 'in-the-last-instance').

Kantians, and their heirs, are not immune from this decisional structure either, for even as they humbly disavow all pretensions to metaphysical intuition, their deduction that we cannot know reality at all can only come from 'on-high', from a transcendent point of view that measures what *might be* real, directly or indirectly (by some means that are a part of the decision, i.e., that the concepts of absolute space and time are antinomical, that negativity is real, that the Real is differential, and so on). Laruelle, though, is not deciding (for) the Real in any contentful way – not because it *can or cannot be known*, but because all decisions are immanent to it, are a part of it already. The Real is in-different (and so One or identical) to all decisions because it is more than all decisions, though not in such a way that it becomes a mystery, *ad hoc*, or superfluous. And to realise this, if only for a moment, is not *another* decision (or even a meta-decision) but a revision of what all decisions are, that is, immanent material parts rather than transcendent immaterial representations. Or, at least, this is Laruelle's hypothesis or axiom. This axiom *itself*, of course, can be taken as simply one *other* decision – such is the philosopher's prerogative and even essential trait.

Hence, there are still those post-phenomenological or non-Kantian realists who claim to bypass the general Copernicanism and anthropomorphism of Continental philosophy (the self-styled 'object-oriented' or 'speculative' realists), and yet who, all the same, unwittingly abide by a decisional, representational structure for their own thought – that is, they still believe in the power of philosophy to account for the Real. Indeed, they might well regard anyone who would beg to differ as wholly 'arrogant', misreading the non-philosophical hypothesis of the invariant structure of decision for a self-attribution of even greater representational powers than those allowed to philosophy. However, their judgement can be traced back to an inability to *see* a rejection of arrogance as anything other than simply more arrogance, a blindness due to the fact that they prefer to think in only one mould, that of representational thought, even as they disavow it.[10] In contrast to the verdict that condemns Laruelle's 'arrogance', therefore, there is the option to see his approach as what it hypothesises itself to be – a thought that is part of the Real. He invites us into this view in order to allow us to experiment, scientifically, with the effects that follow from this in knowledge. Because his thought is *incomplete*, it claims to be genuinely scientific or experimental, an open-ended experiment in what thought is, or a new experience of thought as immanent (*'expérience'* understood here in two of its French senses).

The mention of 'abstract' above is also crucial. Laruelle begins with an abstract hypothesis that, somewhat like a figure-ground switch, revises how we see philosophy, and so also all other non-philosophical practices such that the latter can also be seen as thoughtful. This 'axiom' is necessary, he says, in order to avoid the usual *circular* arguments of philosophers: their resultant represen-tations (captures) of reality being always premised in a question-begging fashion on their chosen method of thought (whatever it may be). For here is the catch: as an expressed thought (communi-cated on paper, by word, but not, per se, *as the revision itself*) this axiom also implicates Laruelle's own thought (or at least it should) such that any transcendental insights it gains are only momentary (again, just as a switch in the figure-ground is). Hence, the form of non-philosophy *must* always mutate – it can never stand still, it is open-ended.

In fact, Laruelle's postulate, or posture, could be described as an *auto-affective* hypothesis, that is, a conjecture that all thought, including itself, is material, a kind of thing, and not a representa-tion (understood as a successful capture of reality). *Think this*, he says: thought is a thing. Now what follows from that, if we take this thought seriously, that is, as consistently, or persistently, as possible (at least for us)? And taking this seriously means not agreeing that this is *merely* speculation but rather that this thought too is a thing (is a part of the Real). The thought implicates itself – thus the 'auto' – but it side-steps that *tu quoque* response from philosophers (that this is merely 'more philosophy') by seeing itself as a performative thought and not a representational one (cer-tainly not a higher-order *reflective* thought or metaphilosophy). Again, non-philosophy is an action, a doing and a showing, rather than a saying or a representing. One might say that it is a philoso-phy of the look rather than the book (hence, its rejection of *Greco/ Judaic* claims on the exclusive power of thought).

Certainly, then, Laruelle's is a strange thought,[11] but its strange-ness partly stems from its attempt to be utterly consistent. What for some appears to be a *reductio ad absurdum* is for Laruelle embraced as the rigorous conclusion that any thought of abso-lute immanence should accept, were it to be consistent.[12] And to be consistent it must include itself, though not reflexively – as if mirrors reflect without distortion, without always refracting too – but more as a fractal, a 'self-similar' part.[13] As Wittgenstein might admit, the apparent absurdity of throwing away the ladder one ascends becomes here the necessary evil of consistency. Or rather, each person must construct his or her own ladder should he or she adopt this stance, this posture or vision of non-philosophy, or of the non-philosophies. If this leads to mysticism, so be it – but it would be the mysticism, or rather the Gnosticism, of a kind that is the logical destiny of 'consistency' – the value of philosophy so often proclaimed though so little discussed. Laruelle's logic is double-edged, then, as it comes with a concomitant strangeness. And yet this strangeness is just its consistency toward immanence – consistency *being a kind of logic and thing itself* (see the essay by Mullarkey below).

Does all of this make Laruelle special, or utterly ordinary? Or might such an ordinariness, a call to the ordinary, make Laruelle's ideas special, when so many are looking for the *recognisably* 'extraordinary', 'radical', 'transgressive', and so on? If so, it is a special status that is open to all, because what it says is that philosophy – *the* discipline that appropriates for itself the exclusive right to think at the highest levels of thought – does not have a monopoly on these powers. Being ordinary, seeing philosophy in ordinary practices, is not, despite the term's associations, easy or simple. It involves a huge effort to reverse, or 'invert' our intellectual habits, to *perform* the democracy of thought, and refuse to try to explain the Real, and to 'dominate' other forms of knowledge. Non-philosophy is not 'a "model" or "system" closed in on itself', he says: it is 'a practice of – and in – thought' and is thereby open to all the mutations and corruptions that come with such practice (which, contrary to proverbial opinion, never 'makes perfect' but always remains open).[14] Non-philosophy needs to be re-invented, to mutate anew all the time: each practitioner constructs his or her own ladder. As a consequence, one cannot say that there is a clear transferable method in non-philosophy that must be adhered to rigidly. There is only a set of suggestions, or a recipe that, if followed, invites a revision of what we see thinking and philosophy to be.[15]

The essays that follow in this collection all explore, in one way or another, this mutable and performative thought, with a view to its claim of being ordinary, pluralist, and embodying a democratic conception of philosophy without 'domination', without 'authority'. Anthony Paul Smith's essay, 'Thinking from the One: Science and the Ancient Philosophical Figure of the One', examines Laruelle's claim that to think radically is to think *from* the One, placing it within its historical context and revealing how it provides the ground for the entire non-philosophical methodology. It is noteworthy that in late twentieth-century French philosophy, many thought that simply accusing another philosopher of being a thinker of the One was tantamount to polemic, as evidenced by Badiou's critique of Deleuze and the strong reactions it provoked. For Laruelle, however, such debates ultimately cannot escape turning all philosophy into a kind of negative theology, the negative philosophy of transcendence, which can be found at philosophy's core. Marjorie Gracieuse's contribution, 'Laruelle Facing Deleuze: Immanence, Resistance and Desire', continues in this same historical vein, by analysing Laruelle's response to Deleuze with respect to the nature of immanence in order to evaluate the relevance and limits of Laruelle's critique. Both thinkers commit to a non-foundational understanding of thought, but whereas Deleuze conceives of desire as an immanent power capable of purging philosophy of any form of transcendence, Laruelle assimilates philosophical desire to a desire for transcendence, denouncing Deleuze's approach as a betrayal of radical immanence. Gracieuse contrasts Deleuze's commitment to ontology and metaphysics with Laruelle's affirmation of the immanental process as radically *non-ontological*. Doing so leads to another distinction between Laruelle's 'man-in-person' (*l'Homme-en-personne*) and the crowned anarchy of Deleuzian impersonal singularities. Though the former may look like a return to humanism, it is, on the contrary, a reorientation of thought *de hominem*, to an undefined concept of 'man', one *without* any humanist or anthropological mediation.

In 'Laruelle and Ordinary Life', Rocco Gangle looks beneath the formidable language and abstract nature of much of Laruelle's work to its simple insight that leads, albeit with difficulty, to a perfectly ordinary experience by opening up new modes of thinking. Ironically, however, it is the very simplicity of this mode of thinking – one that is ultimately *for those who are in the world* – that necessitates its stringent conceptual labours. In pursuing this line, Gangle contrasts the concept of the ordinary in Laruelle with those of the *Lebenswelt* in the late Husserl and 'ordinary language' in the Analytic tradition. The ordinariness of non-philosophical thought emerges as both an alternative to philosophy and as a 'positive' use of philosophy itself. Joshua Ramey's essay turns to non-philosophy's relationship with religious thought, though still in connection with this idea of the ordinary. His contribution,

'The Justice of Non-Philosophy', explains how, for Laruelle, the non-philosophical is consistently situated in relation to religious experience, specifically, within a heretical, materialist appropriation of religious experience. In particular, Laruelle evokes a mystical or esoteric apprehension, an awareness of a presence that cannot be fully named or imagined or otherwise brought into discourse, and yet is essential to thought. Yet this mystical or esoteric apprehension, for Laruelle, is displaced from its status as a movement toward the transcendent into a radically immanent mode of existence: the immanence of the Real (unthinkable imperative) of thought itself. Unlike for most of the philosophical and theological tradition, this mystical presence is not the object (or subject) of an extraordinary or superhuman experience, but is precisely the radical immanence of experience to what Laruelle calls the ordinary life. Yet, ordinary as it is, this life is not immediately given, either in phenomenological intuition or in a *sensus communis*. Rather, the radically ordinary is a life discovered, through the non-philosophical operations, to be the life of the Stranger, a life identifiable with the Real, a 'man-in-the-last-instance'.

Ray Brassier's essay, 'Laruelle and the Reality of Abstraction', begins with an examination of Laruelle's analysis of the problem of Finitude in Heidegger, travelling via Kant's critical philosophy and Wilfrid Sellars on the 'myth of the Given' along the way. Laruelle, he writes, identifies 'unobjectivizable transcendence with the dimension of withdrawal that Heidegger takes to be inseparable from Being's disclosure of the entity'. However, for Laruelle, it is not Being itself that withdraws but rather the 'entity-in-itself'. As such, Heidegger's conception of Finitude is stuck within a 'fatal equivocation'. However, Brassier also accuses Laruelle of an equivocation in his own work between 'realising abstraction' and 'abstracting the Real'. If, as seems to be the case, Laruelle has simply identified the Real itself with abstraction, then it will be hard for him 'to discharge himself' of the need to justify this identification without either regressing to Michel Henry's phenomenological idealisation of radical immanence or accepting the arbitrary, abstract and ultimately 'decisional' nature of his own categories such as 'the human-in-person' or gnosis.

Following this line of epistemological enquiry, Anne-Françoise Schmid's essay 'The Science-Thought of Laruelle and its Effects on Epistemology' asks how Laruelle's conception of science, or 'non-epistemology', differs from standard epistemology as found in diverse figures such as Carnap, Popper and Feyerabend. Beginning with a comparison of their respective vocabularies concerning science, which differ wildly, Schmid is able to locate the following fundamental difference: all standard epistemologies are organised by way of a tension between opposites, but non-standard philosophy's conception of science is not organised as such, but rather modelled in the lived experience of science that dissolves or 'forgets' about this tension in its practice. Schmid's essay can be seen as a non-philosophical response to the standard epistemological demand for justification, in focusing on the central place of the lived in non-philosophy's conception of science. For, by modelling itself on science's heterogeneous lived experience, non-epistemology declares its autonomy to universal criteria as well as the generic proliferation of disciplinary dimensions for any scientific problem whatsoever.

Turning now to other non-philosophical fields, John Mullarkey's essay, '1 + 1 = 1: The Non-Consistency of Non-Philosophical Practice (Photo: Quantum: Fractal)', examines the development of non-philosophy's expansion across other subjects – photography in particular – and looks at how it differs from the other domains, such as fractal geometry and quantum physics, that have been *used* to articulate Laruelle's thought. Given that non-philosophy is *already* a practice, *already* performative, he asks: is non-philosophy always already an *applied* thought such that there can be no distinction between the applied and the 'pure' theory? The pure is the applied. And, if such is the case – if everything thinks and thought is *already* democratic – what is the purpose in *commending* it? Mullarkey also investigates how self-similar, or fractal, the different implementations of Laruelle's thought are, as we move from quantum, to photo, to fractal. The problem is that, if they are consistently implemented, then what value does mutation really have in his work? Furthermore, is it judicious of Laruelle to insist, as he so often does, on his views concerning non-philosophy being consistent throughout? Might it be that his insistence on consistency, or rigour, in formal argument is a legacy from philosophy that he cannot do without?

Michael Olson's piece, 'Transcendental Arguments, Axiomatic Truth and the Difficulty of Overcoming Idealism', elucidates the value of Laruelle's axiomatic materialism within the Kantian transcendental tradition. Just as the axioms of geometry, for example, compel the geometer's thought through their consistency, Laruelle's transcendental axioms force a non-philosophical realisation of the foreclosure of the Real to the reflexively self-grounding structures of philosophy. This axiomatic compulsion or forcing thought underwrites Laruelle's response to the philosophical problem of materialism. Olson then goes on to gauge the success of Laruelle's attempt to grasp the necessary idealism of philosophy as such on the basis of an axiomatic assertion of the radical immanence of the unity of the Real. Though this endeavour is not wholly fruitful, Laruelle does show how the mutual reinforcement of the structures of material existence and self-consciousness are an exemplary moment of thought's tendency to mistake its own self-sufficiency for a guarantee of the sufficiency of its own structures to the Real they purport to comprehend.

The next two essays engage with the political dimensions of Laruelle's thinking, especially with regards to his engagement with the anti-philosophical thought of Marx. Alexander R. Galloway's essay, 'Laruelle, Anti-Capitalist', looks at this encounter through Laruelle's book *Introduction au non-marxisme* from 2000, which focuses on a non-Marxism that pervades all of Laruelle's thought. In this work, Galloway sees an attempt to describe an immanent kernel in Marx that would be 'devoid of all rationality, all shells, all mystifications'. Yet, though in 'profound deviation from the Marxian tradition', for Galloway Laruelle remains a Marxist, and even produces one of the most 'profound critiques of capitalism hitherto known'. Moreover, Laruelle realises that Marx himself was seeking a true non-philosophy 'by breaking with philosophy and shifting toward the practical science of political economy'. Katerina Kolozova's essay, 'Theories of the Immanent Rebellion: Non-Marxism and Non-Christianity', also tackles this non-Marxism, but does so this time through Laruelle's theories of 'radical concepts' and 'rebellion' rather than an historical enquiry. In *Introduction au non-marxisme* Laruelle argues for a revision of Marxism by virtue of rendering it devoid of the tenets of Transcendentalism. This will allow it to be guided by radical rather than philosophical concepts, ones engendered by recourse to the 'syntax of the Real'. However, Laruelle's non-Marxism does not address in any direct way the question of resistance or political revolt: these are tackled instead in *Future Christ*, where 'Man-in-person' is defined as radically open to the world in the form of ceaseless, immanent rebellion. Kolozova goes on to examine the possibility of intersecting the two projects – non-Marxism and non-Christianity – in order to arrive at a mutable discourse endowed with the immanent possibility of action that evades the disciplinary hold of a political-philosophical doctrine.

The collection ends with an essay from Laruelle himself – 'Is Thinking Democratic? Or, How to Introduce Theory into Democracy' – as well as an interview with Laruelle commissioned specifically for this volume. Both of these pieces address the guiding theme of *Laruelle and Non-Philosophy*, that of the possibility of philosophy's becoming plural (and pluralist), that it might embrace non-philosophies as no less thoughtful than itself, and thereby acquire a 'blind or deaf' thought with no prejudices, no hierarchies – the 'flat thought' that belongs to a democratic science rather than an exclusive and elitist decision that fails to see that thought happens everywhere, not just in itself. Even so, Laruelle's essay uncovers a paradox at the heart of egalitarian philosophical thinking: to think equality is not to practise it. This is because democracy is always thought in relation to some state of exception, some perceived inequality between the democratic ideal (theory) and the play of politics (practice). More important than this inequality, however, are the problems *for thought* that underlie it, problems that Laruelle attempts to solve by introducing theory into practice. He thereby creates a duality between the two, though one that is forever open and without combination. This duality has a unilateral character in the generic subjects that must think both the democratic ideal and political existence. Non-philosophy proclaims a democratic gospel in developing a theory of the generic subject. This generic subject is necessarily, in-the-last-instance, a *living utopia*, because the generic subject is always a stranger, *xenos*, or one without-place, within a world inequitably distributed amongst places that exist, but are not real.

One failing, if that is the right word, of this collection is its relative lack – with the exception of a discussion of non-photography – of engagement with those other non-philosophies that are not also using (at least overtly) philosophical texts as their raw material. The thinking present in cinema, for instance, might well be examined in light of Laruelle's work on photography. This would, of course, be a mutation of his ideas, but it would be no less consistent for being so (in fact, it would be thoroughly consistent just for being so mutable).[16] For even if Laruelle claims that philosophy and science are the two major sources of thought – as he does at one point below – they are already-mutated conceptions of science and philosophy. Science is the lived experiences or living experiments of knowledge and philosophy. It is the 'hermeneutic' or bearer of a knowing that has no need for meaning or justification.[17] Science is the practice of understanding, and philosophy is the creation of fiction that is – as Schmid writes – 'a method of renewing understandings and knowledge'.[18] So what would the other mutations of generic science and generic philosophy that are *already* present in other fields look like? Alongside a noncinematic thinking, how does thought appear in non-literature or non-theatre (a film, book, or play)? It will be the objective of a future volume to examine the thinking within *other* non-philosophies in all their non-Laruellean guises – always remembering that the 'non-' here is not the negation, but the amplification and mutation of thought.[19]

We wish to express our gratitude to a number of others whose amazing efforts helped make this collection possible. Firstly, we wish to thank Marjorie Gracieuse and Nicola Rubczak for all the labour they put into organising the interview that closes this volume, as well as its subsequent translation. We are greatly indebted to them both. Our appreciation is also due to the editor at Edinburgh University Press, Carol MacDonald, for commissioning the volume as much as for her assistance all along its path to publication. The copy-editor (Tim Clark) at Edinburgh improved upon the work in equal measure. Lastly, we thank François Laruelle, both for creating this strange and lovely thing called non-philosophy and for his co-operation throughout the production of this book.

Notes

1. François Laruelle, 'Is Thinking Democratic?', p. 232 below.
2. See François Laruelle, *Philosophies of Difference: A Critical Introduction to Non-Philosophy*, translated by Rocco Gangle (London and New York: Continuum, 2010), p. xviii, for the allusion to 'the same old game'.
3. See François Laruelle, *Philosophie et non-philosophie* (Liege/Bruxelles: Pierre Mardaga, 1989), pp. 8, 99 ff; François Laruelle, *En tant qu'Un: La «non-philosophie» expliquée aux philosophes* (Paris: Aubier, 1991), p. 247.
4. See John Mullarkey, *Post-Continental Philosophy: An Outline*

(London and New York: Continuum, 2006), Chapter 5, for an attempt to materialise metaphilosophy through a use of the diagram that would move metaphilosophy away from being a higher-order reflection and come closer to a non-philosophical material fractal.

5. See Laruelle's essay '"I, the Philosopher, Am Lying": A Reply to Deleuze', which also discusses Spinoza and non-philosophy, in François Laruelle, *The Non-Philosophy Project: Essays by François Laruelle*, edited by Gabriel Alkon and Boris Gunjevic (New York: Telos Press Publishing, 2012), pp. 40–74.

6. François Laruelle, *Le Concept de non-photographie/The Concept of Non-Photography* (Bilingual Edition), translated by Robin Mackay (Falmouth: Urbanomic, 2011), p. 53.

7. This includes the anti-philosophies like Lacan's, certain Analytic thought, and Marxism, simply because they are 'anti': a rejection of philosophy in the name of a higher-order thought (representation of the Real) is still philosophical for Laruelle.

8. The question as to why this 'needs' to be done, why the non-philosophical stance *needs* to be commended if, as it also claims, everything *already* thinks, is addressed in the essay by Mullarkey below.

9. The reference here to the mysteriousness present even in how ordinary reference can seemingly succeed is an allusion to Paul Grice, 'Meaning Revisited', in *Studies in the Way of Words* (Cambridge, MA: Harvard University Press, 1989), pp. 283–303; pp. 297 ff.

10. See Graham Harman, 'Review of *Philosophies of Difference*', in *Notre Dame Philosophical Reviews*, 8 August 2011. Available at <http://ndpr.nd.edu/news/25437-philosophies-of-difference-a-critical-introduction-to-non-philosophy/> (accessed 6 February 2012). In this review of the translation of *Philosophies of Difference*, Harman refers to 'the remarkable arrogance with which Laruelle's theory is presented' on account of it reducing all philosophy to one decisional form. Another aspect of Harman's rather uncharitable review (which, as he himself indicates, comes from a position of relative ignorance about Laruelle) is its implied faith in only specific forms of rhetoric or 'prose style' such that Laruelle's writing is castigated as unclear and 'generally abominable'. Much could be said here in reply, but the crucial point to be made is that, contra Harman's faith in the transparent singularity of notions such as 'clarity', a non-philosophical approach would contest whether their meaning is singular at all. Do we have a clear and universal concept of 'clarity', for example (that would avoid the obvious circularity of

the question in its answer – see W. D. Hart, 'Clarity', in David Bell and Neil Cooper [eds], *The Analytic Tradition: Meaning, Thought and Knowledge* [Oxford: Blackwell 1990], pp. 197–222, for more on this)? Harman misses the force of such questions, seeing clarity, as well as 'method' and 'form' as issues concerning effectiveness (in capturing reality) and communicative facility (in convincing others of one's mastery). A helpful inference one can make from Harman's review, though, is that it shows the general tendency of philosophies to take representationalist form, to mediate everything through a limited perspective, and so to leave unexamined how a complete 'insight' into reality is possible.

11. For more on the role of the 'stranger' (in every sense) in Laruelle, see Anthony Paul Smith, *A Stranger Thought: An Introduction to the Non-Philosophy of François Laruelle* (forthcoming).

12. This is, perhaps, the perennial philosophical virtue *and* vice: think only of Peter Singer's highly consistent implementation of the utility principle: for some, it leads to a more moral, fairer, practical ethics; for others (usually humanists) it leads to absurdity and monstrous immorality.

13. For the concept of 'refraction' and non-philosophy, see John Mullarkey, *Philosophy and the Moving Image: Refractions of Reality* (Basingstoke: Palgrave-Macmillan, 2010).

14. François Laruelle, *Future Christ: A Lesson in Heresy*, translated by Anthony Paul Smith (London and New York: Continuum, 2010), p. x.

15. Laruelle's construction of non-philosophy contains its own set of revisions traced in the periodisation of non-philosophy into five waves (Philosophy I–V). This history is traced in Anthony Paul Smith's essay below.

16. For a first attempt at a non-cinematic philosophy, see Mullarkey, *Philosophy and the Moving Image*.

17. On Laruelle's conception and mutation of hermeneutics see François Laruelle, 'The Truth According to Hermes: Theorems on the Secret and Communication', translated by Alexander R. Galloway, *Parrhesia: A Journal of Critical Philosophy* 9 (2010), pp. 18–22.

18. Anne-Françoise Schmid, 'The Science-Thought of Laruelle and its Effects on Epistemology', p. 134 below.

19. See John Mullarkey, *Reverse Mutations: Laruelle and Non-Human Philosophy* (forthcoming).

I

Thinking From the One: Science and the Ancient Philosophical Figure of the One

Anthony Paul Smith

'Beyond the Idea, there is the real.'[1]

Without a doubt the non-philosophy of François Laruelle frustrates and agitates both philosophers and the philosophically aware theorists who read him. Such reactions arise from the sense that one should easily be able to place Laruelle's non-philosophy in the usual constellation of philosophical positions. This feeling that it should all make sense comes from the familiarity one has when reading him – of this concept seeming like Kant, of that move hearkening back to Heidegger or Deleuze – but for all that, this familiarity is never sufficient to get one's bearing within his thought. In an intellectual milieu crowded with any number of brands or ideas, often conflated or blended together, Laruelle's non-philosophy sticks out, like an unwanted tangled root or an unmovable stone waiting for philosophers and theorists to trip up on. For there is no easy way to classify non-philosophy within the now familiar and moribund debates. Non-philosophy is not vitalist, but neither is it mechanistic or determinist. It is not a subjective phenomenology, nor is it a scientistic reductionism. It is not a Christian meditation, but it cannot simply be called an atheistic philosophy either. It seems to be a kind of realism, but one that speaks always of the Real and the One rather than the usual discrete units, substances, or even material patterns of standard philosophical realisms. And so the reader of Laruelle often gives up on non-philosophy, frightened off by the difficulty of its formalism combined with the strangeness of his appeals to gnosis and the mystical.

This is true of new readers of Laruelle, but also of some luminaries of the Francophone philosophical world, such as Derrida, Deleuze, Nancy and Badiou, all of whom have expressed some frustration with Laruelle. The most famous example of this comes from Derrida (ironically, considering his own ability to frustrate his interlocutors), who we find exclaiming that only Laruelle knows the rules to his game and that he terrorises his readers.[2] Laruelle's response remains frustrating and he seems almost to revel in refusing to surrender an inch to Derrida during this debate. While I appreciate this refusal, constituting as it does a struggle against philosophy's resistance to non-philosophy, I recognise that for those who meet Laruelle's work with confusion and agitation a number of questions still remain: what is the basis of the claims he makes? what about that basis marks non-philosophy out from standard philosophical discourse and practice? and what difference does it make for the usual concerns of philosophy? We may begin to answer the first of these questions in a manner that will remain as frustrating as it will at first appear enigmatic. The answer is simply that the basis (Laruelle would prefer to say 'posture') of non-philosophy comes from the One, which is to say the Real itself. The purpose of this chapter, then, is to explore how the One functions as a name for what remains not unthought, but rather always insufficiently thought, what is radically immanent and foreclosed to thought, but infinitely effable. I begin by discussing the philosophical background for discussion about the One, looking first to the ancient philosophical One and then to contemporary debates surrounding the One. This brings to the fore the real issues surrounding the use of the One in non-philosophy, which is centred around the focus on a radical immanence that encompasses what philosophy calls transcendence, as well as the absolute or pure forms of immanence. It is upon these that the non-philosophical One operates. Finally, I turn to the way this description of the One lies at the heart of non-philosophy's valorisation of scientific posture, but in turn mutates the image of science as the unitary judge of all knowledge. This connection between the One (a strange and mystical, almost hermetic name in the history of philosophy and retaining some of that in non-philosophy) and science (taken to be a sober practice of reason, one drained of colour and blood, almost with disdain for the subjects that produce it) is forgotten in some of the recent Anglophone presentations of non-philosophy. But the One and science are always thought together in Laruelle, and it is his thinking from the One, in its radical essence rather than as a skin for Being or Alterity, that differentiates his valorisation of science from an all-too-easy scientism that has very little to do with anything interesting at work in the sciences.

The One in Ancient and Contemporary Philosophy

Before turning to our discussion of the importance of the One for non-philosophy, it will help orient us if we survey the relationship of this non-philosophical One to the standard One found in the ancient and contemporary philosophical material Laruelle draws upon. In his 'Glossary Raissoné', Laruelle defines the One thus: 'An ancient transcendental utilised as a first name under the forms One-in-One, One-in-person, vision-in-One.'[3] That there is then a relationship between non-philosophy and ancient, primarily Neoplatonic philosophy, is clear, but what is the nature of that relationship? Nick Srnicek deftly and succinctly outlines the similarities and differences between the two traditions along six lines:

1) For Neoplatonists, the One is singular and simple. For nonphilosophy [sic], the One is foreclosed to the one/many divide and is instead already-given prior to any conceptualisation.

2) Unlike the Neoplatonist's One, the nonphilosophical One is not ineffable, but rather infinitely effable. It provides the basis for an infinite number of names for itself.

3) For Neoplatonists, the One operates through emanation. For nonphilosophy, the One operates through determination-in-the-last-instance.

4) For the Neoplatonists, the One is beyond Being. For nonphilosophy, Being is beyond the One. The relation of immanence and transcendence is reversed between them. Nonphilosophy's radical immanence *encompasses* the separation of immanence and transcendence that philosophy institutes.

5) This entails that while Neoplatonism has to strive to reach the transcendent One, for nonphilosophy we are always already within the immanent One.

6) And as a result, Neoplatonists aim to know the One. Nonphilosophy meanwhile aims to think in accordance with the One.[4]

With this summation, Srnicek shows that Laruelle's relationship with ancient philosophy is ultimately one of mutation.[5] Ancient philosophy, too, operates along a decisional axis, separating the One and the Many, but Laruelle's use of ancient philosophy entails extracting from it the material of the One and deploying it in a framework outside of the one/many distinction as that which is pre-conceptual, always foreclosed as such to philosophy's standard operations. As he puts it in an early work: 'Beyond the immanent frontiers of Being, the Idea, the tolerated space of multiplicities, *there is* . . . something, perhaps even an aliquid, like the One.'[6]

The philosophical trope of the One is, as Laruelle himself says, an ancient philosophical name and, as such, it can appear anachronistic to try and speak of it on the contemporary scene. In fact, that a contemporary philosopher may be thinking of the One functions now as an accusation, one serious enough that it provides the authority for one contemporary philosopher to drag another before the acephalic tribunal of philosophy and demand an account. The paradigmatic case for such prosecution is Badiou's polemical book *Deleuze: The Clamour of Being*, and the further criticisms of Deleuze it spawned, most notably in Peter Hallward's *Out of This World: Deleuze and the Philosophy of Creation*, but also the less-well known *L'Exercice différé de la philosophie. À l'occasion de Deleuze* by Guy Lardreau, which explicitly builds on Badiou's book. In the first two cases, Deleuze's philosophy is questioned on the basis of its relationship to the One and thus its assumed Neoplatonic character. The impetus behind these prosecutions is not, however, to challenge the basis of Deleuze's philosophy, but to question its *radicality*, the utility of Deleuze's philosophy for radical political projects. For, according to all these Badiouian critiques, a truly radical politics is *only* and *absolutely* supported by materialist philosophy.

Setting aside the accuracy of these claims regarding Deleuze, this criticism reveals something endemic to philosophy: its decisional character. This characteristic of philosophy, as uncovered by Laruelle, is one of always grounding itself within an arbitrary decision that ultimately turns out to be only itself as an operation of thought. It is a self-grounding, a making of philosophy that turns it, and it alone, into a divine being, self-constituting and self-sufficient unto itself. The point of this description of philosophy in Laruelle has little to do with an anti-philosophical project, but rather locates philosophy's own mode of production which can then be reappropriated by the non-philosopher for what Laruelle calls human usage.[7] Rather than submitting humans-in-person, and arguably any other kind of immanent lived experience, to philosophy, philosophy must be submitted to the lived: 'philosophy is made for man, not man for philosophy'.[8] In this case the decision is always for materialism; it is a decision, then, for a philosophy, bearing down on these humans-in-person and other strangers to the philosophical world, forcing them either to submit or to put their backs up against the wall. But, ask these philosophers, 'why materialism?' Will they not then go on to speak of events and fidelity? This is always then an appeal to aspects of lived experience, what we can perhaps simply call 'the lived', outside of philosophy, but that are nonetheless only able to speak when given voice by philosophy.

The purely and arbitrarily decisional character of this prosecution by one philosopher against another can also be seen in the defence raised for Deleuze against Badiou's assertions. While Deleuze referred to himself at least once as a materialist philosopher and not a spiritualist one, the more interesting line of defence has been taken by those who put the prosecutor on trial and make the claim that the truly radical philosophy is always that of a spiritual philosophy.[9] The argumentation here, most notably as found in a special issue of the journal *SubStance*, is predicated on the notion that there is something that outruns human rationality; that there is something, call it a power if you will, that is at work in the universe which operates in a way not unlike what used to be called spirit.[10] This defence is perhaps closer to non-philosophy's own constructive mode, since within Laruelle's development he too assumes a kind of 'spiritual element', which he calls relative transcendence (to differentiate it from the absolute form of transcendence found in standard forms of philosophy, *pace* Levinas, as well as in theology), in addition to something that outstrips philosophy, that is foreclosed to philosophy: this is what he calls the One. However, the difference between Laruelle's philosophy and this Deleuzian-Spiritualism is that Laruelle attempts to provide a more developed axiomatic description of the One, which non-philosophy then uses to think *from*. This attempt to think the One marks a significant difference from both the decisional character of philosophy as well as the metaphysical super-rationalism of Deleuzian-Spiritualism.[11]

After these two short descriptive detours through the original source material for non-philosophy's One and the Badiou-Deleuze debate concerning the One, the question of the real issues raised by ancient philosophy and this contemporary debate remain. After all, if non-philosophy is ultimately unconcerned with the war between philosophies, then what concern would a seemingly purely philosophical argument have for non-philosophy? In short, it comes down to the deployment of philosophical immanence and transcendence within philosophy's operation of thought. The standard philosophical One, to be differentiated from the non-philosophical One, brings to the fore the functions of both philosophical immanence and transcendence, while the non-philosophical One reveals itself as the means by which these philosophical forms can be deployed once they are turned into plastic materials rather than hallucinations of absolute positions of thought, oases in the philosophical desert. How does the non-philosophical perform this operation of turning these hallucinations into materials? In so far as the One is already given, pre-conceptual, the given-without-givenness, and radical immanence, but infinitely effable, then philosophical deployments of concepts like immanence and transcendence are both equal, and thus equally of use, in terms of their relativity to the One.

The Non-Philosophical One and its Axiomatic Operations

Laruelle's taking up of the One as the central term in non-philosophy is an attempt to speak in a familiar philosophical idiom, though perhaps this is done in a cruel way since the One is notoriously strange within philosophy itself. But what Laruelle does with that One is very different. As he himself says, 'There are innumerable philosophers who speak of the One', but these philosophers always speak in some sense of the figure of the One which is then always reduced in some way to some other philosophical concept and so none of them 'know what the essence of the One is', and moreover this is 'because they have first *refused* to elucidate its essence'.[12] These philosophers, Laruelle charges, never attempt to think the essence of the One, to think the One-in-One, the One as an identity that cannot be mixed with Being or Alterity (the two main philosophically transcendental concepts traditionally spoken about in relation to the One). This will be the task Laruelle sets up for himself in relation to the One: to describe the essence of the One without any appeal to ontology (Being always coming after the One) or to transcendence (as Alterity is always caught in some kind of mediating dialectic, even if it is the mediating term, to which the One is also prior). In this way, the

One and the Real are equivalent. The two words are sometimes written together as the 'Real-One' and clearly, within non-philosophy, there is a central connection between the Real and the One. To put it simply, the Real is non-conceptual; it is always already foreclosed to thought, to any absolute circumscription, to any philosophical determination, to any ontological or ethical determination. And so Laruelle takes up this descriptive task in a number of books, but it is perhaps most clearly laid out in *Philosophie et non-philosophie*, where we find six descriptions of the Real-One, expertly summarised by Ray Brassier in the following way:

1. The [R]eal is phenomenon-in-itself, the phenomenon as *already-*given or given-*without*-givenness, rather than constituted as given via the transcendental synthesis of empirical and a priori, given and givenness.

2. The [R]eal is the phenomenon as *already*-manifest or manifest-*without*-manifestation, the phenomenon-without-phenomenality, rather than the phenomenon which is posited and presupposed as manifest in accordance with the transcendental synthesis of manifest and manifestation.

3. The [R]eal is that in and through which we have been *already-*gripped rather than any originary factum or datum by which we suppose ourselves to be gripped.

4. The [R]eal is *already*-acquired prior to all cognitive or intuitive acquisition, rather than that which is merely posited and presupposed as acquired through the a priori forms of cognition and intuition.

5. The [R]eal is *already*-inherent prior to all the substantialist forcings of inherence, conditioning all those supposedly inherent models of identity, be they analytic, synthetic, or differential.

6. The [R]eal is *already*-undivided rather than the transcendent unity which is posited and presupposed as undivided and deployed in order to effect the transcendental synthesis of the empirical and the metaphysical.[13]

These six axiomatic descriptions are referred to by Laruelle in *Philosophie et non-philosophie* as an axiomatic matrix concerning the Real-One. The One, a name taken from philosophy but ultimately forgotten by it in favour of Being and Alterity, becomes a privileged name for the Real in non-philosophy because it is beyond Being and Alterity. It refuses to split and is at the root of other words that name radical immanence. Keep in mind that in French the One is *l'Un* and that this definite *Un* is as the indefinite article of those other words that bear witness to the radical immanence of the lived, meaning here the 'lived-without-life' or the actuality of the lived without the transcendental guarantee of life: *une vie* or *une vécue* without *la vie*. There is something important to the syntax of non-philosophy operative within the French language here and this operation is difficult to translate into English. Life is determined by the lived, and it is only from the perspective of a transcendental understanding of life that the lived is another thing. Thus, within non-philosophy it is the indeterminate that is primary. Not the indeterminate as what is sometimes referred to pejoratively as 'postmodern flux', but the indeterminate as that which escapes any determination; that which remains relatively autonomous and equal before the Real. It is the indeterminate of the '*un/e*' carried in French as the indefinite article. Thus, there is a certain similarity between Deleuze's focus on *a* life (*une vie*) as the name for immanence in his last essay and Laruelle's obsession with the philo-fiction of the One. That is, Laruelle's particular conception of immanence is as radical immanence. Radical immanence refers to the practical actuality of immanence: rather than its metaphysical character as a plane, an objective, or a proclamation, immanence is a 'manner of thinking'.[14] Immanence is thus always singular; it is always prior to any determination by transcendence; transcendence is never transcendent to immanence, but always determined-in-the-last-instance by immanence.

The One then comes to be the site where non-philosophy develops its principles of style; where it experiments with thinking from the Real, or looking at its material from the vision-in-One. And so to understand non-philosophy's One is largely to understand formally the practice of non-philosophy. To begin with, since the Real-One is foreclosed to thought it comes to be referred to also as the One-in-One. Non-philosophy clones its transcendental organon from this One-in-One.[15] Or, in other words, it clones a (non-)One which will be used as an organon of selection when applied to its material and which will operate on the philosophical resistance to the foreclosed nature of the Real, formalised as non(-One). The dualism, as a thought, is in a unilateral causal relationship with the One where one aspect of the dualism, the one most often taking the place of transcendence, will correspond to a non(-One), while the other, generally taking the place of a relative philosophical immanence, will correspond to a (non-)One. The non(-One) indicates that the transcendent element of thought is a kind of negation, a hallucinatory aspect of thought that arises from the foreclosed nature of the One-Real. It is that aspect of thought that responds to the trauma of the foreclosing by negating the radical immanence of the One, reducing it to some hallucinatory transcendence of Being, Alterity, Difference, etc., but this aspect is at the same time *actually transcendent* within that philosophical occasion, but only as rooted in the radical immanence of the One.[16] The (non-)One is the suspension of negation or the negative of philosophy and thus it does correspond to those conceptions of immanence, found for example in Henry and Deleuze, that resist, in a philosophical way, the philosophical negative, but these are radicalised here so that the (non-)One indicates its mutation of the radical immanence of the One. Yet, within these philosophies the function of immanence can slip from this (non-)One to a kind of transcendental immanence as a non(-One) that resists what non-philosophy identifies and uses as relative transcendence or non-thetic transcendence. In such cases these philosophies actually split absolute immanence itself, turning it into an object that can be mapped on to the formalism Laruelle develops. But the last vestiges of philosophical transcendence (i.e. thetic or self-sufficient transcendence) have to be identified within these philosophies *of* immanence in order to create an immanental style of thought. A thought that is, in its very practice, performative of this radical immanence.

Laruelle does this by developing the various axioms of the One-Real that direct and drive non-philosophy generally and specifically in relation to science or rather as a 'unified theory of philosophy and science'. This attempt to think science and philosophy together is not hidden in his work, and is given a central place in his own history of non-philosophy as outlined in his important *Principes de la non-philosophie*. Here, he explains the periodisation he has given his own work and which is to be found in nearly every one of his books; on the page typically reserved for 'Books by the Same Author' you will find a division of his 21 books into categories labelled 'Philosophy I' to 'Philosophy V'. Recently, he claimed that he had 'finally understood the principle of this endless classification; they are not movements or stages, perhaps they are phases, but most certainly they are waves, nothing other than waves, it is always the same form with slightly different water each time'.[17] I have discussed at length Laruelle's own presentation of this history, but the general shape of these different waves in relation to the axiomatics of the One can be summed up here.[18]

The general aim of non-philosophy is to think a transcendental realism that fosters a certain equality among objects and discursive materials. Non-philosophy posits a Real that is foreclosed to philosophical thought, meaning that philosophy does not have any effect on the Real; the Real is radically autonomous from thought, but thought, as ultimately Real in-the-last-instance, also contains a certain relative autonomy and so any particular expression of thought can be taken as a simple material for an occasional theory. Occasional in this sense refers to the lack of self-sufficiency in those theories, a positive lack that protects against philosophical illusions of correlation with the Real. Laruelle's early work, which includes the books listed under the heading of Philosophy I, was undertaken in large part as that of a standard philosopher writing works on the history of philosophy, political philosophy and deconstruction. Philosophy II marks his break with what he calls the 'principle of sufficient philosophy' after he comes to recognise an invariant structure to philosophy that limits thought by taking philosophy as, in some sense, unlimited. In this period Laruelle aims to break this sufficiency by way of a confrontation between philosophy and science, and during this period there is a simple reversal and overturning of the dominant hierarchy between philosophy and science as identified by Laruelle. Thus Philosophy II was founded on two complementary axioms: '1) The One is vision immanent in-One. 2) There is a special affinity between the vision-in-One and the phenomenal experience of "scientific thought".'[19]

In the period under the heading of Philosophy III, Laruelle moves beyond a mere reversal of this hierarchy, making actual the declaration of peace to the philosophers at which he had hinted in the previous period by way of his conception of a unified theory of philosophy and science. This theory was unified, rather than a unity, because of the general philo-fiction structure (rather than metaphysics or metaphilosophy) that theorised both discursive practices as relative before the Real. So axiomatically Philosophy III begins with the suspension of this second axiom of Philosophy II in order to begin thinking from the radical autonomy of the Real – not as a reversal of Philosophy II's valorisation of science, but in order to free the Real from all authority, even that of science.

In Philosophy IV, Laruelle deploys this unified theory in a

number of investigations of other non philosophical material (in the sense that they lie outside of 'philosophy proper', hence my leaving out the hyphen), returning to questions about politics and turning for the first time to a serious investigation of religion, thereby deepening his concepts, like heresy, and elements of style that he had lifted from various religious traditions and which were already operative in his earlier works. What, though, is the change in axiom here? Does the change from Philosophy III to Philosophy IV constitute a change in axiom in the same way that Philosophy II changed to Philosophy III? The answer to this question may be found in the text *La Lutte et l'Utopie à la fin des temps philosophiques* where he again turns to the axioms that allow non-philosophy to function. Here they take a slightly modified form. To be more precise, they are modified in that they are now more generalised: '1. the Real is radically immanent; 2. its causality is unilaterality or Determination-in-the-last-instance; 3. the object of that causality is the thought-World, more exactly philosophy complicated by experience.'[20] For Laruelle, the World and philosophy are one and the same; the World is the form of philosophy. Whereas the move from Philosophy II to III was effectuated by the suspension of the axiom of science's privileged relationship to the Real, Philosophy IV begins with the intensification of attention given to the *complication* of philosophy in experience. That is, Philosophy IV is concerned with what might be traditionally called philosophical problems, but because philosophy's attention, for Laruelle, is always distracted (that is, philosophical problems are always a mirror for philosophy to gaze back upon itself), here these problems are the complication of philosophy in the experience of the lived human. This experience resists carving up human experience, including in the realm of thought where the conditions for human thought are separated into something empirical (for example, a living human brain with adequate material support, including nutrition and the material conditions of a society that allows for such thought), and the traditional transcendental conditions that post-Kantian philosophy has attended to. Instead of complicating experience by philosophy, start from the axiom that human experience is real and one and complicates philosophy. This is an axiom, ultimately, concerned with the human (itself always an indefinite name that lacks any transcendent meaning) as radical immanence, the human as one equivalent to the One-Real amongst an infinite range of equivalences.

Finally, the practice of non-philosophy, Laruelle claims, is accomplished at its fullest in Philosophy V with *Philosophie non-standard*. Philosophy V's main axiom is ultimately a corollary to the third axiom of Philosophy IV, the one which stated that its material is philosophy complicated by experience. First, a mutation of the third axiom, where the 'complication' is philosophy 'being introduced' to some other regional knowledge (like Gnosticism or science). The corollary axiom may perhaps, following this mutation, be rendered something like this, the object of the causality of determination-in-the-last-instance, the thought-World (philosophy complicated by experience), may be mutated into a different form, a generic (i.e. non-universal) truth or utopia. In this way the hallucinatory transcendence of the thought-World is reduced to a symptom and when known in this immanent way is productive of generic truth.[21] This thought-World, that is 'Philosophy', ultimately comes to be 'marginalised' in the name of this generic truth. So standard philosophy is understood by Laruelle as 'a method that is productive of "thought" and certain effects which accompany it, but it has that fate of wanting to give a specific image of the Real, like the positive sciences'.[22] By mutating, in this work, standard philosophical practice through the specific scientific material of quantum physics, Laruelle creates a non-standard philosophy that is

> precisely not constructed 'in the margins' of the philosophical model; it is rather that model which systematically cultivates the margin or even the marginality, whereas the generic is, if we can put it thus, the margin as something somewhat 'turned around' [*retournée*] or rather *turned-toward* philosophy; a space of welcome and intelligibility for philosophy itself.[23]

In other words, non-standard philosophy uses material from science alongside the productive powers of philosophy to produce generic spaces that reject marginality, hierarchy, and all other forms of transcendent judgement used against the human as Real.

The Division of Labour Imposed Upon Science

Thus far I have discussed the function of the One as being prior to philosophical determinations and thus lying outside of philosophy's general decisional structure. This status creates a relationship of equivalence between the operative terms most fundamentally at work within philosophy; namely, transcendence and immanence. I then examined the non-philosophical One by looking at the changing axiomatic description found in Laruelle's work and how this axiomatic structure organises non-philosophy's constructive projects. In these final sections, I will look more directly at the way this intra-philosophical debate concerning transcendence and immanence over-determines standard philosophy's relationship to science (philosophy *of* science) and then how, once this is disempowered through a simple identification and naming, non-philosophy is able to think immanently with science without falling into the philosophical trap of scientism.

A basic theme running throughout Laruelle's work is that philosophy only ever sees itself in a grounding role for science; as a philosophy of science that tends to make *thinking* about *thinking philosophically*, about its own philosophical practice. Thus epistemology is philosophy's philosophy of science in those forms of philosophy that are not even explicitly about science as such, because they place themselves in a position to speak for science, to *think for it* since science does not think. We will see that this is true if we return to Badiou and Deleuze, who, in addition to their debate concerning the one and the multiple, share an attempt to construct a more fruitful relationship between the sciences and philosophy. And though this is somewhat rare in twentieth-century Continental philosophy, in both thinkers there is still an unequal division of labour. For Badiou may think that mathematics is ontology, but he regards other forms of science as non-thinking and even as pretenders to the name of science. He thus sets up a hierarchy within science, where some particular science, mathematics, is said to attain the status of *thought* but others do not: 'physics provides no bulwark against spiritualist (which is to say obscurantist) speculation, and biology – *that wild empiricism disguised as science* – even less so. *Only* in mathematics can one unequivocally maintain that if thought can formulate a problem, it can and it will solve it.'[24]

We find in Deleuze's philosophy a marked difference. Whereas Badiou's philosophy is always a quadruple object, split four ways between the domains of science (mathematics), art, love and politics, Deleuze's is an agonistic plane of immanence without these strict demarcations. Badiou understands philosophy necessarily to think Being mathematically in a way that erases Nature, thus undercutting the status of the natural sciences. But Deleuze hews a bit closer to the 'wild empiricism of biology', accepting that is not merely *masquerading* as a science but actually *is* one. For Deleuze, in fact, that judgement is not for the philosopher to make, but he makes this decision (though it is somewhat egalitarian) on philosophical grounds separate from the science itself. Iain Hamilton Grant has traced how this exclusive disjunction between animal and number has dominated philosophical debates concerning the metaphysics of nature and ultimately how this distinction between pure formalism and organicism provides 'the alibi . . . for the preservation of the "ancient (Greek) division of philosophy into physics and ethics".'[25] For Grant, following Schelling and Deleuze, what is needed is a 'physics of the All'. As we have seen this is, ultimately, Deleuze's philosophical problem: how to think the All, both what is formal and what is organic, which is called in his philosophy the plane of immanence.[26] But ultimately this plane of immanence is given the first name of 'chaos' and chaos is the common milieu that science, logic, art and philosophy deal with each in their own way. Deleuze and Guattari define chaos as that which makes chaotic, undoing every consistency in the infinite, rather than as an inert or stationary space.[27] In other words, chaos is not simply some 'thing', but an infinite process that, in some way, differs fundamentally from the way we think. Thus, unlike Badiou (as well as Badiou's great enemy, Heidegger), Deleuze allows for different forms of thought in response to this experience of chaos. In other words, for Deleuze and Guattari, the division of labour is more horizontal than it is in Badiou. So, within each domain there is located some essential practice that constitutes its response to chaos. Yet, this sense of essentialism is presented by Deleuze in a way that is ultimately inconsistent with other, wilder aspects of his and Guattari's philosophy. For *What Is Philosophy?* is a book that proposes to provide a kind of metaphilosophy, as well as a philosophy of science and a philosophy of art within that metaphilosophy. Yet, that theory, despite its basis in an agonistic plane of immanence, is ultimately presented as one of limits. For the book spends most of its time discussing the barriers between philosophy and science (as well as philosophy and art), such that, when a discussion of the interaction between the two is finally offered, there is only the suggestion of a wider theory to explain that interaction. Thus, they claim that the lines of philosophy and science are 'inseparable but independent, each complete in itself', going on to say that if they are 'inseparable it is in their respective sufficiency'.[28] Here science is found to be productive of thought, but there is no user-manual for that productive activity. A more productive theory that would allow for a more intentional engagement with science and philosophy is lacking.

Axioms of the One and the Posture of Science

What we find in Laruelle is a very different form of thought precisely because of its coming from the One. His thought, as has been said before, aims to break out of the circle of self-sufficiency endemic to philosophy in order to form unified theories of thought that move outside of standard philosophy. Yet that difference is to be found in the way it fills out the practices of figures like Badiou and Deleuze and Guattari. In this way, Laruelle's non-philosophy incorporates elements of the division of labour found in both Badiou and Deleuze. Laruelle valorises science in a similar way to Badiou's raising of mathematics to ontology, but he generalises that in a non-hierarchical way to include a general posture of science rather than the conclusions of a single scientific practice. From Badiou then, there is this deep connection with the sciences that is theorised within the very practice of his thought. While Laruelle also presents a theory of science that focuses on its productive element like Deleuze and Guattari, this theory of the production of thought is given within a wider development of its lived production. This element keeps non-philosophy from falling back on a certain spontaneity of the Event or *eventus ex machina* that we find in both Badiou and Deleuze and Guattari. But, along with Deleuze, Laruelle thinks from immanence, but no longer as chaos, for in non-philosophy immanence is the radically lived, the Real itself, and thus must be thought *from*. Laruelle, in short, is able to break from the weaknesses of these thinkers and push forward their more radical elements.

In *Théorie des identités*, the work that marks the end of Philosophy II before the transition to Philosophy III, Laruelle performs what he claims philosophers have not – a transcendental, 'which is to say rigorously immanent', description of the essence of science, one which is, as non-philosophy, non-epistemological.[29] Laruelle marks a path unlike any other, seemingly avoiding the problems inherent in scientistic philosophies (that, ironically, are akin in many ways to Christian philosophy in their practice and obsession with teleology, albeit in a negative mode) and the anti-scientific discourses that are more common in Continental philosophy. This is because Laruelle grants science its autonomy by radicalising a certain strand of philosophy that claims 'ethics as first philosophy', and thereby recognises science as philosophy's Other. Laruelle claims, though, that philosophy is *unable* to accept science as its Other, wishing instead to reassert its own identity by treating science with the same philosophical structure of division that it treats everything else that it deems philosophisable. This means that it must rend science apart, separating out a brute factual and transcendent existence (the mixed philosophical identity of science) and the practice of objectivity, which is philosophy's denial of the realist character of science.[30] In Laruelle's mutation of Levinas' ethics of the Other to the abstract level, where the demand is made of philosophy that it recognise science as its Other and acknowledge the autonomy of science, he thereby makes philosophy the hostage (in the Levinasian sense) of the sciences. Philosophy must submit to science here: 'Our hypothesis takes the postural or "subjective" realism of science for a transcendental guide or rule of its immanent theory.'[31] This is a certain abstract openness to the Other; one that attempts to move from the closed and circular vision of the philosophical to that of a non-philosophical *hypothesis* which opens up a *possibility* within philosophy to think alongside its Other, science. This being the case, philosophy must understand science from the position of science; its hypothesis must be one of a certain abstract empathy.

> It is the scientific attitude that consists in entrusting to science itself the elucidation of its essence; entrusting to science the recognition all the way through of its radicality and deriving all the consequences of its autonomy: science is for itself, at least in its cause – the Identity-of-the-last-instance – an emergent theoretical object, a 'hypothesis', or an 'axiom' in the 'hypothetico-deductive' sense.[32]

His critique here is ethical (again ventriloquising Levinas and putting that philosophy to another use); it is a certain recognition that science and philosophy cannot be reconciled in a synthesis, but that philosophy's crimes against science must be recognised and understood. Science becomes both the internal enemy of philosophy, threatening meaning, and that which philosophy strives for as a seemingly apodictic knowledge: 'Our experience of science is at the same time marked by a devalorisation (as devoid of meaning and absolute truth) and overvalorisation (as factuality and efficacy) which are characterised by its philosophical and "cultural" interpretation.'[33] This image of science arises out of an alienating structure of intellectual labour, a division of intellectual labour into three parts. First, the philosopher admits that science produces knowledge as understanding. In French, there are two words that can be translated into English as knowledge: *connaissance* and *savoir*. Science is said by Heidegger and a host of other post-Kantian philosophers to produce knowledge of the first kind, which is, roughly speaking, a kind of 'know-how' or 'understanding'; it is deemed not to be knowledge of the essence of things; not true philosophical knowledge, but mere understanding. The second, *savoir*, is what philosophy aims at, the kind of knowledge that is sure and absolute. Knowledge (as understanding) is produced by science, but not philosophical knowledge; not philosophical *thought*. For, from Plato through Kant and up to Heidegger, the claim is that 'science does not think'. Science dreams; its dream is to think even as it produces blind knowledge. The second division rips science in two, separating the multiple empirical sciences, that produce knowledge, from 'an absolute, unique and self-founded science – first philosophy as ontology or logic'.[34] This separation is the condition for philosophy's concept of science; 'philosophy splits the concept of science after having separated understanding [*connaissance*] and thought'.[35] Finally, the third division divides up the objects proper to philosophy and science: 'To philosophy Being or the authentic and total real; to science not even beings, but the properties of beings or facts; the object of knowledge [*savoir*] is now that which is divided.'[36]

What differentiates Laruelle from post-Kantian philosophy of science and from the general post-Kantian posture toward science (including those in the Anglophone world who deploy aspects of science as philosophical arguments and positions about reality taken to be the Real), and what differentiates Laruelle from those philosophers engaging in a war over the status of science, is that he accepts the autonomy of science, he accepts that it is free in its practice from philosophical conditions. He opposes this to the tripartite division discussed above in order to show 'that every science, "empirical" or not, is also a thought; that it is absolute *in its way* [genre]; that it bears – at least "in-the-last-instance" – on the Real "itself"'.[37] To quickly summarise, in this early work

Laruelle rejects the philosophical-epistemological tripartite division of labour, which results in philosophy's invariant approach to science or its separation of the transcendental and the empirical. Rather than following some variant of this usual philosophical approach to science, which may differ in terms of what is valued in this split (but still accepts *some* form of this split), Laruelle proposes a thought experiment where philosophy is mutated. This thought experiment is, as I have said above, ethical, and demands that philosophy practise in the face of its Other (mutated from its Levinasian sense to refer to science). The essence of philosophy is to break up its object and then to take this break as constitutive of the Real, rather than localised in philosophical practice. Philosophy renders the object into a dyad, an empirico-transcendental doublet, that is always united (not unified) by some third term, whether that term be named transcendence or immanence, and follows the different paths the chosen name determines. By contrast, the posture of science, which underlies the various scientific practices, does not split its object. Even when it breaks up an object into its constituent parts, these then become new objects with identities, so each breakdown occurs under the realist thesis that the object is One-in-the-last-instance.[38] This thesis, Laruelle claims, is incomprehensible to philosophy because philosophy requires some third term; some transcendent (in its operation) unity to the object, rather than the radical immanence of the One-in-the-last-instance or One-in-One.

Laruelle especially rejects the second division within the tripartite division – the division of science into empirical and transcendental.[39] This division is the vehicle for the philosophical doublet of 'empirico-transcendental' that is maximalised by philosophy in its splitting up of the One-Real in the philosophical Decision. What Laruelle locates in science, and the reason he initially gives in to the temptation simply to reverse the post-Kantian hierarchy, is its non-decisional relationship to the One, such that science practices the vision-in-One rather than the philosophical splitting of the One into condition and conditioned; empirical and transcendental. Laruelle therefore claims that 'Every science, even "empirical" ones called such by philosophy in order to denigrate them, are in reality also "transcendental": they bear upon the Real itself and, more than that, know that it bears a relation to it there.'[40] This is, of course, and as Laruelle makes clearer in subsequent works, only a general or abstract resemblance, which he will later call generic.

Moreover, in the Real there is no separation between the empirical and the transcendental, there is no separate 'thing-in-itself' outside of the radical immanence of the Real. In Philosophy II, outlined above, Laruelle reversed the post-Kantian hierarchy of philosophy and science, raising science to the status of thought: against those philosophers who claim that 'science does not think'; science is seen here to be a thought that moves beyond itself – beyond the vicious circle of deciding upon itself – to the thought that practises vision-in-One. While the mere reversal of the hierarchy is ultimately rejected, this thought experiment is what leads Laruelle to the discovery of the vision-in-One as underlying science's practice, and as that which can modify philosophical practice. What the vision-in-One does is think *from* the One rather than *about* the One. The One is foreclosed to thought; the relationship between the One and thought goes in one direction, it is unilateral, such that thought has no effect on the One but is determined by the One. This means that any thought of the One can only be described via axioms – statements that cannot be thought directly in so far as their truth cannot be falsified, but are necessary and provisional for thinking into the future. This can be understood if one recalls Laruelle's description of science as 'hypothetico-deductive'. There is a simple reason for identifying the 'hypothetico-deductive' as science's identity: it names science as a practice, and, moreover, it names it as a heterogeneous practice. Even when a scientist stops to falsify her findings, she does so within a unified practice that *includes* falsification, rather than one that is determined by it. It is not an *ex cathedra* pronouncement by Laruelle that the One is foreclosed to thought, but rather a deduction from the way practice happens within the lived, within radical immanence.

It should be clear already that this is not a scientism. Even though, during this wave of non-philosophical practice (Philosophy II), Laruelle gives philosophy over to science in an attempt to take on the same posture found in the identity of science, this is clearly not in an attempt to speak for science, to think for science, or to present science as the only human discipline that can speak with any authority in which we human beings may trust. Even science, as a regional knowledge, is always outstripped by the One-Real; indeed this may be its immanent, if unacknowledged, practice. A certain respect for the One as infinitely effable. Rather than a scientism, non-philosophy – thinking from the One – is thought made stranger.

Notes

1. François Laruelle, *Le Principe de minorité* (Paris: Aubier, 1981), p. 111. (All translations are mine unless otherwise noted.)
2. This confrontation between the deconstructive philosopher and the non-philosopher was reproduced in the journal *La Décision philosophique* 5 (April 1988), pp. 62–7, and has been translated into English by Ray Brassier and Robin Mackay as 'Controversy Over the Possibility of a Science of Philosophy', in *The Non-Philosophy Project: Essays by François Laruelle*, edited by Gabriel Alkon and Boris Gunjevic (New York: Telos Press Publishing, 2012), pp. 75–93. Reading this confrontational exchange with the elder philosopher Derrida, whom Laruelle credits in the course of the exchange with teaching him much, the former demanding that Laruelle answer for his misbehaviour, I could not help but think of a ubiquitous anti-drugs commercial from my childhood. The commercial, preserved for the sake of nostalgia and easily found on-line, features a father confronting his teenage son with a box of drugs and demanding, 'Who taught you how to do this stuff?' The son bursts out, 'You, all right, I learned it from watching you!' Deconstruction horrified the philosophical world because it was able to tease out structures and traces that philosophy felt were better left unknown. But deconstruction is horrified when a science of philosophy claims to make it too understandable. The cracks forming between the standard deconstructors, who we now know are the guardians of philosophy's honour, were evident in an earlier confrontation between Jean-Luc Nancy and Laruelle that can be found in the appendix to Laruelle's early work *Le déclin de l'écriture* (Paris: Aubier, 1977). This work, one which Laruelle now would say comes prior to non-philosophy proper and so is purely philosophical, was published in a series edited by Nancy, Sarah Kofman, Derrida and Philippe Lacoue-Labarthe, and the appendix includes a short conversation between the four editors and Laruelle. Nancy opens the questions up in a way that is not so different from Graham Harman's own contemporary complaints: 'My question will be one of readability. First of all, from the most superficial point of view, your text is very difficult to read' (Laruelle, *Le déclin*, p. 245). *La plus ça change . . .* Laruelle's response? To affirm the difficulty as a way of escaping the philosophical tribunal: 'My response will be one of illegibility – a way of throwing back your question, displacing it: I only displace it as an interrogation, for a better position' (ibid., p. 246).

3. François Laruelle, *Future Christ: A Lesson in Heresy*, translated by Anthony Paul Smith (London and New York: Continuum, 2010), p. xxvii.

4. Nick Srnicek, 'François Laruelle, the One and the Non-Philosophical Tradition', in *Pli: The Warwick Journal of Philosophy* 22 (2010), pp. 194–5.

5. I have some minor disagreements with Srnicek's description here, but a focus on disagreements about the influence of the history of philosophy on non-philosophy is not really in the spirit of non-philosophy's productive project. That said, here I simply want to nuance the description of Being as beyond the One. This is only true in an ironic sense, where the 'beyond' is a philosophical beyond. From the perspective of the One, Being is only a quasi-transcendental and so it is only truly quasi-beyond the One.

6. Laruelle, *Le Principe de minorité*, p. 92.

7. Regarding anti-philosophy, there are certainly similarities between non-philosophy and anti-philosophy, the term coined by Lacan and developed by Badiou to describe diverse thinkers like Pascal and Wittgenstein. But only in the same sense that major critical, anti-philosophical projects like that of Jacobi or Kierkegaard are also taken as a kind of material that non-philosophy can make a usage of.

8. François Laruelle, *Philosophies of Difference: A Critical Introduction to Non-Philosophy*, translated by Rocco Gangle (London and New York: Continuum, 2010), p. xvii.

9. See the letter Deleuze wrote to Philip Goodchild and reproduced in part in Philip Goodchild, *Gilles Deleuze and the Question of Philosophy* (Madison: Fairleigh Dickinson University Press, 1996), p. 185, n. 8.

10. See the special issue of *SubStance* entitled *Spiritual Politics after Deleuze*, edited by Joshua Delpech-Ramey and Paul A. Harris, *SubStance: A Review of Theory and Literary Criticism* 39.1 (2010). Note that this 'spiritual politics' is not an anti-materialism and is shared by equally political philosophers like Adorno. The difference between Adorno and Deleuze on this score comes to choosing negative dialectics over positive univocity and as a difference it is worth exploring, but it shows that the turn to spirit is not necessarily a reactionary stance, tied to actually existing religious institutions, as some philosophers suppose.

11. I say super-rationalism, a term that Laruelle himself uses in *Le Principe de minorité*, because it uses reason to understand what lies outside of reason, the same kind of practice of philosophy that

originates powerfully in Spinoza. This is a form of rationalism that is more powerful than a kind of naive, humanist rationalism that confuses its own operations, bounded by the specific form it takes within the human subject, with the whole of Being.

12. François Laruelle, *Philosophie et non-philosophie* (Liege/Bruxelles: Pierre Mardaga, 1989), p. 37 (my emphasis).

13. Ray Brassier, *Nihil Unbound: Enlightenment and Extinction* (Basingstoke: Palgrave Macmillan, 2007), p. 128.

14. 'In philosophy, Marxism included, immanence is an objective, a proclamation, an object, never a manner of thinking or a style' (François Laruelle, *Introduction au non-marxisme* [Paris: PUF, 2000], p. 40).

15. See Erik del Bufalo, *Deleuze et Laruelle. De la schizo-analyse à la non-philosophie* (Paris: Kimé, 2003), p. 40.

16. Laruelle, *Philosophies of Difference*, pp. 198–202. See also ibid pp. 219–23 for an early formal schema of the One, as well as François Laruelle, *Dictionnare de la non-philosophie* (Paris: Kimé, 1998), pp. 202–5, and François Laruelle, *Principes de la non-philosophie* (Paris: PUF, 1996), pp. 168–92.

17. François Laruelle, personal communication, 2 May 2010. Waves and phases, in the sense these words have within physics, become important concepts in his most recent *Philosophie non-standard. Générique, Quantique, Philo-Fiction* (Paris: Kimé, 2010) Some may be wondering why these different waves are named 'Philosophy I–V' and not 'Non-Philosophy I–V'. As Laruelle makes clear throughout his work, one can't simply replace philosophy. A theory that is assumed to lie outside of philosophy all too often has the same structure, and thus the same problems, as philosophy. So taking on this name of philosophy is, to be somewhat dramatic, non-philosophy in the mode of Christ. Non-philosophy doesn't negate philosophy, but it takes on philosophy with some difference (i.e. thinking from the One) and the wager is that this difference is in some way salvific in its amplification of thought.

18. See Anthony Paul Smith, 'Philosophy and Ecosystem: Towards a Transcendental Ecology', *Polygraph* 22 (2010), pp. 65–82.

19. Laruelle, *Principes*, p. 39.

20. François Laruelle, *La Lutte et l'Utopie à la fin des temps philosophiques* (Paris: Kimé, 2004), p. 43.

21. Laruelle, *Philosophie non-standard*, p. 135.

22. Ibid., p. 137.

23. Ibid.

24. Alain Badiou, 'Mathematics and Philosophy: The Grand Style and the Little Style', in *Theoretical Writings*, edited and translated by Ray Brassier and Alberto Toscano (London and New York: Continuum, 2006), p. 17 (my emphases).

25. Iain Hamilton Grant, *Philosophies of Nature after Schelling* (London and New York: Continuum, 2006), p. 17.

26. Gilles Deleuze and Félix Guattari, *What is Philosophy?*, translated by Hugh Tomlinson and Graham Burchell (New York: Columbia University Press, 1994), pp. 33, 37.

27. Ibid., p. 42.

28. Ibid., p. 161.

29. François Laruelle, *Théorie des identités. Fractalité généralisée et philosophie artificielle* (Paris: PUF, 1992), p. 56.

30. Ibid., p. 57.

31. Ibid., p. 58.

32. Ibid. I explain the reason behind this identification below.

33. Ibid., p. 54.

34. Ibid.

35. Ibid., p. 55.

36. Ibid.

37. Ibid., p. 59.

38. Ibid., p. 60.

39. Ibid., p. 100.

40. Ibid. One must keep in mind here that transcendence, the transcendental, and the relative immanence of philosophy are all included in non-philosophy's radical immanence. And moreover that the transcendental, as an operation of thought, is not the same thing as transcendence, as a condition of thought. In his most recent works Laruelle tries to avoid this confusion by referring to the transcendental operation of thought as immanental.

2

Laruelle Facing Deleuze: Immanence, Resistance and Desire

Marjorie Gracieuse

'To meditate on the essence of Being, on the forgetting of Being is a task that has lost its sense of urgency'[1]

In this chapter, it will be a question of elucidating the main lines of divergence that separate the respective visions of Deleuze and Laruelle concerning what they both name 'immanence'. I will also identify Laruelle's conception of resistance and explore the lineaments of Laruelle's critique of Deleuze's micropolitics. This will enable me to shed light on the reasons that have led Laruelle to distinguish his trajectory from that of Deleuze, but also to show why Deleuze has, on the contrary, attempted to assimilate Laruelle's non-philosophy to a philosophy of 'pure immanence', whose main goal consists in wresting the vital potentialities of humans from the artificial forms and static norms that subjugate them.

The Rediscovery of Immanence and the Neutralisation of Transcendence

In contemporary French philosophy, Laruelle and Deleuze stand out as the two thinkers who have invoked immanence in the most obstinate way, presenting it as a material realm that can be explored and must be protected from belief in autonomous and transcendent orders of reality and truth. For these two thinkers, transcendence constitutes the most detrimental yet entrenched 'transcendental illusion' of traditional philosophy. If faith in transcendence is seen as the source of all alienation, it is in so far as it introduces artificial yet effective divisions between humans and their productive forces, enslaving practices to established orders and preventing beings from fully realising their immanent power of singular and collective transformation. When it is caught up in the belief in transcendence and supra-signifiers, philosophy becomes abstract hermeneutics, that is, a self-centred doctrine that privileges interpretation over experimentation and despises humans' intrinsic potentialities in favour of obscure principles of explanation such as the Unconscious, Being, Power, etc. Moreover, when appealing to forms of transcendence, philosophy tends to become a rigid system of judgement. Beings are judged by philosophy according to positivist and non-human criteria and philosophy overlooks humanity's unpredictability and richness. This is why both Deleuze and Laruelle seek to neutralise transcendence, conceiving the latter as an abstraction, an illusion which is produced in thought when the logos negates the material and ever-new moving realm from which it emerges and to which it belongs, namely the living – and not simply organic – matter or 'immanence'.

However, Laruelle's and Deleuze's common struggle against transcendence should not prevent us from appreciating their radical divergence when it comes to their account of what they both call 'immanence'. Whereas Deleuze presents immanence as a vital force or matter-energy that is not reducible to the finitude of human materiality but is said of being itself as 'non-organic life', Laruelle refuses to apprehend immanence as an ontological infinite or vitalist absolute. Rather, the non-philosopher speaks of a finite immanence, which merges with humans as generic humanity and with the solitude of each human being, as immediately given and non-exchangeable individuality. What non-philosophy calls 'the One-in-One', 'the Real' or *radical* immanence' does not refer to life as ontological principle, but simply designates the living identity of Man-in-person, both singular and generic, whose flesh and blood are unthinkable through the speculative and logical categories of philosophical thinking. As a consequence, to the Deleuzian ontology of generative difference, Laruelle opposes the radical primacy of individuals' singular identity, as first and ultimate flesh that forever remains hermetic to, and not affected by, philosophy's various modes of idealisation of matter. Whereas Deleuze privileges the pre-individual singularities of a life as the 'superior form of all that is', Laruelle thinks the individual as the sole real origin of all multiplicity, as 'One-without-Being' or 'minority principle', next to which any philosophical syntheses, divisions and deconstructions look like sterile and artificial forms of authority.

One can see that, if Deleuze practises a form of 'metaphysical entryism', believing in the possibility of creating new modes of existence by getting out of philosophy by philosophy, Laruelle refuses either to enter philosophy's speculative and specular circles as well or to adopt a prescriptive standpoint with respect to the Real or Man. In many of his books, Laruelle has ceaselessly criticised the implicit Deleuzian way of conserving a hierarchical approach toward regimes of thought. This way of thinking, which privileges a differential and ideal principle over the real experience of lived identity, fails to introduce democracy in thought and to account for the generic and idempotent essence of humanity.

In fact, Laruelle rejects the Deleuzian ethical distinction, of Spinozist origin, between an ethics of potency (*puissance*) and a morality of Power (*pouvoir*) as much as the Nietzschean injunction of human self-overcoming. For non-philosophy, the human does not have to be overcome; neither does he have to move from a 'moral vision of the world' toward an ethical existence of life's immanent intensification. Rather, human kind needs to be protected against the authoritarian conceptions of man and of the world, into which philosophy continues to lock it, even when it becomes, as with Deleuze, an 'ethology' or a 'micropolitics' of life. Thus, Laruelle does not limit himself to arguing that philosophy is always philosophy of power and that power is of philosophical essence; he also identifies philosophy with the very form of transcendence itself, presenting it as a conservative and totalising thought that lives at the expense of the One, appropriating the One's effects to make the latter serve its own utilitarian ends. What Marx used to say of the bourgeoisie is now applied by Laruelle to any type of philosophy: the latter prospers by dividing a classless and generic humanity into classified subjects and objects, with the help of transcendent principles by which it codifies practices, deploys its reign over humans and maintains its self-sufficiency. Philosophy is characterised by its excessive use of the form of infinite dyads or mixtures (i.e. Being and becoming, the One and the Multiple, etc.) which leads it to combine abstract contraries through a series of contingent 'decisions', each time ignoring or negating the human's non-decidable and inalienable essence. As institutional and cultural discipline, philosophy remains dominated by a 'spirit of hierarchy', which prevents it from thinking the radical alterity of the Real as Man-in-person and the antecedence of lived identity over any type of difference. Laruelle's problem is thus to 'de-potentialise' or disempower philosophy's self-sufficiency and authoritative arguments, in order to turn it into a means of safeguarding humanity. It is philosophy that must serve the human, and not the reverse: hence Laruelle's desire to introduce democracy in thought and among human practices, as a way to neutralise the abstract hierarchies and the spontaneous idealism that govern philosophy's approach of reality and that codify the Real that we are into rigid and incomprehensible schemes of organisation.

Laruelle's Critique of Differential Immanence: The One-Without-All

According to non-philosophy, philosophers of difference such as Nietzsche and Deleuze have been deluding themselves. By deploying a materialism of forces at all levels, positing the ontological primacy of pure relations, they diluted the identity of beings in an ontologically pure becoming and rendered 'the real genesis of ideality and of its forms impossible'.[2] This culmination of idealist contemplation, first performed by the Nietzschean identification of being and becoming, is found repeated by Deleuze and Guattari when they define immanence as 'unlimited One-All' or '*omnitudo realitatis*', positing the reversibility of being and thinking in an encompassing gesture that identifies the philosophical logos with the Real itself.

Indeed, for Deleuze, immanence immediately enjoys an ontological, absolute nature: it designates the infinite recurrence of the differential becoming of life in all beings. The latter are the multiple singularisations (i.e. 'multiplicities') of a life that is immediately present to all, as virtual power of differentiation, renewal and resistance. Such is the reason why Deleuze speaks of a 'One-All' to qualify the plane of life as plane of matter and plane of thought. This formula is the translation of the Greek expression '*Hen-Panta*', which does not mean the unity of the whole (it is not a numerical totality) but the unity of all beings, a unity that can only be said of the immanent and living relations that unite multiplicities and by which they compose, by their thoughts and actions, an ever-new and common plan of being. With Deleuze, therefore, the old Platonic 'second principle' of the indefinite dyad, which first defined a passive materiality informed by an active One or Monad, finds itself deprived of any unitary transcendent principle and become active by itself. The formula of Deleuzian multiplicities is 'n-1', that is to say that the sole unity Deleuze acknowledges is that of life or being as 'strange unity that can only be said of the multiple'. It is the unity of vital and multiple differences, of living individualities that are never fully individuated or actualised, but remain inseparable from a virtual reserve, a universal becoming which dispossesses them of any foundational or intrinsic identity.

Moreover, philosophy, for Deleuze, is an art of multiplicities and an ethics of events. It entails 'becoming equal' to a life that is often greater than us, by extracting, from the lived actuality of bodily existence, the incorporeal and virtual 'events of life'. There is, in Deleuze's thought, an ethical injunction to detach oneself from bodily mixtures and reach the subtlest degrees of matter, as the ideal signs of the universal presence of an impersonal and powerful non-organic life. This reintroduces a prescriptive stance at the heart of immanence, namely a 'becoming-equal to the event', a 'becoming-infinite of thought', which precisely makes all the hierarchical difference between an ordinary existence and a philosophical life. By becoming infinitely philosophical, thought learns to take the events of life onto itself, reaches a higher power and a more intense existence by extracting the important, the remarkable, the 'eternal truth of the event' from the ordinariness of everyday banality, and by this, each existent can learn to actually overcome one's structural, organic stupidity (*bêtise*).

Contrary to Deleuze, Laruelle refuses to speak of immanence as an absolute plane of life to which the human would belong as a mode of life, for this way of accounting for the essence of the human remains committed to a metaphysical standpoint from which emerges an intensive hierarchy of modes of existence. The problem of a hierarchy of forces, thematised by Nietzsche and explored further by Deleuze, supposes to think human individuality as a complex of forces in relations of tensions with one another, and to make of 'hierarchy' or 'difference' the motor of thought, the philosophical operation by which an individual becomes more and more capable of elevating himself to higher planes of perception. This is even clearer when it comes to Deleuze's account of individuality: the living body is the site of a struggle between an organisation of bodily forces by a representational consciousness and a disorganisation of perception by way of the dissolving ground of the body. This supposes a perpetual 'combat between oneself', by which one learns to 'become the master of one's speeds' and escape the organicity of a purely material body. In

Difference and Repetition, Deleuze argues that only the 'abstract thinker of the eternal return' can be considered as the 'universal individual', for he only becomes equal to life by losing his identity and affirming the eternal repetition of the forces of difference in thought and in existence.

For Laruelle, the Deleuzian theory of the superior form of individuality through the figure of the thinker of the eternal return is nothing but a new way of presupposing that humans need philosophy to live more intensely. In fact, by promoting life as non-human principle and superior form of all that is, Deleuze conserves the presupposition of philosophy's self-sufficiency and confuses the necessary critique of humanism with a contemptuous approach to ordinary human existence: 'once again under the mitigated form of unlimited becoming, we find here the distinction between man and philosopher, their hierarchy despite it all. The philosopher who constructs the system and the idiot to which he refers and who certainly stumbles over the detours of the system, are no longer adequately distinguished. Once again the philosopher does not truly want stupidity, he limits it.'[3] This is the reason why Deleuzian immanence is just a partial and relative immanence for Laruelle, whose full experimentation remains reserved for the 'initiated' (i.e. the clan of philosophers). Once again, the ordinary man finds himself marginalised and expelled by philosophy's self-enjoyment and self-sufficiency. The philosophical indifference to the Real is reinforced, and becomes even more apparent when it comes to analysing the political consequences of Deleuze's philosophy. According to Laruelle, Deleuze's thought would be a thought of 'what is happening between democracy and aristocracy', which is another way of saying that the Nietzschean thinker of immanence conserves, like all philosophers, the privilege of philosophers over ordinary men, by glorifying the 'superior' decision to overcome the humanity in man toward a non-human life and an impersonal politics of pure forces and capacities: 'the essence of philosophy achieved as becoming is therefore certainly not "democracy" – it seems to us in every sense of the word, and not only in the sense of liberal democracy or the ethics of the Other man'.[4]

Besides, hierarchy or difference is not only the motor of Deleuze's philosophy but also appears in his own conception of 'ontology' as an ontology of unequal forces or modal powers of one single life. From the Deleuzian ontological perspective, life is indeed a non-human hyletic continuum that traverses all beings and cancels their self-identity. However, if all beings are ontologically equal from the point of view of their vital and virtual essence, an equivocity of beings is reintroduced at the level of the actualisation of life, one that allows for a hierarchy of modes of existence and of the various planes of immanence as planes of thought. Indeed, if life is pure or absolute immanence and the intensive matter of all that becomes, it is never fully embraced by the multiplicities of planes of thought that attempt to think it.[5] Such is the reason why each philosopher selects certain movements of this infinite life, so much that thinkers differ by their ways of 'making immanence'. The universal plane of life is for Deleuze 'folded' into a multiplicity of planes of immanence; they are regimes or planes of perception that imply very distinct ways of feeling, thinking, perceiving and evaluating. Thus, Deleuze's philosophy of immanence does not abandon the project of selection or hierarchisation of modes of thought but consists in interrogating the capacity of each philosophical perspective to affirm and intensify life.[6] This scaffolding of planes of thought, Laruelle argues, 'masks the Nietzschean spirit of hierarchy; the auto-position of the concept as surface or absolute volume; the stratigraphic piling of the layers of the plane; all the forms which suppose the fold'.[7]

This is why, particularly in his early works, Laruelle has ceaselessly denounced the circle of difference and repetition, as a philosophical 'game of ink and paper' which reinforces the forgetting of the essence of the One and alienates the human to the ontological game of being and becoming. The decision, at the roots of Deleuze's thought, to privilege difference over identity is denounced by Laruelle as being a contingent decision which denies the real cut and foreclosing of the One to thought. Deleuze remains bound up within a thought of decision, attempting to think the ontological and hierarchical difference between life and the living, continuing to onto-logicise the Real by measuring the greatness of the latter by its immanent capacity to intensify life 'more or less'.

In order to abandon any type of ontological difference or decisional posture, Laruelle argues, against his predecessors, for the *non-ontological* nature of the One:

> the One's radical autonomy, its real indifference with regard to being and to thought . . . invalidates a fundamental thesis of ontology: that of the convertibility between the One and being . . . It also limits the

putatively primary pertinence of the thesis of another convertibility: that of the ontological difference between being and beings.[8]

Thus, Laruelle seeks to think the One outside of its convertibility with Being. It is a question of thinking a One that is deprived of any fold, which is immediately given, radically open and forever unfoldable. By confusing the logic of sense with that of Being, Deleuze would have overlooked the human non-thinkable essence and its foreclosure to Being. The Deleuzian plane of immanence, as 'absolute survey', is thus an idealisation of the chaotic becomings of materiality for Laruelle, it is

> position and transcendence: their pairing is the passage or becoming of the between-two . . . the plane is the continuous passage to self, thus survey or overposition. Not of transcendence in immanence, undoubtedly, at least in Husserl's sense, but their co-intension, that which happens between the one and the other. Consequently, the One is always Other and identity always marginal.[9]

A One Not Alienated in Becoming: The Dispersive Matter of the Real

To the Deleuzian reversibility between thought and being, Laruelle opposes the radical irreversibility of the order of the One, which denies any kind of reciprocal determination between thought and the Real or between the Real and the world. The Laruellean One-Real is a lived immanence, a transcendental and internal experience of identity that always already precedes the logical identity of the logos and the empirical feeling of difference and becoming. It is simply human and generic, that is, a non-ontological matter whose positive identity cannot be confused with the ideal self-position or differential repetition of life in the living and the lived. Identity will be now defined 'as the flesh of the One rather than as the remainder of a gesture of abstraction'.[10] The Deleuzian One, on the contrary, is always the index of an impersonal life that always exceeds the life lived by an individual. Immanence as *a* life or as 'singular essence' is essentially non-human for it is populated by the differential virtualities of life. Immanence is both '*Homo tantum*'[11] and '*Eventum tantum*', obeying the dyadic mixture of singular and universal and whose infinite movement continuously dissolves any identity and reduces the human to a form of life amongst others, a contingent crystallisation of living matter. The Laruellean non-ontological One, as One-in-One or One-without-All, neither includes nor requires any ideal disjunctive synthesis or active reprise, but on the contrary is non-problematic. It is the sole *real cut* (*divisio realis*) between the One and 'Being', it is a One-without-Being to which philosophical thought has no access and that it cannot reduce to a modal differentiation of a differential life. This internal difference, this line of demarcation between the One and all types of idealities is itself produced by the One internally, who is the unique and true differentiator of difference: 'it is the determined, the real as matter-without-determination, that makes the determination'.[12] Contra the unifying vision of differential philosophy, which gives way to dispersed experience and sensory fragmentation, Laruelle discloses the One as material dispersivity and its absolute precedence over ideal interpretations and the horizontality of appearance that presupposes a totalising plane of perception. The One is the uninterpretable from which all interpretations emerge, and which never reaches consciousness or vanishes when it becomes an ideal 'plane'. It is strictly human and does not need to presuppose a transcendent principle such as life or difference to think. The 'dark thought of the One', Laruelle says, does not need any mirror and is not a plane of absolute survey, for it is capable of enlightening itself from within and by its own means.

However, despite the imperturbable critique Laruelle has continued to address to philosophy as a whole and to Deleuze in particular, one cannot help grasping a disruptive resonance between the two thinkers of immanence. This theoretical echo risks going unheard as long as one does not read Laruelle and Deleuze as being, first and foremost, the creative explorers of corporeal immanence, for which they have created a multitude of concepts capable of helping to shed new light on what it means to be human. Indeed for both thinkers, the living body is 'the Real in person' and the genetic base of a force of thought, which can never be reduced to its logical, artificial effects of sense. Beneath Laruelle's creative syntax and Deleuze's conceptual constructivism, one must retrieve the presentational immediacy of an ever resisting instance, an 'immediately given multiplicity', which is not the result of an operation of division and thus has always represented the most persistent disruption of philosophical logocentrism.

This force of resistance (Deleuze) or this force of vision (Laruelle) is above all the living body considered in its darkest materiality, that is, as the 'imperceptible of all perception', the 'unreflected One' into which philosophical thought must plunge or be introduced, if it is to renew itself and transform its vision of reality. Perhaps it is useful to come back to the materiality of the body, as that which produces thought without getting out of itself. Thought distinguishes itself from the body, but in the last instance the latter does not distinguish itself from the former. Such is the reason why the body as One is the real essence of thought, it is a heretical force of vision whose drives escape the ideal codifications of philosophy and the technical structure of what is called the world:

> Which body? That which is defined by the lived experience of an undivided identity or of a radical immanence: not alienating subject, nor an object alien to instrumentation. This immanent, undivided body, unshareable, cannot, then be subjected to the recurrence of teleological circuitry, and neither is it affected by technical causality and is not a 'subjective piece' of a machine or a greater system . . . Hence the immanent body is really a 'return' or a 'transcendence' (though undivided), i.e. difference. It is, then, a drive that we will call non-positional (of) itself. The body acts on the world without leaving it; without miming the type of efficacy of the world itself, without identifying itself with the world as all technical philosophies do. This type of causality signifies that the cause remains in itself, does not alienate itself in the object 'upon' which it acts, or in the instrument it uses.[13]

If the undividable body is indeed for Laruelle the Real in person, it is not simply a 'body without organs', but a non-objectivising vision, a worldless identity within which Laruelle's thought dwells and from which it refuses to get out. This is why non-philosophy is above all a 'vision-in-One' that apprehends the humanity of Man as an open, unfolded intimacy, as a secret that is so immediately obvious that it can but only escape the abstract mediations of philosophical logic: 'the essence of the secret knows nothing of the play of veiling and unveiling, of the structure of difference in general. It is the One, understood in an absolutely immanent and finite way: it excludes the play of Being and play in general.'[14] The secret is ordinary humanity, inalienable in a hierarchy of planes of thought or existence. It is a truth that does not need meaning or interpretation, even if the latter always need truth, as their radical prerequisite without which they would not even emerge. It is an undivided body, deprived of scission and the real a priori and essence of ideality.

To the philosophy of difference, Laruelle opposes the 'dual' thought of the One, in order to give up the philosophical illusion according to which language would be co-constitutive of the Real. Instead of bringing about some mixture, as in the dyad of the ontologically infinite in the 'super-All' of an unlimited becoming, one must conceive the One as one-sided, as a One that is always already withdrawn from Being or from the World, the latter being just contingent idealities which are capable of being transformed immanently. The One is radically independent from the dyad, even though the latter is derived from it as immanent 'secretion' or 'non-thetic' transcendence. The vision-in-One is therefore not a differential vision-in-the-Other: the Other is not the immanent content of the One, but just the symptom of a non-positional and non-reflexive alterity. Non-thetic transcendence, if it distinguishes itself from the one and constitutes the radically contingent basis of 'philosophical decision', is nonetheless an effect produced by the One whose indivisibility is immediately given to itself.

The Radical Resistance of the One Against the Imperium of Philosophical Desire

With non-philosophy, and contra the philosophical ontological 'rumour' and the privilege Deleuze seemed to grant to 'surfaces', it is now a question of getting attuned to the 'transcendental noise of the depth' ('*bruit de fond transcendantal*'),[15] and reaching a purely immanent standpoint that no longer differentiates between surfaces and depth but thinks according to the given identity of a non-conceptual thought and the radical indivisibility of the body. Such is the reason why the One, Laruelle argues, is the 'degree zero of thought' and the 'black continent' of philosophy. It is the material real before all thinkable matter (materiality), the thinking force before all thought and which, as generic experience that all humans immediately share in so far as they are material beings, does not need ontology or philosophy to be known as such. This new practice breaks with the syntax of an operational transcendence by suspending philosophical hierarchies and circular couplings in order to attain the radical individuality of man and universality of the human as points of no return. The Real is indeed always already abstract from thought without there having been an ideal gesture of abstraction: Man, in his essence, is radically given without-image, it is non-reflected and does not need to be in order to be described. It is, therefore, against the philosophical images of mirrors that non-philosophy inscribes itself: the One is the matrix of all duality, without self-reflection and yet animated by a virtual flux, a force (of) thought that can be turned against the speculative and specular fascination of philosophy (its narcissism) to retrieve the unity of water and earth, of thought and the body, and prevents the flow of thought from becoming a static position, an oppressive instance.

To 'radicalise' immanence instead of rendering it absolute means to retrieve the non-philosophical roots of philosophy and to reduce the latter to a simple ideal material that the One can use without being affected by it. There is an irreversible relation between the One and the world: the One is not the horizon of an infinite differentiation but the finite and radically indifferent requisite of a difference by 'dualisation' or 'unilateralisation'. Uni-laterality means that the One is radically without relation to the symbolic order of the logos even if it produces it immanently, as his effect, but remains radically separated from it. Such is the reason why philosophy is given in the mode of the One, but rejected out of the latter's essence. If the One does not need philosophy, philosophy on the contrary needs the Real to become effective. One must start from the One and conceive the ideal distinctions from his immanence, instead of reaching a unitary standpoint that would synthesise two terms posited as facing one another (dyad). Non-philosophy remains in One; it is a thought of a generic humanity that is founded on the radical and material individual that is never preceded by a differential processes of individuation, but is the one who precedes individuation and renders it effective.[16] Man is the real base, the infra-structure of any discourse about materiality, that is why it is a positive 'nothing' whose essence is not decidable by philosophy (man is not a concept). Laruelle's science 'does not start with God or the things or man: it starts from *nothing* – before Being and nothingness – that is by a cut (*une coupure*), the Real as such (*tel quel*) anterior to ideality in general'.[17] Dualisation is the act of the One and the operatory principle of non-philosophy: it separates the Real and the philosophical, the generic and the transcendental rendering irrelevant the 'dice-throw' of philosophical thought, the fragmentation of Being into beings in dyadic and triadic forms. Thought for Laruelle is just a flow that acts as unique face of the One and that apprehends beings without Being and thus cancels the problem of hierarchy and of the power distribution that fuelled ontology from Plato to Deleuze.[18] The latter's philosophy, by trying to move beyond the human condition, remains in fact embedded in an idealist vitalism which leaves us with a new problem of hierarchy, a hierarchy of desire which privileges the 'non-human becomings' of man and the latter's dissolution into the flow of life. Contra Deleuze, Laruelle argues: 'that thought could even be a "superior" or "transcendental" ethology only inspires disgust – man is neither plant nor animal, terrestrial nor celestial, not even a becoming-plant or a becoming-animal: it would still be necessary to feel it rather than resent it and allow it to be lost in resentment and repression.'[19]

Laruelle criticises Deleuze not simply for having conserved the philosophical passion for ontology, but also for having kept 'desire' as the privileged affect of philosophy. Consider this passage, which I must quote at length, from *Le Principe de minorité* in which Laruelle reactivates an old 'war of principles', and opposes the primacy and positivity of the desireless One to the Deleuzian priority of desire and of a differing difference over any forms of identity:

> Desire is the first and the last word; the height of Greco-Occidental contemplation; the identity of becoming and Being. But it determines the absolute transcendental condition, the One, in exteriority and in an insufficient manner. Its experience of Essence is not sufficiently determining as it is founded above all on testing everything. It determines the One insufficiently by confounding it with the one-upmanship of unity, synthesis, ideality which crown being. Crowned being, crowned anarchy, these are what techno-metaphysics has done with the One, just as it has made multiplicities into an impressional diversity, the diversity of an empirical passivity, or even and simultaneously the variety of an activity, a synthesis submitting them to the powers of logos or its essence.[20]

Thus, to the Deleuzian conception of individuality, which thinks the body as a complex of intensities, on the side of which identity is just an effect or a simulacrum, it is a question, with Laruelle, of thinking the human as *homo simplex*, whose identity is radically devoid of duplicity and yet really distinct from the sphere of ideality that the One unilateralises. The 'dual' is not a duplex for it is not a state, but the very operation of the One, the very force (of) thought which produces knowledge as its own phenomenalisation. This is why Laruelle underlines the necessity of a transcendental science of the One, capable of describing the non-positional positivity of the One as immediate and unreflected experience: 'the real of science is in fact the One who is only One, nothing but the One and that describes himself as non-positional and non-decisional (of) himself (without the decision and the position that characterise Being).'[21]

Science, Laruelle argues, is 'the absolutely undivided identity of the surfaces and of the internal, of horizontal platitude and the immanent Real'.[22] The posture of Laruellean science entails considering human individuality in its indivisible and immediate oneness, that is, prior to any logical division and organisation. Already in *The Logic of Sense* Deleuze proposed a new way of understanding the relations between the heights, the surface of thought and the depth of bodies. In this book, the philosopher of immanence focused on the regimes of sense and non-sense that the logos can produce and conceived these different levels as the ontological effects, in thought, of the infinite dyad of becoming. Ontology no longer referred to transcendent hierarchy, which unites yet separates Being and beings, but simply designated the logic of sense and its various levels of deployment, in thought and language. However, the Deleuzian exploration of immanence and of its 'events' ultimately privileged the surfaces over the depths, the incorporeal dimension of thought over the mixtures of bodies.

Moreover, if the One is untaught science, unknowledge or gnosis, it does not need the help or the grace of an ontological 'desire' to be as such. Such is the reason why Deleuze's philosophy of desire is for Laruelle still grounded on a certain resentment toward the human, which condemns the latter to the circular movement of a desire that unceasingly seeks its own repetition and reproduction as creation of new differences in the world and in thought: 'resentment is temporality folding back onto itself, the internalisation and the doubling of transcendence in itself that refuses its immanence and simplicity . . . if resentment is the return of the felt (*senti*), its reflexivity, we oppose to it . . . the non-recurrent flux of affectivity or the lived without return but not without the appearance of a return.'[23]

Contra Deleuze, Laruelle argues that desire does not characterise the radical resistance of the One, but only the relative resistance of philosophy to the simplicity of a One whose desire is not thetic: it is a pure 'jouissance' that is not submitted to the vital imperative of creation. This is why Laruelle defines the One or the dispersive as being-without-desire, as an absolute resistance to relations and divisions, which globally excludes all ontico-ontological structures and which is in fact more powerful than them: 'There is a shadow (of the) One rather than a sun of Reason, and the shadow of the One is stronger than the sun of Reason.'[24] Thus, Laruelle criticises the Deleuzian approach of minorities as differential multiplicities or desiring machines, for by reducing them to pure relations between forces and as parts of a universal differential machine (a rhizosphere or mecanosphere), Deleuze presupposes an antecedence of the relations over the terms and thus dissolves identities in the powerful fluxes of desire that now act as an ontological principle that governs individual identities. The philosophy of difference does not liberate the human from the transcendence of power, but only the non-human virtualities in man, preventing us from truly grasping what really differentiates authoritarian from minoritarian regimes of desire. The non-philosopher argues, against Deleuze, that minorities are not differential but strictly unary: they are not syntheses of forces but indivisible multiplicities and are the sole measure of thought and the world. Thus, Laruelle opposes the 'minoritarian' principle to the 'unitarian' and differential principle of Deleuze's philosophy, which gives itself two regimes of desire (minor and major) and thinks their ontological synthesis a priori (as modes of the same desire). For the non-philosopher, minorities are not differential but undivided multiplicities and must be thought outside of the decisional regime of difference: 'there is no minority difference. Minority is an immanent and unreflexive multiplicity before all difference, differend or differance. The minority = relative or "different than" equation is a thought of the State and the State's last ruse.'[25]

For Laruelle, therefore, Deleuze's minorities are still 'statist minorities', locked into the system of power relations as a differential system of desire that is an ontological continuum. The Deleuzian monism of desire fails to grasp the non-ontological that is strictly human, as well as the finite nature of the a priori and immediate resistance of unary multiplicities to mixtures or authorities such as the World, Power, Philosophy, etc. The Real is indifferent to power and desire, this is why it can exert itself as a primary resistance to the occasional cause of the world and thereby breaks out of the circle of reciprocal determination or interactivity. The sole requisite of authorities is therefore just minorities, as the unique instances capable of modifying immanently the economy of Being and of the State. The primary resistance of the One is not a reaction to the World, but the suspension of its absolute authority and the instauration of an irreversible order that goes from the One to the other instances. If politics is science of the world, it is a part of the transcendental science of man, which describes the primacy of man over the logos and its doublets, each time depriving the world of its self-sufficiency. Man is the non-mundane essence of the World, the non-historical essence of history who breaks the empirico-transcendental parallelism: his acts are really distinguished from the world on which he acts.

We have seen that whereas Deleuze seeks to potentialise philosophy by turning it into a means to liberate life within and outside the human forms, Laruelle chooses the reverse path, namely that of diminishing philosophical *hubris*, by recalling it to the order of the One and of a generic humanity. However, one can ask if these two trajectories are not, in the last instance, complementary, despite their different posture and divergent use of philosophical language. For ultimately, if the immanental non-philosopher distinguishes himself from the philosopher of immanence, their respective thoughts share the same corporeal base, that of a living matter which, if it is necessarily non-philosophical in its essence and always singular, nonetheless constitutes the singular essence of philosophy and non-philosophy, for it is the flesh and blood of a generic humanity from the perspective of which the humanness of the philosopher and the non-philosopher is, in the last instance, indiscernible.

Notes

1. François Laruelle, 'The Truth According to Hermes: Theorems on the Secret and Communication', translated by Alexander R. Galloway, *Parrhesia: Journal of Critical Philosophy* 9 (2010), p. 21.
2. François Laruelle, 'The Decline of Materialism in the Name of Matter', translated by Ray Brassier, *Pli: The Warwick Journal of Philosophy* 12 (2001), p. 37.
3. François Laruelle, 'Response to Deleuze', translated by Taylor Adkins, *Pli: The Warwick Journal of Philosophy* 20 (2009), p. 155.
4. Ibid., p. 142.

5. Gilles Deleuze, *Difference and Repetition*, translated by Paul Patton (New York: Columbia University Press, 1994), p. 48: 'with univocity, it is not the differences which are and must be: it is Being which is difference, in the sense that it is said of difference. Moreover, it is not we who are univocal in a Being which is not; it is we and our individuality which remains equivocal in and for a univocal being.'

6. Gilles Deleuze, *Essays Critical and Clinical*, translated by Daniel Smith and Michael Greco (Minneapolis: University of Minnesota Press, 1997), p. 137: 'Every reaction against Platonism is a restoration of immanence in its full extension and its purity, which forbids the return of any transcendence. The question is whether such a reaction abandons the project of a selection among rivals, or on the contrary, as Spinoza and Nietzsche believed, draws up completely different methods of selection. Such methods would no longer concern claims as acts of transcendence, but the manner in which an existing being fills itself with immanence (the Eternal Return as the capacity of something or someone to return eternally). Selection no longer concerns the claim, but power; unlike the claim, power is modest. In truth, only the philosophies of pure immanence escape Platonism – from the Stoics to Spinoza or Nietzsche.'

7. Laruelle, 'Response to Deleuze'.

8. François Laruelle, *Principes de la non-philosophie* (Paris: PUF, 1996), p. 24. (Unless otherwise noted, all translations have been made by Marjorie Gracieuse and Nicola Rubczak.)

9. Laruelle, 'Response to Deleuze', p. 153.

10. François Laruelle, 'What Can Non-Philosophy Do?', translated by Ray Brassier, *Angelaki: Journal of the Theoretical Humanities* 8.2 (2003), p. 175.

11. See Gilles Deleuze, 'Immanence: A Life . . .', in *Two Regimes of Madness* (New York: Semiotexte, 2006), p. 387, where he writes, 'Pure immanence is A LIFE and nothing else . . . the life of an individual has given way to a life that is impersonal but singular nevertheless, and which releases a pure event freed from the accidents of inner and outer life; freed, in other words, from the subjectivity and objectivity of what happens: "*Homo Tantum*" with which everyone sympathises and which attains a sort of beatitude . . . The life of such an individuality effaces itself to the benefit of the singular life that is immanent to a man who no longer has a name yet cannot be confused with anyone else. Singular essence, a life . . .'

12. François Laruelle, *Introduction au non-marxisme* (Paris: PUF, 2000), p. 45.

13. François Laruelle, 'L'essence de la technique: entretien avec François Laruelle', *Art Press* 12 (2001). On the status of the body in non-philosophy, see also François Laruelle, *Le Concept de non-photographie/The Concept of Non-Photography* (Bilingual Edition), translated by Robin Mackay (Falmouth: Urbanomic, 2011).
14. Laruelle, 'The Truth According to Hermes', p. 21.
15. Laruelle, *Le Principe de Minorité* (Paris: Aubier Montaigne, 1981), p. 27.
16. See François Laruelle, *Une biographie de l'homme ordinaire. Des Autorités et des Minorités* (Paris: Aubier, 1985), p. 209, where he writes, 'finitude is intrinsic: present from the beginning, it determines everything in an irreversible manner, not in the circular manner of an ideal. Just as there is an individual before all processes of individuation, there is a finitude before all processes of finitisation.'
17. Laruelle, *Le Principe de Minorité*, p. 53.
18. See François Laruelle, 'The Generic as Predicate and Constant: Non-Philosophy and Materialism', translated by Taylor Adkins, in *The Speculative Turn: Continental Materialism and Realism*, edited by Levi Bryant, Nick Srnicek and Graham Harman (Melbourne: re.press, 2011), p. 254: 'on the reflected side of the philosophical One-All or bifacial transcendence, idempotent lived experience detaches or subtracts a single face, a uniface.'
19. Laruelle, 'Response to Deleuze', p. 161.
20. Laruelle, *Le Principe de Minorité*, p. 136.
21. Laruelle, *En tant qu'Un* (Paris: Aubier, 1991), p. 59.
22. Laruelle, *Le Principe de Minorité*, p. 104.
23. François Laruelle, 'Lettres non-philosophiques: Resistance ou Affectivite – comment le monde est donné'. Available at <http://www.onphi.net/lettre-laruelle-resistance-ou-affectivite---comment-le-monde-est-donne-10.html> (accessed 13 December 2011).
24. Laruelle, *Une biographie de l'homme ordinaire*, p. 168.
25. Laruelle, *Le Principe de Minorité*, p. 77.

3

Laruelle and Ordinary Life

Rocco Gangle

Philosophy *Ad Hominem*

The formidable technicality and abstractness of much of Laruelle's
work may mislead some into seeing it as merely another variant
of formalism or pure theory, an attempt to escape the world and
its life. But this would be a mistake – the abstract nature of non-
philosophy is wholly positive and far from denying the world is in
fact ultimately *for* what in the world is truly real (and not merely
empirical or concrete). A primary impetus of Laruelle's thought
at least since the period he calls Philosophy II has been the desire
precisely to open new modes of thinking that would not repeat
the basic philosophical gesture of transcendence in so far as this
latter implies a movement – implicit or explicit – of turning against
and denigrating X (where X may range over quite an extensive
domain: the world, God, gods, human individuals, *doxa*, the
empirical, ideality, madness, content, form, religion, philosophy
itself . . .). Even if grounded in an ultimately illusory notion of
thought's transcendence, such gestures themselves possess a real
dimension and produce real effects. Without simply identifying
acts of philosophical transcendence and worldly violence or, still
less, asserting some dubious intra-worldly causal claim from the
one to the other, it is imperative to understand the effective essence
intricating this canonical philosophical gesture to forms of actual
violence in the world and to grasp the precise limits of this intrication's generality and necessity. Is philosophy capable of thinking
the ordinariness of its violence? We must be careful not to reject or
denigrate philosophy by the very posing or even the answering of
this question, as this would risk repeating the very gesture at issue
in attempting to know it. What matters is the effective essence of
thought's perhaps unnecessary movement of transcendence and

denigration as well as access to the reality of a mode of knowledge that would stand unaffected by such a movement as wholly ordinary or generic.

In one of its most important aspects non-philosophy is engaged with how ordinary human beings tend to be denigrated by authoritarian structures in and of the world with both implicit and explicit philosophical legitimisation. Such cases (and above all their common structure) form a special object for non-philosophical thought. While non-philosophy's at times highly technical engagement with philosophical materials may be understood at one level as a form of resistance to and even effective suspension of these denigration-legitimising dispositions, more fundamentally non-philosophy is a rigorous discipline in the experience of non-denigrating thinking itself, less a forceful opposition or resistance to philosophical violence than a real, disciplined indifference to it.

Thought individually or according-to-One – that is, without problematising the second-order relation of access to the relation at issue – the essence of philosophy as dyadic decision and synthesis is known immanently to miss the essence of the ordinary real, which is *inter alia* the unmediated, non-reflexive essence of each human individual, such generic individuality having nothing whatsoever to do with a differential or liberal individualism. For non-philosophy, the *ordinary human* is not 'that everyday or common being of a bad sociology or an "existential" philosophy', as Laruelle says in *En tant qu'Un*, but rather an undivided thought, a static, solitary invulnerability and unbroken calm into which philosophy's denigrating aspect may be generalised and thus relatively, but also radically, neutralised.[1] The simple possibility of such an ordinary or generic science remains occluded and overwritten by the ontico-ontological positioning of human beings in the world. From the theoretical stance that en-visions the real essence of ordinary humans, the world itself as the philosophical enfolding of Being and beings appears as utterly contingent, and so does every such philosophical interpretation. Taken in its real but restricted generality, the field of these world-interpretations appears structured so as to deny this very contingency and to attribute either negativity or incompleteness to what is in fact wholly, positively and ordinarily real, in particular whatsoever may be real and (therefore) non-philosophisable in and of ordinary humans themselves. The philosophical organisation and legitimisation of the world as a mixture of immanence and transcendence (or as a correlation of reality and thought) would thus involve, in particular, an *ad hominem* attack against what such a world cannot encompass. From this perspective, one of the primary motivations for non-philosophy is or can be ethico-political in a certain still-to-be-determined sense, a sense itself available only as real-in-the-last-instance, or ordinary.

To witness the essential philosophical gesture of decision as an intelligible pattern of worldly denigration is to think non-decisionally, that is, *from* (and not toward) a real democracy – a purely generic subject-form like that implied by scientific inquiry – the structure of which is a transcendental and yet perfectly ordinary, first-order knowledge. This is in one sense the very trial of finitude and precariousness known to every human being in a thoroughly immediate and immanent way, although – and this will be a key point – without precarious finitude becoming thereby a human *eidos*, a foundation for existential analysis, or the substance of some universal common world.[2] Rather than being attributed to the human-being-in-the-world, precariousness is attributed by non-philosophy to the world itself. The two philosophically distinct levels of the transcendental and the ordinary (a category which philosophy generally reduces to the empirical) are in non-philosophy no longer coordinated, correlated or differentiated. There is thus a real, non-philosophical democracy of thought. Strangely, perhaps, the very simplicity and directedness of this democratic mode of thinking which is ultimately *for us here in the world* necessitates stringent conceptual labours. At any rate, by emphasising at the start the unavoidability of technical and conceptual sophistication for elaborating non-philosophy's relation to ordinary experience, we will avoid any possible equation of the real human ordinary with a vulgarism or an anti-philosophy.

Across its history, philosophy has always maintained an uneasy relationship with the ordinary world and its generally non-philosophical life. From the ancient Greek differentiation of *doxa* and *episteme* and the subsequent formation of localised philosophical schools (Academy, Lyceum, Stoa) to the professionalisation and division of labour of philosophy in contemporary academic ghettoes, philosophical thought across its history has tended at least to condescend to if not wholly to disparage ordinary human life, philosophy's primal non-philosophical Other. To be sure, there is a long and varied history here, one touching upon issues of language, gender, power and all the immediate concerns of contemporary thought, and it is by no means a simple or one-sided history. It should be equally recognised that as common inhabitants of the City, ordinary humans have often nursed a symmetrical distrust and even poisonous hatred for philosophy and philosophers. The challenge for a rigorous non-philosophy of the ordinary will be to understand both these sets of animosities as well as their mutually determining differences without thereby deciding for or participating in either side, simply to see the relative necessity of such taking sides from a standpoint no longer subject to this necessity, a standpoint that generalises rather than opposes both the philosophical and the ordinary as well as their various systems of relation and disjunction (theoretical, practical, theoretico-practical). Prior to any such systematics we pose a question of the immanent discovery of a non-philosophical subject who would be neither opposed to nor identified with essential structures of philosophical subjectivity, in particular those of transcendental constitution and linguistic pragmatics. This task will be both ordinary and difficult, and philosophical concepts (indeed the only kind we have) will prove both useful and necessary for it. But the relative necessity of such philosophical support will not enter into the essence of what is thereby uncovered.

Non-philosophy is a discipline of thought that works to sustain a certain affect within thinking that is at once rigorously theoretical and radically indifferent to philosophy and thus supportive of a scientific, experimental use of philosophical materials that is itself neither philosophical nor anti-philosophical. In Laruelle's *Biographie de l'homme ordinaire*, there is an explicit call 'to create a non-philosophical affect: to render sensible what there are of immediate givens, of non-hallucinatory reality, of finite transcendental experience in humans'.[3] How is such an affect generated and sustained? How is it transmitted or relayed? With philosophical materials but not philosophical means; it will be rather by means of a new theoretical practice that takes the materials of philosophy as experimental data. In the present context we will work with a pair of discrete philosophical instances drawn from two texts engaging the problematic of the ordinary. These texts are extracted from distinct philosophical standpoints: Edmund Husserl's late phenomenological turn to the experiential life-world in the *Crisis of European Sciences and Transcendental Phenomenology* and Gilbert Ryle's therapeutic examination of self-knowledge via language in *The Concept of Mind*. We will see that in both texts, despite every intent to include its own activity in the range of its object of inquiry and determination, to problematise – and thereby resolve – itself, philosophy remains blind to the very ordinariness of what it really presupposes, the flat or ordinary real, and is nonetheless obsessed with the irreducible exteriority of its operational act to its powers of sufficient determination. Experience and language are not meant here to exhaust the fields into which philosophy may insert itself according to this structure, but together these should be sufficient to indicate the concrete generality at issue. Thus, the following two sections should be read not primarily as logical arguments but rather as simple representations, indicative cases or diagrammatic lines of force extracted from an objective philosophical continuum or field.

Husserl: The Ordinary Life-World

When philosophy considers the ordinary in terms of a typical pre-philosophical form of experience, the problem it sets for itself is to account both for the emergence or self-distinguishing difference of philosophical from ordinary experience and the determinative force of philosophical thought with respect to the latter. The Kantian transcendental turn codifies the dominant response to this problem for the subsequent Idealist tradition up to its transformation and relative overcoming in phenomenology and hermeneutics. These latter developments render *effective* the circular and self-grounding structure already evident in Kant's transcendental method. With such effectivity inevitably come questions of the historical deployment of philosophy as a determinate human tradition – this is foregrounded already in Schelling and Hegel – and the concomitant historical envelopment of transcendental human concerns (those of culture, politics, language, religion. . .). Here we will take the turn toward the life-world in Husserl's *Crisis of European Sciences and Transcendental Phenomenology* as an index and experimental support for investigating this general problematic.

In this late, unfinished work Husserl treats the problem of the life-world (*Lebenswelt*) as the origin and unsurpassable horizon of the transcendental philosophical project. In response largely to existentialist and historicist critiques, Husserl reconfigures in the *Crisis* the philosophical enactment of phenomenology's key method of transcendental reduction not as a simple methodological step but as a culturally and historically sedimented potential of and for European and ultimately human civilisation as such. Without rehearsing the complex inner structure of the argument of the *Crisis* as a whole, we look only to the investigation in Part III that sets forth the life-world as a new basis for and methodological entrance into transcendental phenomenology from an existential-historical perspective. The rich pre-predicative experiential field of the life-world consists of strata of active and passive synthe-ses, at the ground of which churns the pure passive synthesis of time, which serves as the ground of both empirical history and transcendental subjectivity. If Husserl's earlier analyses of phe-nomenological experience in *Ideas* and *Cartesian Meditations* were characterised by the subjective transcendence-in-immanence of intentionality, the phenomenology of the *Crisis* takes place within a more complex transcendental-from-and-for-immanence of the life-world's own irreducible concrete-ideal temporality. In Husserl's late work, phenomenology thus becomes both more fully rooted in and teleologically oriented toward the world and its history, although its transcendental status continues to guarantee a relative cancellation of merely empirical, worldly objectivity.

From this insight into the transcendental bracketing of histori-cally constituted knowledge, Husserl draws radically democratic consequences for institutional philosophy: the technical expertise of the academically trained philosopher, like that of every tra-ditional expert, is radically suspended. The accrued knowledge and methods of the philosophical tradition are revealed to be synthetic products and sedimentations grounded ultimately in the temporal syntheses of the life-world itself, and like all other historical, cultural and scientific phenomena, philosophy thus appears as a constituted product and not a self-sufficiently consti-tutive act. Without the stance of radical questioning opened by the transcendental reduction, all apparently universal philosophical results remain conditioned by certain presupposed syntheses of the life-world that necessarily go unthematised. Recognition of the unsurpassable ground of the life-world thus places the thinker in a new precarious relation to tradition, one in which tradition cannot itself provide support or succour:

> We are absolute beginners, here, and have nothing in the way of a logic designed to provide norms; we can do nothing but reflect, engross our-selves in the still not unfolded sense of our task, and thus secure, with

the utmost care, freedom from prejudice, keeping our undertaking free of alien interferences.[4]

Phenomenology's transcendental reduction provokes a paradoxically radical experience of uprootedness. Yet is this experience not in fact a perfectly ordinary condition, and as such no longer paradoxical? Husserl never fails to maintain the universal validity of transcendental phenomenology's results for the projects and values of its pre-philosophical inhabitants, we ordinary humans, such scientific, non-decisional universality being possible only because

> the life-world does have, in all its relative features, a *general structure.* This general structure, to which everything that exists relatively is bound, is not itself relative. We can attend to it in its generality and, with sufficient care, fix it once and for all in a way equally accessible to all.[5]

The enactment of transcendental reduction, what becomes in the *Crisis* a civilisational and no longer merely individual or even simply intersubjective task, thereby makes visible a genuinely pluralistic universality under which the differences and disjunctions of the life-world may be equally preserved and subsumed. In this way the life-world – or rather its philosophical recognition and reflection – appears to open thought up to a profoundly democratic possibility, the possibility of an event both inside and outside philosophy, civilisational in nature, that would effectively determine the theoretico-practical relation of philosophical reflection to the general structure of the life-world itself and would do so in a universally accessible way. This is a globally democratic and scientific vision in which the overarching goals of a phenomenological rebirth of the West would be a universality and openness far more extensive than any narrow Enlightenment rationality. Yet the movement from the natural attitude of ordinary human beings in the life-world to the phenomenological attitude of the practising philosopher involves both a continuity and a disjunction – ultimately, an undecidability between continuity and disjunction that opens the phenomenological field of infinite tasks as equally an unending repetition of infinite beginnings. It is thus the possibility of this repetition itself that becomes the effective content of Husserl's democratic universality.

Such an infinitely open, yet irreducibly chiasmic relation between transcendental historicity and factical history represents in the late Husserl already what Derrida and Derridians will later develop and institutionalise under the name of the quasi-transcendental.[6] No doubt the relation in the late Husserl of phenomenological reflection to the life-world and its ordinary denizens is subtle and complex: a perhaps too-simple distinction of the phenomenological from the natural attitude in earlier works is more fully differentiated and topologised in the *Crisis*, qualified as continuous and immanent as much as disjunctive and transcendent. Yet if anything, this revised conception of phenomenology's rootedness in the life-world only makes all the more evident the extent to which something in the very essence of the ordinary experience of human beings remains outside the purview of phenomenological philosophy.

For all its internal complexity and despite its overarching drive toward the unity and immanence of the life-world, Husserl's *Crisis* still takes the form of a logical or quasi-logical synthesis between two levels that must be held both distinct and inseparable. Even if this disjunctive synthesis is not external (formal) but rather internal (transcendental) to experience itself, the subject who alternately enacts and undergoes it remains excluded in principle from the at once scientific and socio-political unity and resolution it (half-)promises. If the Greco-European and hence global crisis diagnosed by Husserl in the 1930s is not merely epistemological or scientific, but equally ethico-political and even world-historical, there is nonetheless a certain provinciality of the diagnosis: who indeed are the humans undergoing this crisis? More pointedly, in what sense are its victims even in principle secured by any possible phenomenological securing of its foundations? For all the continuity linking acts of transcendental reflection to the historical time of the life-world, the philosophising subject remains effectively split – as Husserl himself says explicitly – between an empirical human being who 'is not merely an ego-pole but an "I" with all its accomplishments and accomplished acquisitions, including the world as existing and being-such' and a transcendental subject in which 'nothing human is to be found, neither soul nor psychic life nor real psychophysical human beings'.[7] Even as radically transformed by phenomenology, philosophy still functions here as a decision, a political decision *inter alia*, to take as the universal image of thought the form of such a split as coordinated to some possible

synthesis or suture. Even and especially in response to real, historical crisis, the philosophically (in this case, phenomenologically)
transformed subject cannot in principle coincide with the ordinary
human whose need would appear (at least to philosophy) to call
for philosophy in the first place.

Ryle: Ordinary Language

When philosophy restricts itself to the domain of language (or at
any rate claims to do so), the constitutive philosophical problems
of reflexivity and exteriority are at once epistemologically clarified
and ontologically obscured. Even without recourse to philosophical reflection, the relatively autonomous space of language appears
already structured through orthogonal axes of sense and reference.
Rather than attempting to account for its own transcendental constitution (out) of this field, philosophy is thus left with the seemingly straightforward and strictly derivative tasks of clarification
and explication. On this basis, the relation of philosophy to the
ordinary is reconfigured in terms of levels or regions of linguistic
usage.

Accordingly, we draw a second philosophical index from the
broad project of linguistic analysis that has predominated in
Anglo-American philosophy for some decades. Our aim is to
identify a purely pragmatic-linguistic variant of the structure we
saw manifest in phenomenology as the problem of transcendental
constitution. While Husserl's *Crisis* is clearly set in a mainstream
Continental philosophical tradition stretching from Descartes and
Spinoza to Derrida and Deleuze that arguably finds its central
problematic and spiritual trial in the concepts of immanence and
transcendence and their social-political expressions, it would seem
that any such magnetism toward political metaphysics is largely
missing from the broadly analytic tradition that breaks away
from Idealism for the logicism of Frege and the analytic method
of Moore and Russell.[8] Yet at least some forms of the analytic
linguistic turn, particularly in the line of the later Wittgenstein,
harbour a strange analogue to such a drive: a pragmatic method
of grammatical immanence with a deflationary stance toward traditional philosophical pretensions. The sub-tradition of ordinary
language philosophy originating in Wittgenstein's lectures of the
1930s and the *Philosophical Investigations* and taken up by philosophers such as Ryle and Austin may be understood as a practice

of immanence in its own right, methodological and pragmatic rather than metaphysical or ontological, with its own generally unthematised politics.

Ordinary language philosophy rejects as a point of order any necessity to construct a theory of language or to compile a formalisation of ordinary linguistic syntax in order to engage philosophical questions. Indeed, the ordinary language philosophers tend to view such theories and formalisations (even and especially when they arise naively and pre-philosophically) as themselves the culprits in generating philosophical false problems. Ordinary language philosophy thus does not proceed via the production of a meta-language and is not a philosophy *of* ordinary language so much as an immanent usage of ordinary language *for* ordinary life in so far as philosophical puzzles trouble it and reveal its lacks, its therapeutic needs.

We take Ryle's work as exemplary here. Ryle, like both Wittgenstein and Austin, conceives of philosophy as a form of discursive practice, and his basic method consists in distinguishing in any given philosophical dispute those stakes which are real from those which are merely apparent. Attention to the grammar of philosophical disputes makes this possible: for Ryle, logic is internal to natural linguistic practice; it is something we do implicitly before it is ever thematised critically and explicitly. To produce a philosophical argument in a Rylean mode is not a matter of honing logical distinctions in order to talk more finely of the reality of the objective world as opposed to its merely subjective phenomenality or to theorise the reality of transcendent reference with respect to the immanence of propositional sense, but is instead the counter-technical or ordinary demonstrative distinguishing of the (real) ordinary grammar or first-order usage of language from its (phenomenal) sophisticated effects of second-order, reflectively aporetic or paradoxical meaning. If anything, there is in Ryle as in the late Wittgenstein very nearly a complete reversal of the traditional privileging of *episteme* over *doxa* in terms of philosophy's standard and aim. It is ordinary *doxa* – conceived grammatically, or practically – which function here as the real substrata and criteria of epiphenomenal theoretical dilemmas. Common linguistic exchange serves as a pragmatic ground of last resort to which such dilemmas become reducible, and aporias at the theoretical level of meaning are resolved at the practical level of ordinary grammar.

In his key work *The Concept of Mind*, Ryle argues that

apparently intractable philosophical dilemmas dissolve when they are reduced to – that is, made manifest as – category mistakes. Philosophical error results when two or more statements belonging naturally to separate categories are linked together through either conjunction or disjunction into a single statement, as though they shared the same grammatical world. Ryle himself cites the absurdity: 'She came home in a flood of tears and a sedan chair', in Ryle's view such a statement being akin, formally, to the philosophical (Cartesian) claim that there are both physical and mental causal processes.[9] In both cases, an apparent synthesis is effected at the level of syntax or grammar that is in fact categorically foreclosed: 'in' diverges here just where it ought to synthesise and 'causal' imports precisely what it needs to produce. In such instances, the natural separation and relative autonomy of diverse grammatical worlds is treated as a pre-philosophical datum, and thus in Ryle philosophy's clarifying labour must work strictly *ad hoc* within given linguistic and conceptual practices; it is not first secured by means of any methodological or axiomatic foundation that would order such worlds a priori. Philosophy begins and operates in the middle of the thing, in the middle of language itself, and Ryle proceeds from the assumption that the direct use of language is naturally prior to language's self-reflexivity: the practice always precedes and diverges from the theory of language. As he says in *Dilemmas*, 'it is one thing to employ a concept efficiently, it is quite another to describe that employment'.[10] Ordinary language philosophy puts this priority of linguistic practice to philosophical use.

The essential method of philosophy becomes that of analogical transference: one solves an apparently insoluble conceptual dilemma by shifting ground strategically to a separate but relevantly similar case, generally a more concrete and ordinary one, and distinguishing clearly in the analogous case what remains relatively hidden or unapparent in the initial, philosophical synthesis of grammars. Such analogies become necessary because what genuine philosophical inquiry aims to think is always one degree more formal (in the sense of the Scholastic/Cartesian distinction of *realitas formalis* and *realitas objectiva*) than what one can say, which is not at all to suggest that philosophy's aim is intrinsically more sophisticated or complicated than language can express – indeed to the contrary.

A usefully self-interpreting instance of Ryle's method appears at the close of the chapter on 'Self-Knowledge' in *The Concept of Mind*, the explicit purpose of which is 'to show that the official theories of consciousness and introspection are logical muddles', certainly a noteworthy task.[11] Ryle here addresses in particular the philosophical problem of 'the systematic elusiveness of the notion of "I"', philosophy's reflective call for a metaphysical 'Ghost in the Machine' to explain the experience of self-consciousness. He first translates this problem into a purely pragmatic-linguistic register: self-consciousness corresponds simply to a second-order linguistic operation, and since a 'higher order action cannot be the action upon which it is performed', the metaphysical 'I''s apparent elusiveness is shown to be a simple false problem, merely a bad mix of distinct grammars.[12] This strictly logical point (the abstract dissolution of a misleading abstraction) is then made effective through an analogical concretion, an ordinary if artificial illustration:

A singing-master might criticise the accents or notes of a pupil by mimicking with exaggerations each word that the pupil sang; and if the pupil sang slowly enough, the master could parody each word sung by the pupil before the next came to be uttered. But then, in a mood of humility, the singing-master tries to criticise his own singing in the same way, and more than that to mimic with exaggerations each word that he utters, including those that he utters in self-parody. It is at once clear, first, that he can never get beyond the very earliest word of his song and, second, that at any given moment he has uttered one noise which has yet to be mimicked – and it makes no difference how rapidly he chases his notes with mimicries of them. He can, in principle, never catch more than the coat-tails of the object of his pursuit, since a word cannot be a parody of itself.[13]

Here, it is not just a matter of exemplifying the general by means of the particular and concrete, but of utilising the concrete and familiar as against certain muddling tendencies intrinsic to the general and abstract. The relevant logical point is not formally elaborated but rather immediately displayed and more importantly felt. The practical utility of Rylean *ad hoc* analogy does not depend upon any logically consistent theory of analogy that would have to find application in any given case. Philosophical discourse – like consciousness – simply cannot catch its own tail or account fully for its own practice and need not bother to try on either count. This is not to pose a theoretical problem but to acknowledge the absence of a (real) practical problem. The analogical method simply works – except when it does not. To seek non-analogical grounding for the success or failure of the method is to pose precisely the wrong problem, the very problem the method itself is designed to solve.

Both the analogical method in general and the specific point made in the example above carry certain democratising, anti-specialist consequences. While Ryle is careful to defend himself against the attribution of some sort of behaviourism or metaphysical rejection of consciousness, the linguistic and analogical reduction of first-person, conscious 'phosphorescence' nonetheless serves to equalise epistemological access to oneself and to others. Knowledge of self and of others are brought into structural and methodological parity. In a similar way, Ryle's method makes use of a distinction of 'natural' from 'sophisticated' modes of speech and enforces a structural dependency of the latter upon the former. Such dependency is logical, but not in the sense of a formal condition that in principle may or may not be met. It is rather the logic internal to the grammar of the modes of speech themselves, their ordinary condition. Ryle writes:

> In a certain sense of 'natural', the natural thing to do is to speak one's mind, and the sophisticated thing to do is to refrain from doing this, or even to pretend to do this, when one is not really doing so. Furthermore, not only is unstudied talk natural or unsophisticated, it is also the normal way of talking. We have to take special pains to keep things back, only because letting them out is our normal response; and we discover the techniques of insincerity only from familiarity with the modes of unforced conversation that are to be simulated.[14]

A kind of faith in ordinary speech finds itself subtly entangled here with condescension. The priority of the natural is also its enforced humility.

Ryle himself emphasises in this context that 'Camouflage and gravity are only intermittent necessities.'[15] One immediately grasps the gulf separating Ryle here from someone in the Continental tradition such as Derrida who is equally interested in the phenomena of secrecy and camouflage. Where Derrida will include an element of secrecy at the heart of all manifest speech and the possibility of duplicity in the very essence of sincerity, Ryle will insist upon the unambiguous priority of sincerity to duplicity and of open speech to secrecy. Ryle, who like Austin may thus appear naive in contrast to deconstruction, does not reproduce the difference between the reticent and the candid at the heart of each term. Instead, in each case he treats the two terms at issue as definitively hierarchised and linked through an irreversible dependency relation. In this respect, Ryle appears 'pre-differential' relative to Derrida's sophisticated philosophical employment of difference/*différance*.[16] But it would be too hasty to disqualify Ryle in this way: there may be from Ryle's side an equally penetrating sophistication, a relatively esoteric or secret simplicity. In any case, the practice of philosophy itself for Ryle implies at the very least a special, second-order linguistic and analogical activity.

Non-Philosophical Dualysis and Ordinary Strangers

It will not be a matter here of critiquing Husserl and Ryle nor of offering a competing account of philosophy's proper relation to ordinary life and language. It is first of all simply a matter of noting the following:

1. The ordinary, far from being denigrated in Husserl and Ryle, is if anything *prima facie* valorised in both philosophers (at the very least in Husserl as a necessary basis for the historical accomplishment of transcendental philosophy and in Ryle as an endless source of philosophically effective analogies and deflationary strategies).

2. This valorisation of the ordinary comes in each case with a relative immanentisation and democratisation of philosophy as well as a critique of its technical and institutionally sedimented forms.

3. Nonetheless, in each case the democratic tendency still involves a form of relation between necessarily distinguishable strata and thus involves a logical or quasi-logical exclusion. The immanent tendency is at once balanced and qualified by a transcendence or semi-transcendence.

Both Husserlian phenomenology and Rylean ordinary language philosophy may legitimately make claim to a certain relative immanence of philosophy to ordinary experience, an immanence which nonetheless underwrites the very operations of transcendence or semi-transcendence by which philosophy distinguishes itself from the ordinary. Clearing away a myriad of accidental details and qualifications, what matters for us essentially is the way both philosophers conceive the ordinary as a pre-philosophical stratum, in some sense a necessary presupposition and foundation for philosophy, while at the same time asking that philosophy hew close to ordinary experience and be drawn into the ambit of its life. Two contrary and conflictual tendencies are thus at work ambiguously in both projects. Will it then be a matter of a new and better attempt at the same problem? No, precisely not an attempt but rather an acknowledgement. Non-philosophy does not offer a new solution to the problem of the relation of philosophy to ordinary life, but relativises and generalises this problem itself by showing it to be no more than one manifestation of an intrinsic philosophical structure that is universal and necessary for philosophy but arbitrary in itself.

At the most general level, non-philosophy relativises in a new mode the typically philosophical form of thinking that itself proceeds by way of relations and correlations. The method through which non-philosophy accomplishes this is called dualysis. The method of dualysis makes new use of a constitutive structure of philosophy, the general form of relation that consists of a combination or mixture of two contrary relational aspects or tendencies, one relatively immanent that tends to reduce the difference between the related terms to a synthetic continuum, one relatively transcendent that allows one of the relation's terms partially to escape the relation itself and thereby to problematise the simple, first-order synthesis or unity of the relation as such. Viewed under the former aspect, a relation becomes essentially a synthetic unity relatively interiorised to each of the poles or terms of the relation; viewed according to the latter, it becomes primarily a cut or exteriority typically giving rise to a second-order problem of the relation-of-the-relation. Philosophy effectively subsists by repeating and re-inserting itself within the higher-order problem of relation or access to this very form of mixed relationality, which is itself already redoubled as self-similar/self-differing. Such an indefinitely reproduced mixture of immanence and transcendence may be understood as characterising the very essence of philosophy, its own structural a priori or transcendental. One canonical example of this structure is given by the relation of thought to the real, where the thought-pole serves the function of immanent-synthesis and the reality-pole that of the transcendent-cut. Another is found in the phenomenological analysis of intentionality, where the correlation of noesis and noema manifests the relatively immanent aspect and the infinity and exteriority of the noematic core presents the relatively transcendent aspect. In both these cases, philosophy itself is clearly at stake; more generally, the effective self-inclusion of the philosophical form within the very relations and problems with which it deals tends to produce a fractal-like reproduction of similar structures at all levels of philosophical thought.

The problem of immanence and exteriority within relation is a perfectly general problem which philosophy rightly treats as necessary and unavoidable for all thought. What is not necessary, however, but purely decisional, is the transformation of this problem (or structure) into a redoubled and self-participated method for thinking. Philosophy is obviously highly aware of this difference or duplicity built into the very concept of relation – even to the point of obsession – and makes use of it in various ways, above all to pose the problems philosophy addresses. In contrast, non-philosophical dualysis undoes the duplicity and allows transcendence and immanence simply to rest as what they essentially are without submitting these to the second-order reflection of a problematic, a relation, a correlation or even a mere juxtaposition. The terms of all such relations are thus unilateralised, which means that instead of being problematised and redoubled, the first-order synthetic function of their relation is left entirely to one side (the only side that requires one to take sides), thereby freeing both immanent and transcendent tendencies from second- and higher-order reduplication.

Unilateralisation involves neither the reception nor the constitution of an object, and for this reason its subject-form is no longer philosophical. The subject of dualysis is no longer the pole of a relation but instead a unilateral identity, precisely the real exteriority of the relation as thought on the basis of its transcendent aspect or tendency, but now unilateralised as simply or only transcendent (that is, not transcendent *with respect to* a correlative immanence) or – identically – simply or ordinarily immanent. In this way, non-philosophical immanence is not opposed to transcendence as such but only to a false and compromised correlative transcendence. Thought in this fashion, the comparative difference of transcendence and immanence in every such relation is made indifferent to thought, but without advantage to either side as such. 'Stranger' names the new condition of the previously philosophical and philosophisable subject, now dualysed in a simple, non-self-scaling manner and thus no longer constituted by any relation of the philosophical, semi-transcendent/semi-immanent type or problematised by any meta-relation of disjunction and synthesis between effectivity and identity, or act and substance. All philosophical problems and solutions at every level of abstraction and detail then become available as data to such Strangers, and yet the Stranger is in no way subject to these or determined by them.

In particular, the irreducibly political dimension of philosophy no longer constrains the Stranger to participate in a contested field that would be at once semi-philosophical and semi-political. Laruelle's thought, from the early studies of Nietzsche, Heidegger, deconstruction and machinic desire (Philosophy I), to the most recent installations of non-philosophy within theological, scientific and mathematical materials (Philosophy V), has been concerned in one way or another to address the worldly denigrations of the human and their philosophically legitimated, generalised inhuman politics. Dualysis is a perfectly general method, applicable wherever philosophy is operative, that is, wherever thought situates itself within a problem, relation or correlation mixing a relatively transcendent with a relatively immanent aspect, including within political action and reflection.

As a final philosophical index, then, consider a brief extract from an incisive philosophical text by Pierre Klossowski on the Marquis de Sade and the French Revolution:

> Apparently the Revolution could break out only because of a vast combination of contradictory demands. If the existing psychic forces had identified one another at the start, their unanimous mobilisation would never have come about. It was because of a kind of confusion between two different categories of demands that the subversive atmosphere could take form. There were, in fact, two groups in collusion.[17]

The constituents of these two groups are then specified. Comprising the Revolution, there was on the one hand 'the amorphous mass of average men who demanded a social order in which the idea of *natural man* could prove itself', their call for this realisation expressing 'the idealisation of the ordinary man, an ideal that especially attracted that portion of the people who had hitherto lived below the level of the ordinary man'.[18] On the other hand, one finds 'a category of men belonging to the ruling classes and existing at a higher level of life, who, because of the iniquity of this level, were able to develop a supreme degree of lucidity'.[19] As opposed to the masses asking for the unobstructed constitution of a natural humanity, these aristocratic, criminal philosophers 'awaited the Revolution as something that would bring about a complete remolding of the structure of man'.[20] Thus, a mass party calling itself Man and a select class of individuals calling for the Overman: especially intriguing in this sketch is the political productivity of the contradictory and confused relation formed with and between these two parties, the categorical confusion of their respective desires becoming an effective political force. It is neither a matter of criticising nor of validating this particular interpretation of the Revolution, but only of seeing how it instantiates in its own register the problem of philosophy's relation to the ordinary we examined above. Indeed, every philosophical interpretation of the political necessarily involves a similar structure, whether explicitly (constatively) or implicitly (performatively), and in general political problems *qua* problems always take a philosophical form that depends upon both an a priori distinction of thought from power as well as their a priori relation. Philosophy thus inevitably inserts itself into the political as such and should be quite unsurprised to find its own image reflected there.

Despite their decision, in some sense, *for* the ordinary, both Husserl and Ryle (to return to our earlier philosophical instances) cannot help but think according to a form that structurally legitimates a decisional political model. From within the non-philosophical stance of individual thought or thought according-to-One, the Stranger has neither need nor desire to decide for or against the ordinary in the same way. The political contentions internal to philosophy, like the problematic relations and disjunctions of philosophy with its outside(s) or Other(s), are deactivated and reduced to simple instances or tokens of a universal type: the Philosophy-World. Instead of constituting a multilateral and differentiated fight *over* the world, philosophy may be treated as the unilateral identity *of* the world. More than just being an a priori presupposition of interpretative and argumentative struggle, the very idea of the world as a universal container and court of judgement for such differences is equally an unregistered product of this all-too-common agonistic mode of thinking, philosophy's own hallucinated double. Rather than joining philosophy's fight on one side or another, the Stranger merely acknowledges the manifest absurdity of its stakes: the struggle is grounded only in itself. Non-philosophy rejects not philosophy but only philosophy's self-legitimating and hence thoroughly relative circumscriptions of its Other(s). The Stranger thus does not opt out of the real world, but instead sees that the world itself as defined a priori by philosophy as a form of contest and enclosure (however infinite or horizonal in principle) in fact opts out of the ordinary human Real.

Notes

1. François Laruelle, *En tant qu'Un* (Paris: Aubier, 1991).
2. From the non-philosophical stance of Vision-in-One, philosophy itself is the form of the world. It is a world-logic, *the* world-logic. This non-philosophical identification of Philosophy with the World is not by any means a denigration of the World but rather an unlatching of thought and experience from inessential constraints.
3. François Laruelle, *Une biographie de l'homme ordinaire* (Paris: Aubier, 1985), p. 16.
4. Edmund Husserl, *The Crisis of European Sciences and Transcendental Phenomenology*, translated by David Carr (Evanston: Northwestern University Press, 1970), pp. 133–4.
5. Ibid., p. 139.
6. See, for instance, Hent de Vries, *Philosophy and the Turn to Religion* (Baltimore: Johns Hopkins University Press, 1999), pp. 143–4.
7. Husserl, *Crisis*, p. 183.
8. Whether to its detriment: analytic aridity; or its glory: analytic clarity.
9. Gilbert Ryle, *The Concept of Mind* (London: Hutchinson, 1949), p. 22.
10. Gilbert Ryle, *Dilemmas* (Cambridge and New York: Cambridge, 1954), p. 63.
11. Ryle, *The Concept of Mind*, p. 155.
12. Ibid., p. 195.
13. Ibid., pp. 195–6.
14. Ibid., p. 181.
15. Ibid., p. 182.
16. Laruelle's analysis of Derridian deconstruction as one mode of the more general structure of philosophical Difference is found in François Laruelle, *Philosophies of Difference: A Critical Introduction to Non-Philosophy*, translated by Rocco Gangle (London and New York: Continuum, 2010), Chapter 5.

17. Pierre Klossowski, *Sade my Neighbor*, translated by Alphonso Lingis (London: Quartet, 1991), p. 48.

18. Ibid.

19. Ibid.

20. Ibid.

4

The Justice of Non-Philosophy
Joshua Ramey

Obedient to no man, dependent only on weather and season, without a goal before them or a roof above them, owning nothing, open to every whim of fate, the homeless wanderers lead their childlike, brave, shabby existence. They are the sons of Adam, who was driven out of Paradise; the brothers of the animals, of innocence. Out of heaven's hand they accept what is given them from moment to moment: sun, rain, fog, snow, warmth, cold, comfort, and hardship; time does not exist for them and neither does history, or ambition, or that bizarre idol called progress and evolution, in which houseowners believe so desperately. A wayfarer may be delicate or crude, artful or awkward, brave or cowardly – he is always a child at heart, living in the first day of creation, before the beginning of the history of the world, his life always guided by a few simple instincts and needs. He may be intelligent or stupid; he may be deeply aware of the fleeting fragility of all living things, of how pettily and fearfully each living creature carries its bit of warm blood through the glacier of cosmic space, or he may merely follow the commands of his poor stomach with childlike glee – he is always the opponent, the deadly enemy of the established proprietor, who hates him, despises him, or fears him, because he does not wish to be reminded that all existence is transitory, that life is constantly wilting, that merciless icy death fills the cosmos all around.

Herman Hesse, *Narcissus and Goldmund*

In Terrence Malick's *The Tree of Life* (2011) a gesture is made that is highly revealing for the contours of non-philosophy. The film presents a completely ordinary family drama: a father is too severe, a mother suffers in silence, a son chafes. A friend is lost in a drowning accident, a father loses his job, a family is forced to move. The film does not add these events together; in fact it hardly narrates them, at all. Continuity is left at a minimum. Early in the film, when it is revealed that a son has been lost, meditation on this event begins from a distant perspective, that of the grown brother (Sean Penn), who simply takes a moment in his day as an architect to consider his past, and is moved to call his father on a break. This utterly common reverie, however, parallels a sequence of cosmic meditations on the origins of life, cosmic destruction, and the prospects of redemption.

What is crucial, in all of this, is Malick's intense use of parataxis. Rather than using film to narrate, Malick places himself, as *auteur*, alongside a set of human lives, and simply makes himself cinematically present. That is to say, Malick actively resists the temptation to construct a cinematic Whole which might reveal to us some true, hidden reality immanent to life's mute persistence. Rather, in *Tree of Life* a relation to reality is revealed only from the side of cinema. And yet, the intensity of this (non-)relation to life enables the film to be *present* to that which cannot be represented.

In this way, Malick does an almost unconceivable *justice* to human life. If human life is a story, then each life *is* its own story. Thus every telling of that tale is an abstraction, perhaps a kind of distortion. But what kind of a story is a life? The discontinuities in life – including violence, suffering and death itself – seem either ineffable or patently betrayed by narration, the sense of such events betrayed by any sense of continuity imposed upon these events by narrative. What any narrative must do, but seems incapable of doing in good faith, is to deal with discontinuity. For *living* – in pain or pleasure, through loss or ecstasy, and with the constant burden of the past – is different from narrating that living, and it is difficult to see how narration could fail to fail existence, to merely pretend to keep the secret of life by telling it.

But perhaps that way of framing the problem is too coarse. It may be true that to the degree that living is a minimal continuity, any narrative continuity is already a kind of metanarrative, a subsumption of life in something larger than a life. At the same time, however, life – at least human life – *is* arguably a struggle to narrate, a creative struggle for some kind of consistency, however minimal, even if what is narrated are a series of nearly insurmountable challenges to any conception of consistency and coherence. It is Malick's genius that, rather than despair of telling a human story, he manages to be present, with his camera, to those discontinuities (archaic, present, or futural) about which we continue to wonder: those events whose narrative we *are*, but whose story we do not *have*.

Malick manages, that is to say, to be present to the discontinuous in life. In this way, Malick removes himself from a position of authority that would take it upon itself to give sense to the senseless (or 'sense poor', to twist Heidegger). By assuming that a certain level of senselessness, or at least enigma, is both perfectly ordinary and ultimately insurmountable, Malick is able to present the human struggle for comprehension through images of the origins of life and intimations of the afterlife, without for all that needing to pass judgement on the salience or value of these images. By being present to ordinary human life in this way, or to present cosmic levels of destruction and potential redemption as perfectly ordinary dimensions of existence, Malick manages to affirm life in a way that refuses any pretension to a coherence that would do violence to the internal, immanent struggle for coherence itself.

Malick's technique has striking parallels with non-philosophy, especially in Laruelle's efforts in *Future Christ* to disinter an 'in-past' or 'in-man' of humanity, a human essence that is 'heretical' in so far as it is perpetually persecuted, misused and ultimately obliterated by the narratives that enforce the agenda of the world.[1] To begin with, humanity or the 'in-man', for Laruelle, has a heretical relationship to *time*. For Laruelle, there is, strictly speaking, no development in the essence of humanity: all was there from the beginning. This is obviously an outlandish statement, but it cannot be softened or nuanced without diminishing its significance. For the 'Living-without-life' that is the human essence, we are each like the wanderer Goldmund of whom Hesse writes in our epigram. For this wanderer, as for non-philosophy, there is neither decline nor progress in humanity. Taking up this position of the wandering, 'outlandish' vagabond, non-philosophy is a militant insistence that humanity is neither a being in the world swept up in a temporal *ecstasis*, nor a self-consciousness struggling for recognition, but is, in an extremely banal sense, a being that is *persecuted in the world*. Taking up this stance in relation to recent continental thought, the human essence of non-philosophy is neither 'thrown' into the world (as in the early Heidegger), 'to come' (as in Derrida, or perhaps even as in Deleuze), found 'remaining' (as in Benjamin or Agamben), or persisting as 'undead' (Žižek). Rather, the subject is *present* and *persecuted*, present-as-persecuted. As Laruelle puts it, in *Future Christ*:

Our problem remains this: is man an historical and philosophical being, as the *doxa* of intellectuals have it, and who calls for this self-knowledge and recognition? ... From the point of view that is human-in-the-last-identity history is no longer a criteria, not evidently of facts nor even of their signification, but of that which is valuable for man, not as being-in-the-world but as subject-for-the-world.[2]

When it comes to what matters for humanity, the category of history holds no meaning, and the concept of time no promise. By insisting upon the position of the human as a subject *for* the world and not a being *in* the world (or even a being *in* time), non-philosophy produces a 'unilateral duality' between humanity and its world. What is such a unilateral duality? In Laruelle's language, humanity and the world are fundamentally separate. That is to say, they are not distinct by being related, but are different *by* separation. Absolute separation entails that the essence of the human is *not* revealed by its relations with the-World, and that human nature is never revealed through a temporal process, whether world-historical, deconstructive, critical or clinical. The human discovers its essence only 'in-the-last-instance'. What Laruelle means to index through such an instance is a future that is, paradoxically, *not in a process of arriving*. The 'future Christ', or what Laruelle calls 'life in-the-last-instance', is not a process of arrival, but an ultimatum always already here. Put laconically, the human is a past that does not pass. It is in this sense a past in-itself, what Laruelle calls the 'in-past'. The in-past is an existence *out of time*, in the sense that it is that which has always been excluded, despised and rejected by the temporality of the passing World. Hence the proper name of the human essence, according to non-philosophy, is 'Christ', or rather 'future Christ': the stone the builders rejected, the 'in past' despised and rejected by the process of the World.

However, for non-philosophy, the persecution of the human is neither dramatic nor eventful, but utterly ordinary. For non-philosophy, a conception of humanity persecuted, harassed, betrayed and murdered entails neither the radical passivity of the abject nor the radical activity of the revolutionary. Rather, persecution is simply the distinctive mark of that which is in continuous *revolt* against a World whose most basic form of violence consists in the utterly banal attempt to relate or correlate every struggle, need, or concern to a struggle, need, or concern within the World, such as it is. But for non-philosophy, the human struggle is a struggle precisely because it is *not* the struggle of the World, but separate from the World, in the last instance. It is the task of non-philosophy to speak from the position of a subject separate from the World, a subject out of time.

Dualysis

What is the logic of an essence revealed 'in the last instance' or 'by separation'? For surely this is not a temporal 'last' or a spatial separateness. It is, rather, an axiomatic operation Laruelle has christened 'dualysis'. In brief, dualysis is a method of analysing an extremely general form of syntax germane to all of philosophy, or to what Laruelle calls 'the-philosophy'. Writ large, Laruelle's critique is that, across multiple iterations, the-philosophy attempts to think the Real from within the heart of relations, but in a gesture that is self-defeating, since the very setting-into-relation of terms obscures the reality to which the relations are thought to attest. An order of discourse is substituted for an ordering by the Real. Laruelle's procedure of 'dualysis' attempts to disinter any mixture of relatively transcendent with relatively immanent terms, whatever – whether these terms be thought and being, concept and intuition, form and content, empirical and transcendental, and so on.

For example, in *Philosophies of Difference*, Laruelle argues that the thought of difference, championed by Nietzsche, Heidegger, Derrida and Deleuze, brings difference into relation with thought, and thus repeats a fundamental gesture of the-philosophy subject to dualysis.[3] The thought of difference encompasses difference within a discourse of difference, englobing the Real (of difference) and its discourse within a unified whole, an identity of identity and difference. While difference is supposed to be an evental upsurge, unthinkable trace, or multiple Real, it is nevertheless subordinated by philosophical syntax to a One that blends or mixes the immanence of difference and the transcendence of discourse. On the basis of its subordination to any such mixture, the thinking of difference fails to be other than a renewed thinking of the One (even if this One is seen as fractured or split within itself).

Rather than disburden thought of its false transcendence and abstract character, the 'thought of difference' privileges a certain thought-of-difference over difference in itself, and thus fails to be a thinking *from* the Real. By contrast, Laruelle's axiom is that thought must move from a discourse *of* the One to a conceptual axiomatics operating *from* the Real, *from* the 'One-in-person'. The difficulty, of course, is that the One-in-person is radically partial, and the One speaks only from its strangeness. So Laruelle claims that each One, each Stranger, is an Identity and not a Universal, a unilateral identity that speaks from and not of its identity, making use of philosophical materials and concepts in the most ordinary sense of 'use', *without the identity in question being retroactively constituted by the materials of which it makes use.* This last clause, obviously the most crucial, is also the most difficult to carry out, as each deliverance from the One is tempted to identify itself with its relation to its discourse rather than its non-relation to every other discourse, which would be the hallmark of the One in its separateness.

For Laruelle, the gesture of blending or conflating the relative immanence of individual identity and the relative transcendence of identifying structures in the World, is what the World shares with the-philosophy. Both the World and the-philosophy essentially render the Real (One) – unilateral difference and solitary essence – unthinkable. However, it is not the project of non-philosophy to prove that *there is* unilateral (non-relational) difference and solitary essence, but to show that such essence is there by thinking *from* it, in axiomatic fashion. Put somewhat differently, both the World and the-philosophy insist upon 'phenomenalising' every identity – whether human, animal, divine, political, erotic, or otherwise – in relation to some thought-of or use-of such identities, some setting-into-relation that undermines that which is essentially non-related (the Real of the One in each case). But non-philosophy is a thought, using philosophical materials, of a unilateral duality, a strangeness that is not an estrangement, but an identity-in-the-last-instance that can is encountered outside of all process of having-become-estranged, or having-been-identified, beyond any circumstance that mixes or blends transcendence and immanence, discourse and reality, concept and object.

Persecution

To speak from such a position is to speak from persecution, a persecution of essence that is made necessary by the format of the World. Because it is not a mixture, but an identity, the human as such never *appears*. What is revealed in non-philosophy (or non-philosophically revealed) is a 'Living' of persecution, a life hunted down, a Life sought after by the assassins of the Church as much as the World, a life revealed only as destroyed. This heretical inhumanity is the truly universal dimension of human life, but is a life that has nothing to do with the generalities of biology or nature, civilisation or culture. Laruelle writes:

> We call forth 'the living', in this way naming humans as victims and those murdered in the cause of heresy, thereby revealing the nature of it. Their persecution testifies to an experience of the human that is not natural, that is no longer humanist or philosophical; it is a heretical concept of man as in-Person and applies to all men. The other first names like Humans, Christ-subjects, Heretics, etc., do not designate natural men, susceptible to biological life and death, but *insofar as* they exist as Living and are liable to a being-revealed by persecution and assassination. Heretics are living an invisible life, towards which no gaze can turn no matter what its nature, even a spiritual one.[4]

The 'spiritual gaze' of post-war European thought has arguably attempted (in apparent agreement with Laruelle) to affirm the essence of human life as persecuted, as invisible, incapable of being contemplated. It has tended to do this through reflections upon the Shoah. One of Laruelle's most audacious heresies is that he acknowledges the significance of the Shoah by *refusing* to allow it to stand as *sui generis*, as an event in any sense singular. Far from reducing the world-historical significance of this atrocity, by positing the Shoah as an index of global persecution, and not as an ineffable singularity, Laruelle in some sense *refuses to capitalise* on the holocaust. That is to say, he refuses to enrich the transcendental, or to enrich philosophy, by recasting the transcendental and/or the conceptual on the basis of some overpowering empirical phenomenon. On the contrary, Laruelle moves thought to the *side* of this Real, and to an oblique position with respect to the transcendental-empirical doublet. Non-philosophy speaks *from* an essence of suffering given to thought from the holocaust and *from* the multitude of persecutions. In this way the possibility is preserved of an *ordinary* thought, a contingent thought from the Shoah and from the persecution of heretics, rather than a thought *by* or *for* some abstract transcendental category of dereliction, abjection, or suffering, within which the intractable immanence of

the Shoah and heresy might be made to play exemplary or typo-
logical roles.

This is to say that, for Laruelle, neither the victims of the Shoah
nor the heretics offer to philosophy or to religion a material for
contemplation, or for any kind of hermeneutic enterprise.[5] What
the heretics and victims have, or guard and keep 'against the day'
– against the totalising and interpretational gestures of philosophy
and religion – is an experience that is not a matter of memory.[6]
This is the experience of the 'in-past', of something immemorial
that goes ever-unrecognised by the world. This 'in-past' remains
always a Stranger whose demand alone can form the basis for
axioms of a life separable from the World. This in-past, this living-
without-life, is found not in memory, but in an uncanny, atempo-
ral future: 'if the Jews are witnesses it is as survivors in the trial
who must follow their murder in an immanent way'.[7] It is only as
immanently continued, or as 'in-One', that victims are witnesses
to the Shoah. It is only in so far as this event interrupts or breaks
with the present, and not as it is remembered by the present, that
it matters for thought, rather than becoming once again subordinated as simple material for its pacifying mixtures.

Salvation From Time

In *Future Christ*, Laruelle acknowledges that the notion of a
humanity whose essence is separable from its life in the world is
an explicitly Christian and Gnostic idea, one entailed by a view of
the World as fallen and humanity as essentially alienated in and
ultimately murdered by the World. Laruelle writes:

> Those Murdered in the cause of heresy are not dormant in memory
> and buried in history. The murder of human beings reveals, in trying
> to fill it, the gap within the world that *is* Man-in-person. It is in this
> completely positive gap, in this inconsistency of Life, that a new deci-
> sion can be captured under the form of axioms and an explication
> given under the form of theorems, but still practices of those that are
> and those that want, among other things, Christian confessions.[8]

Humanity is, by definition, that which cannot be subordinated to
the World. No matter how intricate, technologically complex, or
full or subterfuge and intrigue, history has no ruse, and humanity
does not discover itself in its historical being. From this position,

in the gap within the world, Laruelle asserts that axioms can be formulated and explanations given in the name of ordinary human life, and asserts that the practice of generating such discourse is of and for those who want and need what Christian confessions have promised, and yet so far have failed to deliver. This is nothing less than the promise of *salvation*.

Laruelle's indictment of Christianity operates on many fronts, but here his critique is extremely precise. Christianity does not fail in so far as it attempts to find, preach, or produce salvation, even the universal salvation of humanity. It fails, rather, in the *compromise* it necessarily makes with the world. When Laruelle criticises the pretensions of both 'Greek Being' and 'Christian Time' to serve as general categories of experience, he argues that 'the World', in a strictly ordinary sense, subordinates both being and time to *functions* within the world in a way that philosophical discourse cannot comprehend. Despite philosophical pretensions to the contrary, being and time are not categories standing outside the world and conditioning it.[9] As Laruelle puts it:

> As for Greek Being and Christian Time, a supplementary mixture in which the philosophy of the preceding century believed to have found its renewal, they are dismissed due to their pretensions and handed over to their rightful place, which is the World. These are no more than the modes of symbolization and formalization of the Man-in-person, but they do not determine him.[10]

What determines humanity in the last instance is neither Being nor time, but a relation to the World of suffering and persecution, a relation that demands nothing less than salvation. Heidegger's conception of the essentially temporal dimension of humanity is obviously Laruelle's opponent here (although, as we will see shortly, the critique has implications for Hegelian views as well). What Laruelle calls 'Man-in-person', or the 'in-man', is not conditioned by any kind of temporal *ecstasis* or distended present, and the rejection of temporality as a determinative category for humanity is meant to displace both the early ('existential') and late ('evental') conceptions of Heideggerian finitude. For Laruelle, Heidegger had determined time in a way that obscurely mixes two notions of time in a single concept. On the one hand there is in Heidegger a sense of temporality that involves the 'immanence of the lived', or what Laruelle calls the 'in-past'. On the other hand, there is a relatively transcendent dimension that Laruelle calls 'the-time', an ecstatic 'present' of the World, a present that cannot be captured as 'presence', but that gives or yields being in its fragile continuity. For Heidegger, it was the positive task of philosophy to dwell or tarry with the poetic density of this mixture wherein beings are let be in their evental upsurge. For Laruelle, there is a singular violence contained in this mixed conception, and indeed in any conception of the human essence as 'temporalised'. (In what follows I leave the validity of Laruelle's critique of Heidegger to the judgement of the reader.)

The human essence, for Laruelle, is always 'unlearned' with respect to the World, and indeed with respect to time. To tem-poralise or historicise the subject, in any way, is to *exclude her unlearned essence*, by folding that essence into the play of the world, its necessary violence. In order to liberate the subject from this violence (at once theoretical and practical), Laruelle insists that the subject is not an evental upsurge [*Ereignis*] within a distended present, but a future-past 'disenclosed' [*désinséré*] in time. What is dis-enclosed is what Laruelle calls the 'in-man', a 'Lived' that is radically 'in-past' in the sense that such a past is that which is never disclosed by the world, but can only suffer in the world. As he puts it, 'because the Lived is without purpose or ecstasy as regards the World, he determines a subject and that subject is for-the-World and Time without being inscribed, even as "future", in the Time-world'.[11] We might even say that, in the last instance, the 'being' of the ordinary is not even 'in the world'. It is simply *for* the world, subject to the world in the most ordinary sense. Man-in-person is not a dimension of temporal *ecstasis*, but an 'in-past' separate from the world, separable from the world in the last instance.

The last instance is the instant of salvation, a salvation that comes by the axiomatic 'cloning' of ordinary human life.[12] Thus, in the face of the persecution of the ordinary, or the ordinary (fact of) persecution, the problem of non-philosophy is that of universal salvation. Considered by non-philosophy, 'saved' simply names 'life-in-the-last-instance', life that is not natural because it cannot be conceived as a flourishing (à la Aristotle) or as a persisting (as in Spinoza), but only as life despised, rejected and persecuted, life crucified by the World. This is the rigorously Paulinian aspect of Laruelle's thought (or Laruelle's usage of Pauline materials) since for Paul eternal life, Life-in-Christ, is not natural life. 'I am crucified with Christ: nevertheless I live; yet not I, but Christ liveth in me: and the life which I now live in the flesh I live by the faith of the Son of God, who loved me, and gave himself for me' (Galatians 2:20 KJV).

But what is the ordinary or non-revealed sense – the non-religious and heretical sense, that is – of saved life? Given the unconditioned reality of universal death, what are the conditions of universal salvation?[13] Put somewhat more strategically, *how* is life in the last instance, the life of 'man-in-man', non-philosophically revealed?

To approach this problem requires a detour through Christology, and more specifically a detour through the passion, the persecution and murder of the Christ. For, to begin with, the heretics are, for all intents and purposes, *how they died*, or how their living was without life, and chafed against the life of the Church and the World, in so far as these lives were despised and rejected by the World and the Church. Ironically, for Laruelle it is the genius of Christianity to recognise *rejected life* as True Life, even if only in the case of its saints and martyrs, not in the case of its heretics. Christianity, starting with Paul, recognised a certain sort of living death or what Laruelle calls 'Living-without-life' as already eternal, even as already-resurrected. As orthodox theologians are rightly proud to point out, this enabled Christian ethics to do away in advance with Stoicism – with an ethic of death or preparation for dying, and with any morbid, let alone merely melancholy attitude to life. From his own heretical position, to this Christian axiom Laruelle adds the Gnostic insistence upon a radical separation and solitude of humanity, a non-relation between human *gnosis* and the ultimate nature of the divine, such that Living-without-life is not a communion with God but a continuous revolt against God-the-World, or against a God complicit with World, the God Laruelle calls God-the-World.[14]

To continue with theological terms, what Laruelle conceives is an argument to the effect that the future Christ, the man-in-the-last-identity or the in-man, is already the first man, the man 'in-past'.[15] That is to say, in heretical terms, if Christ is the second Adam, Adam is also the first Christ.[16] The universal salvation declared by non-philosophy is that, in the last instance, we are all in-Christ because we are all in-Adam. (It might be noted that even for orthodoxy, it is not as if humanity earns Adam through Christ – humanity is Christlike only in so far as it embraces *adam*, dirt, red dirt, earth already ruddy, bloody, the entire 'nature' suffering under the logic of sacrifice, of the sacrificial lamb. Worthy is Adam, worthy is the Lamb).

Biblically speaking, the revelation of the worthiness of the Lamb is made within the apocalypse, the end times. Is not history essential to the revelation of the Lamb? Is not history a salvation history? The interpretation of history, or rather the reading of history as a history of salvation, is perhaps *the* orthodox discipline, in so far as it is constantly incumbent upon theology to make sense of history in terms of the presence of God, the unfolding of an enigmatic yet present divine will in all events. But Laruelle's heresy is a denial of any meaning to history – including to the process or procedure that moves through the sequence creation-fall-redemption, Adam-Christ. It is also heretical in so far as it would deny any dialectical teleology in the Marxist sense to history (as Althusser did already). It is as if Laruelle wishes to think from a totally apocalyptic point, a point *out of time*, where the man-in-the-last-instance is somehow both Adam and Christ and neither, but the One-in-Person. It is at this point that Laruelle's break with Hegelian Christology becomes significant, since his Christology breaks entirely with the process of dialectical revelation.

Toward Non-Hegelian Christology

Laruelle's view of the human essence, and his usage of Christology, directly violates Žižek's injunction not to 'fetishise' the man Jesus. As Žižek puts it in *Living in the End Times*, Christianity is simply an exemplar of a general process of revelation proper to the materialist dialectics of form being emptied of content, then affirmed as such. As Žižek writes:

> emptying the form of its content already takes place within Christianity itself, at its very core – the name for this emptying is *kenosis*: God dies and is resurrected as the Holy Ghost, as the *form* of collective belief. It is a fetishistic mistake to search for the material support of this form (the resurrected Christ) – the Holy Ghost is the very collective of believers, what they search for outside is already here in the guise of the love that binds them.[17]

In Žižek's Hegelian Christology, historical truth is revealed as *aufgehoben* in the dialectical passage from Father to Spirit, within which the death of the Son functions simply as a vanishing moment of mediation. The key moment in the passion is not Christ's literal death, let alone his magical resurrection, but his performative utterance at Calvary: *Eli eli lama sabachtani*, my God, my God, why hast thou forsaken me? For Žižek (following Hegel), this speech act enunciates God's self-rejection, an auto-rejection of the Essence by itself that opens the space for the 'assumption' of the death of God by the universal Singularity that is the ethico-political community of believers (the true Substance).

For Žižek, what is crucial here is Christ as a recapitulation of Job. Job was the first to realise the incoherence at the heart of God, to see beyond the façade of divine consistency, to the inconsistency at the heart of the absolute. Job sees that there is *no reason* for his suffering, and fully assumes this 'lack in the big Other'. Such a lack is, of course, most clearly on display when Job asks for the reason why he has suffered, and is answered by a grotesque and comical display of divine power. God's answer is not an answer at all, but a refusal of the question. It is the very archetype of authoritarianism: who are you to question me? Job's silence, as Carl Jung astutely observed, long before Žižek, represents his moral superiority to Yahweh. Job is polite enough to keep silent at the inability of God to give him an answer. At this moment, the tables are turned: divine impotence is transformed into human strength, becoming the 'divine' human ability to endure suffering, to patiently endure the trial of existence, 'without why'.

Christ's words at Calvary, Žižek asserts, do not express his dismay, but rather the final diremption of God himself, God's complete exile from God. Even Žižek's favourite Catholic apologist, G. K. Chesterton, acknowledges that this is the terrible moment at which 'God is forsaken of God'. Of course, for the orthodox Chesterton, this is simply a moment in the larger narrative of divine *kenosis*, the departure and ultimate return to God that encompasses every cosmic vicissitude.[18] For Žižek, by contrast, when Christ dies, he vanishes. In Hegelian terms, Christ is a 'vanishing mediator'. What is left, the indivisible remainder of the dialectic, is the community, the communion of the Holy Spirit that makes of each believer an 'undead' Christ, a militant subject whose life is already, by faith in Christ, beyond life and death. The Christian subject has fully assumed the death or non-existence of the Father qua Big Other, and has equally assumed the radical freedom entailed by such a position. The militant community of believers demonstrates that life is truly life only as undead, only as having fully assumed – as at the termination, *per impossible*, of successful psychoanalysis – the lack in the Big Other, and the irreducible multiplicity of the *noms-de-Père*, a multiplicity of contingent yet absolute ethical obligations.

What is discounted in this picture, and what Laruelle in some sense insists upon (in an heretical sense), is the role of the man Jesus, his particular death and peculiar resurrection. For Žižek, there is no *sense* in the doctrine of resurrection (let alone a referent). The only sense of 'Christ' is that a certain community has fully assumed the consequences of the revelation of Job-Christ – namely, that there is no God, and all responsibility lies with the human community. But from Laruelle's perspective, this 'atheist' position subordinates the 'future Christ' to a temporal dialectic: man becomes, as it were, a dimension of atheism, reduced to his role as a moment in the World. Žižek thus repeats the fundamental gesture of 'the-philosophy', subordinating Man-in-person to the remainder of a necessary process.[19]

What drops out of Žižek's Job-Christ typology is ordinary humanity, the thing that suffers, the human that is persecuted and abandoned. Žižek makes it seem as if 'we' are God's auto-persecution or abandonment of himself. But such an auto-rejection of God remains entirely *spiritual*: even Žižek's theatrics of calling us divine shit is emperor's new clothes. Truly, from this perspective, we are less than shit, we are nothingness itself. But for Laruelle, the real rejection, and the reality of the Fall, is the alienation between humanity-in-the-last-instance (the in-human, the in-past) and the World. This is Laruelle's Gnostic axiom – the axiom of complete non-relation between humanity and the World, in the last instance. This is the attention to the very Real of suffering that for Žižek is ultimately a kind of temporal passage, a dialectical transition. But it is also, I would argue, what the Biblical notion of Christ as 'Lamb of God' also indicates for humanity, at least for a non-philosophical heresy. Contra Žižek, and from a truly apocalyptic perspective, it is not the Community but the *Lamb* that is worthy. And Laruelle's heresy is that the Lamb is Adam. What is worthy is suffering humanity. If for Hegel, the wounds of spirit heal and leave no scars, then for Laruelle, the spiritual body is the in-past of suffering, itself. Contra Žižek, humanity-in-the-last-instance is not the remainder of the undead *qua* those who Act. Undead is no longer an adjective, no longer the quality of an act, but a genuine substantive: the persecuted Living of an undead suffering servant, the undead Lambs of God, in the hands of the world, the Living-without-life.[20]

Resurrection as Justice

With non-philosophy, Christology moves from a logic of undeath to a logic of *resurrected clones*. What is the non-philosophical and heretical sense of resurrection? In some sense, Laruelle's theory of resurrection is a theory of justice. It is only by enacting a *future* dimension of experience in the past, the experience of the 'in-past', that justice is accomplished. It is, in a sense, only the resurrection, only a kind of immanent insurrection-resurrection of the in-past, that can truly demand justice by becoming identical to justice (that is, to itself). Any witness-to or reading-of the past, any hermeneutic of the past, betrays the in-past, translating the in-past into material for the 'infinite religious urge' to maintain a series of open-ended historical and memorial 'problems' that will require the constant regulation and management by philosophy and religion.[21] Justice cannot be given or rendered to the in-past of persecution without betraying the demand of the human as such, since that demand is not a demand for recognition, but simply for existence. Only resurrection is justice. 'Strictly speaking, the radical past does not exist and does not want to pass into existence, but it determines the old time as existant-Future. The subject is not an existant *in* the future but an existant subject from the mode of the future and exhausts itself in it.'[22]

What is it to exist 'from the mode of the future'? It is at this point that something like the 'practice' of non-philosophy can begin to be clarified, or at least outlined, in so far as it relates to subjectivity. The act of interpretation, mastered by philosophy, by the-Church and the-World, does not usher in the future, but simply elaborates the present, distends it, seeking to make the present large enough, give it enough largesse, to sustain or carry the horrors of the past along with it. By contrast, Laruelle indicates that to exist from the future is to make a certain *usage* of memory, rather than to remember, bear witness, or even mourn. 'To determine memory by a past-outside-time, *no longer cloning as anamnesis* but as future, this is a heretical task.'[23] The tradition of anamnesis – Platonic as much as Augustinian – is that of a re-membering or recapitulation that transforms its materials. The heretical operation of 'cloning' Laruelle wishes to enact precisely does *not* transform the past. It is only in that case – only in case cloning occurs – that a future is produced, a future of the Real in-past, and its insurrection, rather than a simple extension or 'ecstasis' of the World, with its endless cycles and nauseating mirage.

But a cloning of the in-past liberates the in-past from the World and from all temporality. 'The immanent and inecstatic past is inexistent and inconsistent but precisely as capable of determining memory and the present as material for the future.'[24] If it is the hermeneutic enterprise par excellence to render a past consistent (even in its deconstructive phase of mourning or tracing), it is only that which cannot be interpreted, even that which cannot be read, cannot even be indexed, that alone becomes material for the future, and that always already was the only possible future. It is only the 'past which withdraws from every consistency',[25] only the in-past, that can be cloned as future.[26]

Thus non-philosophical subjectivity is a violation of the sacrosanct or *kairological* view of history, a rejection of history as a category of meaningful relevance to subjectivity in the last instance. The subject of non-philosophy is apocalyptic, out of time, and history is the history of *crime*: history is crime, as such, and temporality only ever a false mediation-meditation by the-philosophy. All attempts to subordinate the human to time are so many attempts to gloss the World or subordinate it to a temporal *ecstasis* that only does more subtle and thus more total violence to the essence of in-man, the living-without-Life, the life that represents a radical in-past not subject to any temporalising gloss, destiny, finality, or unveiling. To think from this point of view is to do nothing less than save the world from itself. As Laruelle puts it,

The religious crime is in a parallel situation that resolutely exposes man in the World and alienates him there; it exceeds the simple original error and cannot be made the object of a redemption of the kind of that of man. Because God himself can no longer make sacrifice in order to save himself and man with him from that sufficiency, then we wonder if the crime is not due to an irresponsibility that would have reinforced the irresponsibility of the onto-theo-logians. No new cross is still possible, no Christ is once again situated towards Calvary and it is necessary to invent another salvation for God-the-World himself. The Unredeemed-in-person will be the cause and will be able this time to rescue God from his evil vocation, and from the curse with which gnosis has rightly condemned him.[27]

Here Laruelle effectively sunders the Third Person from the Trinity and replaces it with 'God-the-World', effectively re-asserting the old Gnostic dualism of Unfallen and Fallen divinity. Even God does not find his immanence, his nature 'in-God' as *causa sui*, *actus purus*, or infinite auto-affection, but from the death of Christ and the empty tomb.[28] It is 'God-the-World' as much as the God of the philosophers that must be saved by man-in-man. It is the uncreated in-man, beyond salvation, that saves or redeems God-the-World in the last instance.

The axioms of humanity-in-the-last-instance are the judgements of the resurrected upon the world. These axioms are the voices of the Unredeemed-in-person. The thought of the Unredeemed-in-person is that of the Lamb of God, *Agneau de Dieu*. Such thoughts – multiple, partial, fragmented – are the voices of those who faced the world, receiving its blows but remaining, as murdered, untouched. Only such judgements count, since only the in-past are *without* the determinants of the World, as those who existed *despite* the World. And only such judgements clone the resurrected, or appear as resurrected clones of life in the last instance, ordinary human life. As in *The Tree of Life*, where Malick's camera performs the necessary axiomatic gesture, becoming present to an ineffably enigmatic sequence without masking itself in its own enigma, without glamorising itself through the violence of a totalising gesture. As in camera, so in concept, a struggle for the justice of presence, if not the presence of justice to life. This is the ultimate concern of non-philosophy.

Notes

1. François Laruelle, *Future Christ: A Lesson in Heresy*, translated by Anthony Paul Smith (London: Continuum, 2010).
2. Ibid., pp. 81–2.
3. François Laruelle, *Philosophies of Difference: A Critical Introduction to Non-Philosophy*, translated by Rocco Gangle (London: Continuum, 2010).
4. Laruelle, *Future Christ*, p. 19.
5. It should be said that the understanding of 'hermeneutic' on offer here is not necessarily the philosophical hermeneutics of, say, a Gadamer. Laruelle is thinking more simply of the standard modes of historical interpretation that are aimed at cultivating certain 'virtues' thought to pertain to history, such as 'common objectivity, univer-

sality of comprehension, the establishment of a consensus where men can be recognizable, reconciliation with the past' (Laruelle, *Future Christ*, p. 81).

6. Ibid., p. 78. Here Laruelle is close to Agamben's meditations on *musselman* or Žižek's reflections on Odradek, on the inhuman as witness, but his point is precisely that such figures do not function as witnesses but as *material for the future*, as Life-without-living.

7. Ibid., p. 79.

8. Laruelle, p. 21. With this linkage of subjectivity to a 'positive gap' and an 'inconsistency of life', Laruelle's thinking seems to resonate with that of Slavoj Žižek, who has repeatedly resorted to a Hegelian reading of Christianity to expound the nature of the truly revolutionary collective. But as we will see shortly, Laruelle's usage of Christian and Gnostic themes is a striking departure from that of Žižek.

9. Ibid., p. 28.

10. Ibid.

11. Ibid., p. 29.

12. Ibid., p. 24.

13. Ibid., p. 20.

14. For Laruelle's elaboration of this point, see François Laruelle, *Mystique Non-Philosophique a l'usage des contemporains* (Paris: L'Harmattan, 2007), pp. 35–8.

15. One can see that there is something both heretical and orthodox about Laruelle's thinking. Such a borrowing from both heresy and orthodoxy is in keeping with his stated programme of transforming 'the hierarchical unity of orthodoxy and heresy such that they regain equal right within a new thought' (Laruelle, *Future Christ*, p. 28).

16. I owe this formula to Rocco Gangle, in conversation.

17. Slavoj Žižek, *Living in the End Times* (London: Verso, 2010), p. 118.

18. See G. K. Chesterton, *Orthodoxy* (San Francisco: Ignatius Press, 1995).

19. For Žižek, there is not only no God, but no humanity. There is only the 'undead' ethical community. Living humanity is itself an illusion, an illusion of continuity that should have died with the onto-theological God. For humanism Žižek substitutes a radical voluntarism, an ethos of the will for an ethics of human life sustained through tradition and virtue.

20. In some sense, for Laruelle, the crucified body is the *only* result, the only remainder of the process of salvation. But the crucified body

is *immediately* the resurrected body, because it is the Real. Such a Real Presence is always already subtracted from the world, since the world is always already erected against the suffering body, in so far as suffering is always justified or can always be explained in terms of the World. Laruelle's heresy here is that we are all saved as suffering, as persecuted universally. Adam as East of Eden is already saved. In this way, Laruelle's is a yet more gothic vision than Žižek's, for whom undeath is still an abstraction from suffering and persecution, from man-in-revolt and in exile. But not in the sense of a necessary or fortunate fall, because history has revealed nothing and taught us nothing. That is Laruelle's great anti-Hegelian heresy, his 'unlearned knowledge'. Every advancement in the relief of suffering has been matched by an advance in the rate of exclusion of those who suffer from the means of relief. As Vico, Nietzsche and Foucault already demonstrated, the apparent 'democratisation' of empire has been matched, point by point, with the manipulation of the very defini-tion of humanity, so that power to the people, freedom of or for the people, has been given only at the price of their ever-increasing docility, imbecility and inarticulateness. The consciousness of intel-lectuals has only increased with the increase of the impotence of their discourse and its complicity with power. In a way, one could say that non-philosophy is simply the recognition of philosophy's desperate attempt to seize upon an image of the One and to marshal a counter-violence, a kind of counter-empire, that would displace the political imperium with one that would be philosophical (Plato to Heidegger, with their Kingdoms of Moderation and Authenticity, respectively, and perhaps even to Nietzsche, Derrida and Deleuze, with their various Kingdoms of Difference). But with Christ Laruelle can say, of the in-past, that its 'kingdom is not of this world'.

21. Laruelle, *Future Christ*, p. 78.
22. Ibid., p. 77.
23. Ibid., p. 76.
24. Ibid.
25. Ibid., p. 77.
26. There are affinities here with Bataille's meditations on animality, and on the inaccessibility of animality to all economy, all subjective economy, even that of sacrifice. The animal is the perfect sacrifice because it is that which cannot be killed no matter how much it is sacrificed. No matter how much meaning, truth, interpretation, analysis, introspection, rationalisation goes on within the human animal, it is the animal that *sustains*, that endures every death, every

death-drive. In *The Open*, Agamben recounts his discovery of a thirteenth-century manuscript of the Bible with an engraving depicting the saints in glory feasting on the Leviathan. The saints, however, have the heads of various animals. They have become the animal they eat, they have conquered the beast by becoming the beast they never had yet been. Is this what it is to be a clone of the in-past? We might say, with Laruelle, that the saints have been cloned, if animality in its inconsistency could be taken for the in-past. Perhaps this thought is a mere analogy, or perhaps it is an exercise in non-philosophy, taking revelation, taking mystical imagery, as material. Laruelle does invite us, after all, to follow Husserl in making 'imaginary variations that can "free the essence"' (ibid., p. 75).

27. Ibid., p. 130.
28. Ibid., p. 129.

5

Laruelle and the Reality of Abstraction

Ray Brassier

Perhaps the chief *philosophical* virtue of Laruelle's *Philosophies of Difference* is its remarkable analysis of the problematic of 'Finitude'.[1] Laruelle defines the latter 'in quasi-Kantian terms' as grounded in 'the irreducible distinction between the entity-in-itself and the entity as objectified or present; as ob-ject'.[2] It is on the basis of this distinction, Laruelle maintains, that Heidegger is able to radicalise Kant's critique of dogmatic metaphysics. For Kant, a metaphysical thesis, whether realist, idealist, or materialist, is dogmatic in so far as it disregards the distinction between objects and things-in-themselves. We are affected by things-in-themselves, but we cannot know them independently of our being affected by them. We may of course still try to think them, but for Kant thinking is not knowing. Ignoring this constraint, the claims of dogmatic metaphysics ring hollow because they import into things-in-themselves conceptual determinations that apply only to objects of representation.

But why does Kant insist on this distinction? For Kant, it is sensibility, i.e. our material constitution, that connects us to things-in-themselves. Since we are affected by things-in-themselves through our sensibility, our conceptual capacities are conditioned by a non-conceptual element, originating in sensation. Thus, sensibility limits the reach of reason by tethering the conceptual to the non-conceptual, understanding to intuition. In this regard, sensibility ensures our contact with the in-itself even as it constrains our cognitive access to it. However, if, as Kant himself insists, the category of causality can only be properly applied to objects of representation, then surely it is illegitimate to claim that we are affected by things-in-themselves, given that the concept of 'affection' seems to presuppose a causal relationship between affecting and affected? Contrary to a common misinterpretation invited by Kant's occasionally injudicious use of the word 'cause', things-in-themselves should not be understood as the causes of appearances in the sense in which electrostatic discharges are the causes of lightning. This is not because the category of causation cannot be applied to things-in-themselves; for there is a sense in which it can, provided we bear in mind the distinction between pure and schematised categories. The pure, or unschematised category of causation is simply the logical relation of ground and consequence, and as such it can be applied to the relation between appearances and things-in-themselves, so long as we are clear that this is a purely conceptual rather than a cognitive determination. Thus we can think things-in-themselves as the grounds of appearances, provided that this grounding relation is understood in terms of a modified analogy with the way in which appearances cause other appearances.[3] The relevant modification is that whereas the schematised category of causality always involves a consequence relation between temporal events, the grounding relation between things-in-themselves and appearances involves a consequence relation that operates at the level of transcendental reflection.[4]

Still, we may ask what justifies us in postulating this transcendental and hence purely conceptual analogue of the causal relation. Kant's answer is disarmingly straightforward: 'Even if we cannot cognize these same objects [i.e. appearances] as things-in-themselves, we must at least be able to think them as things-in-themselves. For otherwise there would follow the absurd proposition that there is an appearance without anything that appears.'[5] What is the precise nature of the absurdity Kant seeks to avoid here? On one level, it is obviously absurd to deny that we can think appearances as things-in-themselves if this distinction is simply equivalent to the conceptual distinction between appearance and that which appears. For it is indeed absurd to deny that the concept of appearance implies something that appears. If this is what the distinction boils down to, then it is precisely its purely conceptual status that guarantees its validity. It is secured irrespective of whether or not we are able to know if what appears is like or unlike its appearance, or whether things-in-themselves exist at all. But if the distinction is purely conceptual, then the concept of the in-itself is a pure abstraction: it is simply the concept of something considered in abstraction from the way in which appearances are given to us in sensibility and determined by the concepts of the understanding. This is precisely the view Kant seems to endorse:

it also follows naturally from the concept of an appearance in general that something must correspond to it which is not in itself appearance, for appearance can be nothing for itself and outside of our kind of representation; thus, if there is not to be a constant circle, the word 'appearance' must already indicate a relation to something the immediate representation of which is, to be sure, sensible, but which in itself, without this constitution of our sensibility (on which the form of our intuition is grounded), must be something, i.e. an object independent of sensibility. Now from this arises the concept of a *noumenon*, which, however, is not at all positive and does not signify a determinate cognition of any sort of thing, but rather only the thinking of something in general, in which I abstract from all form of sensible intuition.[6]

The noumenon in this specifically negative sense is not to be confused with what Kant calls 'the transcendental object = X', which, somewhat confusingly, he also describes as 'the entirely undetermined thought of something in general'.[7] The transcendental object is 'that which in all our cognitions is really one and the same = X';[8] it is the ultimate referent of all our objective representations, the pure form of the object in general to which every determinate representation ultimately refers. Thus the transcendental object is still thought in accordance with an ultimate categorial determination: that of substance, not in its schematised, empirical sense as what persists throughout a manifold of appearances, but in its unschematised, transcendental sense as the invariant correlate of pure apperception persisting across a manifold of representations. This is presumably why Kant refers to it as 'one and the same' throughout every representation, and why he refuses to identify it with the noumenon, which, since it plays an entirely negative or limiting role, does not even bear the minimal categorial determination of substance, and so cannot be conceptually determined as one rather than as many.[9]

But the cost of maintaining the negativity of the concept of the noumenon, as devoid of any categorial determination, seems to be to render it a wholly indeterminate abstraction, or as Kant himself puts it 'an empty concept without an object' (*ens rationis*).[10] This 'thought entity', or empty concept without an object, is the concept of the intelligible nothing. Kant distinguishes it from the 'non-entity', the empty object without a concept (e.g. the square circle), which is the unintelligible nothing. These are the two types of empty concept. Kant contrasts them with the two types of empty intuition: the privative nothing as the empty object of a concept (e.g. shade as the absence of light), and the imaginary entity as the pure form of intuition without an object (Kant gives no example of the latter and it is significant that both the objectless empty concept and the objectless empty intuition defy empirical exemplification).[11]

But how can this intelligible nothing be thought of as the ground of appearances? How can we be affected by a wholly indeterminate abstraction? More precisely: How can a wholly indeterminate conceptual abstraction give rise to the kind of determinate empirical experience whose possibility Kant seeks to explain? The difficulty is compounded by Kant's insistence that our intuition, unlike God's, is fundamentally receptive: our minds do not create appearances in Kant's specifically transcendental sense, even though they determine them as objects of representation. Experience is rooted in something affecting us from 'outside'. This is the fundamental meaning of Finitude. Thus it seems there must be 'something' that 'causes' us to have experiences. But in characterising the noumenon as an intelligible nothing, Kant seems to reduce the problematic ground of appearances to a mere thought-entity. Yet it is precisely the reality of this problematic nothing that needs to be accounted for, for without such an account, the claim that things-in-themselves are the source of appearances becomes unintelligible. Thus it seems the absurdity Kant wishes to avoid in acknowledging the necessary link between appearances and things-in-themselves is not merely the contradiction attendant upon the denial of a tautology. The absurdity at issue is more profound, and follows from denying the reality of appearances. The empirical reality of appearances must be rooted in a transcendental reality, albeit one whose determinate characteristics we are barred from knowing. Notwithstanding its role as a purely negative and limiting concept, it seems we are obliged to acknowledge the problematic reality of the noumenon *qua* abstraction. Consequently, on a second reading, Kant's claim about the necessary link between appearances and things-in-themselves can be interpreted as meaning that the *objective* reality proper to appearances in the transcendental (as opposed to empirical or Berkeleyean sense) is grounded in the *formal* reality of things-in-themselves. The distinction at issue is between the empirical reality of appearances qua representables whose being depends upon their being thought (or represented – these are equivalent here), and the transcendental reality of things-in-themselves, which exist independently of being represented. For as Wilfrid Sellars points out, the relation of analytical dependence between represented and representing also renders the objective reality of the represented content conditional upon the formal reality of the representing act.[12] Since every represented implies a representing, the objective reality of a represented entails the formal reality of the representing through which it is represented. Clearly, this argument establishes only that *if* there are representeds, then there must be representings-in-themselves; not that there actually are such representings-in-themselves. While it reveals the degree of conceptual co-dependence between the concept of appearance and that of things-in-themselves, it does not prove that representings exist in-themselves, let alone that non-representings do. This is why the determination of the in-itself in terms of formal reality remains insufficient. If the concept of formal reality as that which exists in-itself remains analytically dependent upon the concept of objective reality as that which exists in representation, the being of the in-itself remains conditional upon the being of appearance. The problem then is that, since an appearance implies a relation to sensibility, this renders the existence of the in-itself conditional upon the existence of appearance, and hence of sensibility, which is precisely the kind of empirical idealism Kant seeks to avoid. Kant's claim is that the existence of appearances presupposes the existence of things-in-themselves, and that the reality of appearances is grounded in the reality of things-in-themselves, not that the existence of the latter is predicated upon that of the former. If this were the case, then the concept of appearance would be intrinsic to that of reality in-itself, with the result that the idea of a reality that does not appear, i.e. that is not representable, would become incoherent. But the claim that to be is to be representable implies precisely the sort of dogmatic idealism Kant wishes to repudiate. Thus, what is required is an account of the reality of the in-itself that grounds the reality of appearances without rendering the former conditional upon the latter. But it is difficult to flesh out the notion of transcendental reality so long as the relation to sensibility in objective representation provides the precondition for cognitive determination. If being is not a real predicate, then the claim that the reality of appearances implies that there is a reality that appears establishes a logical dependency between the concept of appearance and the concept of the in-itself; it does not legiti-

mate any ontological inference, either from the being of appearance to the being of the in-itself, or from being-in-itself to the
being of appearance. It is the nature of the difference between the
reality proper to appearances and the reality proper to the in-itself
that is at issue. Yet the question remains whether it is legitimate to
infer an ontological difference from a conceptual distinction, or to
postulate a domain of being (or reality) independent of the conditions of sensibility.

Contrary to a prevalent caricature, the postulate of the in-itself
does not entail a two-world metaphysics. Indeed, Kant explicitly
denies that the noumenon is another kind of entity, existing in
an intelligible world that transcends experience: 'The division of
objects into phenomena and noumena, and of the world into a
world of sense and a world of understanding, *can therefore not
be permitted at all*, although concepts certainly permit of division
into sensible and intellectual ones.'[13] But then what does it mean to
insist, as Laruelle does, that the transcendental distinction between
appearances and things-in-themselves is to be understood as a *real*,
rather than merely ideal, difference, if this is not the familiar metaphysical difference between two separate kinds of being, such as
the sensible and the intelligible? Clearly, appearances are real in a
sense that goes beyond the objective reality of their representation,
since they are constituted through acts of representing that are not
themselves encompassed within the represented content. The same
point can be made in a phenomenological register by pointing out
that 'objectivating' acts of consciousness must be granted a reality
that transcends the conditioned reality of the objects they constitute.[14] Thus the transcendence proper to formal, as opposed to
objective, reality is not to be understood in terms of the metaphysical transcendence traditionally ascribed to the intelligible object,
but rather in terms of *objectivating transcendence*. What we are
working toward is the suggestion that the reality proper to the in-
itself is neither that of the transcendent object, nor of objectivating
transcendence, but rather that of unobjectivisable transcendence.
This is the key to Laruelle's interpretation of Heidegger.

*   *   *

Once the two-world interpretation of the transcendental difference between phenomena and noumena has been ruled out, it
seems we must acknowledge that the reality of the in-itself constitutes a noumenal dimension within appearance as such; or in

other words, a transcendental difference intrinsic to the entity (the phenomenon) itself. This point can be elucidated by considering the scholastic differentiation between real distinction (*distinctio realis*), conceptual distinction (*distinctio rationis*), and formal distinction (*distinctio formalis*).[15] A real distinction corresponds to a difference in being (i.e. in the 'whatness' or essence of a thing) that does not depend on our understanding because the difference is itself an entity or *res*. A conceptual distinction corresponds to a difference in the definition or concept of a thing, without a corresponding difference in being (i.e. the difference *is not*). A formal distinction, however, corresponds to a difference in the entity that is not a difference in being. It is an inexistent difference that makes an existential difference. This distinction first arose in an attempt to make sense of the difference between essence and existence, a topic to which we shall return below. The difference between the essence of Socrates (the list of properties that make him what he is) and his existence or actuality is not merely conceptual or nominal, and so qualifies as 'real', yet the nature of this 'reality', as well as of its contrast with the 'ideality' of Socrates' essence, both remain obscure. Thus the difference between the definitive concept of Socrates, in so far as it circumscribes his essence, and the actually existing Socrates, is neither a difference in Socrates' definition, since the latter identifies all those attributes that make him what he is, nor a difference between Socrates and some other entity, since Socrates' existence cannot be construed as something separate from Socrates. Consequently, what separates essence from existence is not an individuating difference, since the definition of a thing is what individuates it. But nor is it a specific difference, since what is specific to Socrates is entirely subsumed by his essence. Lastly, it is not a generic difference either, since all of Socrates' generic attributes are encapsulated in his definition. Consequently, the difference between Socrates' essence and his existence falls outside every available ontological rubric. Yet the difference is undeniable, since there would seem to be all the difference in the world between a definition that expresses Socrates' essence by enumerating all his essential attributes, and the flesh and blood Socrates who incarnates these essential attributes. Thus, the difference between Socrates' essence and his existence is a formal distinction in so far as it is a real, as opposed to merely nominal difference; but a real difference that seems to evade all the available conceptual determinations (i.e. of generic, specific, or individuating difference) that render differences in being intelligible. This is why the distinction can be characterised as an ontic difference without any corresponding ontological coordinates.

The distinction between phenomena and noumena is not a metaphysical or (what is equivalent here) an ontological difference, but a formal distinction in the sense we have just outlined: one that is rooted in the entity itself but that does not correspond to a difference in being, understood as *what* something is. This allows us to see how the difference between phenomena and noumena can be construed as a *real* difference, i.e. a difference rooted in the phenomenon as such, and hence one that does not hypostatise a domain of entities transcending the conditions of sensibility, thereby entailing a two-world metaphysics. Moreover, to claim that the difference between phenomena and noumena is real is to insist that the difference between the intelligible form and sensible content of appearances is not just a distinction of reason, since it falls neither on the side of the understanding, nor of intuition.

This is what Laruelle seems to be indicating when he points out that the in-itself is not something other than the appearance:

> the thing-in-itself is the same entity as the phenomenon, as Heidegger says, it is therefore reduced [i.e. it is not dogmatically posited as a transcendent entity existing in an intelligible realm – RB], but at the same time it corresponds to a point of view other than that of the phenomenon: that of the entity's uncreatedness or transcendence relative to Being, the milieu within which Being must be disclosed and illuminated.[16]

By 'Being', Laruelle here has in mind transcendental conditions of objectivation in a Kantian sense, since he views Heidegger's investigation into the being of phenomena as that part of his project which is continuous with Kant's transcendental problematic. Thus Heidegger renders explicit an insight that remains implicit in Kant: that the reality of the entity (i.e. of the phenomenon) is rooted in its transcendence relative to its conditions of objectivation. But this is no longer a metaphysical transcendence. In fact, Laruelle's account requires that we distinguish three varieties of transcendence: first, the transcendence of the intelligible object vis-à-vis its sensible instantiation in dogmatic idealism; second, the transcendence of objectivation with regard to the object in critical idealism;[17] finally, the transcendence of the entity-in-itself with regard to its conditions of objectivation as the key component in the transcendental critique of idealism. It is this latter, unobjectivisable transcendence that is marked by Kant's critical-formal distinction between phenomena and noumena.

This formal distinction is not to be confused with Heidegger's *ontological* difference between Being and beings. For Laruelle, the ontological difference remains metaphysical because it is posited a priori and established in the element of the a priori, i.e., the conceptual: 'Metaphysics establishes itself in the relation between beings and the a priori, a relation which is itself a priori, a prior place of thought.'[18] This relation exposes the correlation between Being and beings as the necessary condition for experiencing the entity as object. In this regard, Being, or more precisely, what Heidegger calls 'pre-ontological understanding', functions as a priori condition of objectivation. However, as an a priori, this ontological distinction between Being and beings remains *ideal*. It is what Laruelle calls an 'a priori factum' for thought, in the sense of that which establishes the correlation between objects and their conditions of objectivation. Such a correlation presupposes an *idealising* reduction of the dogmatic postulate of reality as something existing in-itself (the postulate characteristic of what Husserl called 'the natural attitude'). This idealising reduction preserves the independence of the real, but only as a correlate of the ideal, conditioned by the a priori within the element of ideal immanence (whether that of consciousness, intersubjectivity, or language). It yields what Husserl called 'transcendence in immanence', according to which the real is in-itself for the consciousness (or domain of intersubjectivity) that constitutes it.

But Laruelle credits Heidegger with carrying out a second, more radical reduction; one that suspends not only the transcendence of the object, but also the transcendence that an insufficiently critical idealism continues to attribute to the a priori (i.e. the conditions of objectivation).[19] Thus in Laruelle's reading of Heidegger, Being conditions the entity, but Being itself, i.e. the formal reality of objectivating transcendence, is also conditioned by the entity. It is the relation of objectivation itself, the transcendence of the a priori in so far as it conditions the presence of 'beings as such and as a whole', which is now reduced to the status of immanent *factum*: an a priori fact of reason. The transcendence of Being is affected by the entity, which, since it is not created by Being in the way in which the transcendent Creator produces his creatures, must be given somehow, but in a way that is independent of its objectivation. Consequently, there are two dimensions of givenness: one through which the phenomenon is objectivated, and one through which the phenomenon at once precipitates and transcends its own objectivation. The difference between these two is the difference between the formal reality proper to objectivating transcendence, and the transcendental reality proper to unobjectivisable transcendence. It is this latter brand of transcendence that constitutes the reality of the phenomenon or entity in-itself. Although Laruelle himself never explicitly formulates this distinction as such, it is essential to his interpretation of Heidegger. Moreover, it also sheds light on the grounding relation between the reality of the in-itself and the reality of appearances. The reality of appearances, understood as the mode in which they are given prior to being objectivated, is constituted by the transcendence intrinsic to the entity (or phenomenon) itself. This transcendence is the unobjectivisable dimension immanent to the entity as such in its formal distinction from the present-at-hand object of representation, whether interpreted in terms of the determinate, particular object, or the ideal category of the object in general (*Objekt überhaupt*). It is obscurely prefigured by the metaphysical distinction between essence and existence, usually glossed in terms of the difference between *what* something is, and *that* it is. As we saw above, while the former is conceptually determinable, the latter is a symptom of something in the difference between possibility and actuality that resists conceptual determination. In the theological worldview organised around the distinction between potentiality construed as essence and actuality construed as existence, all formal reality is tributary to the entity's createdness – the actualisation through which God converts potentiality into actuality. As Heidegger himself explains, this process does not involve the addition of something lacking in the possible (i.e. a missing determination), since actualisation is synonymous with creation understood as the transition from essential potency to actual existence:

When in creation [the] possible goes over into actuality, this transition is to be understood, not in the sense that the possible relinquishes a way of being, but rather in the sense that it first of all receives a being. The *essentia* now is not only ... in that potency, namely of being thought by God, but it is only now properly actual ... the being is only now first created by God and as this created being, it at the same time stands on its own in its own self . . . The difficulty of the problem of making the distinction [between essence and existence] intelligible at all depends on how in general actualization is thought of as the transition of a possible to its actuality. Expressed more exactly, the problem of the distinction between *essentia* and *existentia* . . . depends on whether in general the interpretation of being in the sense of existence is oriented towards actualization, towards creation and production.[20]

Heidegger will of course insist that it is the ancient Greek concept of production (*poiesis*) that holds the key to the proper interpretation of the role played by the concept of existence in actualisation. But while he detects in this venerable distinction the seed of the ontico-ontological difference (although pointing out that it remains entirely on the ontic side), the dimension of unobjectivisable transcendence intimated by 'thatness' continues to be occluded by Heidegger's own subsequent characterisation of the ontological difference as distinguishing the 'how' from the 'what' of being, and his claim that the ontological is to be grasped in terms of *how* beings are, i.e. their way of being, rather than what they are. Yet part of Heidegger's remit in exposing and 'destroying' the metaphysical determination of being as presence involves querying this identification of 'thatness' with existence construed as sheer occurrentness, devoid of every determination other than that of its bare presence-at-hand. From Heidegger's point of view, it is precisely this identification of existence with a degree-zero of presence that occludes what is most essential in ontological transcendence, i.e. being's withdrawal from presence, its congenital nothingness as unpresentable condition of presence. This nothingness clearly echoes that of Kant's noumenon, but while the latter remains an intelligible thought-entity marking the porous frontier between the ideal and real, Being marks the juncture of pre-conceptual understanding and supra-conceptual transcendence. Ultimately, the contrast is one between a rationalist and a non-rationalist conception of transcendence. Heidegger's decisive insight comes with the realisation that, just as the metaphysical characterisation of existence as indeterminate occurrentness in contrast to the determinacy of essence leaves the unpresentable ground of presence unthought, it also obscures the real difference between what is given according to the mode of objectivation and its unobjectivisable residue. Heidegger then demarcates himself from Kant's residual rationalism with the claim that this difference remains as unthinkable from the critical standpoint of objectivation as it was from the dogmatic viewpoint of actualisation (i.e. creation). Just as the transcendence of the possible vis-à-vis the actual is a symptom of the entity's createdness, so the transcendence of objectivation vis-à-vis the object is a symptom of the entity's producedness. Both the theological conception of creation and the transcendental conception of objectivation continue to think the absoluteness of being in terms of a notion of formal reality whose transcendence vis-à-vis the created or objectivated shuts out that aspect of the entity which is not conditioned by actualisation or objectivation, because both processes unknowingly presuppose it. The transcendence of the in-itself is the seal of the entity's uncreatedness precisely in so far as it cannot be mapped in terms of the junction of potentiality and actuality. Similarly, it is because the entity is uncreated that its reality cannot be wholly subsumed by its relation to Being, understood as objectivating transcendence. Since objectivating transcendence perpetuates the transcendence of creation (i.e. of actualisation), atheism entails the renovation of transcendental realism; its transformation from a thesis upholding the autonomy of substantial form as existing in the mind of God, to a thesis acknowledging the autonomy of the insubstantial and the formless, understood as that aspect of reality which must be thought in order to secure our knowledge of the reality of appearances. As we saw above, this noumenal ground of appearances is not a substance considered in abstraction from its relation to the subject, but a concept considered in abstraction from its relation to the object. Thus the noumenon as 'thought-entity' or intelligible nothing is not just an abstract concept, but rather the concept of an absolute abstraction, existing independently of its abstraction from experience. In this regard, and contrary to the familiar Hegelian rebuke according to which Kant abandons the in-itself to the domain of the inconceivable, the noumenon as intelligible nothing lays claim to the territory of the in-itself for conceptualisation, without presumptively annexing it to the latter. From Kant, through Heidegger, to Laruelle, the postulate of the in-itself requires that we rethink the metaphysical hypostatisation of being-in-itself, which is an abstraction relative to an empirically given reality, as the absolute reality of abstraction. Laruelle takes his cue in this endeavour from Heidegger's transformation of the concept of essence.

*   *   *

Laruelle identifies unobjectivisable transcendence with the dimension of withdrawal that Heidegger takes to be inseparable from Being's disclosure of the entity. However, in Laruelle's interpretation, it is not Being itself that withdraws – in fact, the very notion of 'Being itself' involves a metaphysical hypostatisation – but rather the entity-in-itself, since Being remains an illuminating projection, and hence an ideal correlate of Dasein's 'thrown projection'; a projection whose function is at once revelatory and objectivating.[21] Accordingly, on Laruelle's account, it is in fact the entity's unobjectivisable transcendence that constitutes the noumenal dimension of phenomena, i.e., that which is in-itself within appearances. This is the immanent dimension of transcendence in which appearances are rooted, and which conditions Being's withholding from presence, its inapparence within appearances. Contrary to those who would interpret it phenomenologically as the 'presencing' or Being of the phenomenon, understood as the non-conceptualisable residue that resists assimilation to metaphysical essence or 'whatness',[22] Laruelle identifies it with the entity's withdrawal from presence and views this as the veritable source of what Heidegger will subsequently describe as the 'essence' (*Wesen*) of Being:

> Essence is no longer a transcendent ideality, in the metaphysical sense. It is rather a real or absolute transcending – not a particular, i.e. objectivized being that is transcendent in the theological style, but rather the transcending of the real *in-itself* that no longer has any object-term and that is an absolute scission. Under the name of Finitude, Heidegger thinks the real, absolute opposite, the 'Other' of every relation of objectivation; the un-objectivizable real that is the essence of Being . . .[23]

From essence as eternal identity to essence as 'absolute scission' or Finitude a remarkable shift takes place. It is this scission of the entity – or rather this entity as real scission – that constitutes the essence of Being understood as disclosive opening (or 'clearing') within which beings can be encountered as present. However, while Heidegger's existential phenomenology tells us what is given and how it is given, the two ontological facets of givenness, it stops short of trying to grasp the given independently of its givenness. This is precisely what Laruelle, radicalising Heidegger, will seek to do. And it is important to note that he does so initially, at that point where he is still providing a philosophical rationale for his dissatisfaction with philosophy's modus operandi,[24] by striving to seize this moment of absolute scission, which he identifies as the hidden wellspring of absolute transcending, and by trying to think it independently not only of the form of the object, but also of objectivating transcendence. This is arguably the pivotal point on which the theoretical cogency of the transition from philosophy to non-philosophy depends, at least in so far as this transition is not to be reduced to some gratuitous and ultimately arbitrary abandonment of philosophy. To wrest this moment of absolute scission free from the horizon of ontological transcendence, Laruelle must think it in its immanence, which is to say non-relation, rather than its transcendence, which here means relation, vis-à-vis objectivation, since to think it as transcendent is to re-inscribe it in and as a mode of Being. The goal is to think scission absolutely, in and from its absoluteness, rather than thinking it relative to what it divides, which would render it relative, and thereby transcendent, once again. But paradoxically, and in an eminently dialectical twist, thinking division absolutely requires thinking it as absolute indivision, uncontaminated by difference or division, which is always relational. This absolutely immanent indivision – not to be confused with unity, which is synthetic and hence relational – is of course what Laruelle calls 'the One', and the entire impetus of his analysis of the 'philosophies of difference' is to demonstrate that philosophy cannot but subordinate the indivisible scission of the One, which for him is ultimately of the order of (non-thetic) experience rather than of the concept, to a division in and of conceptual transcendence. Thus, for Laruelle, Heidegger's conception of Finitude remains mired in a fatal equivocation, using the absolute indivision of the Real to bind Being to beings even as it petitions its power of scission to split the entity from the object. Although this blocks the absolute idealist suspension of ontic transcendence by grounding Being's determination of beings in the transcendence of the in-itself, it stops short of thinking this absolute division in and for itself, independently of its conjunction with division:

What distinguishes finite Difference from the idealist usage of Difference is that this gap, the scission from whence transcendence is deployed, is no longer *relative* to transcendence, as it is in Idealism; is not in its turn a relation or an Idea. It is a non-relation or an absolute 'relation', one that is perhaps unthinkable in itself since one of its 'terms' – the entity in-itself – is real, and hence by definition non-objectivisable and non-manifest; and so it is thinkable only through its other side, that of Being as relation (of transcendence) *to* beings, a relation which is itself ideal. Difference is indeed an indivision or a unity of Being *and* beings, and a real indivision; it is not an ideal and infinitely divisible continuum. Finitude is what gives its reality and consequently its indivisibility to Difference, its repulsion of every division and every integration into itself of new immanent relations. But on its other side, which is no longer the real or ontic origin of transcendence, but transcendence as deployment, as intentional continuity, Difference is divisible and able to integrate new relations into itself; it is the site for the deployment of the analytic of Being or the objectivation of beings, the divisions and new relations that philosophizing thought operates with a view to raising itself up to the essence of Being.[25]

Heidegger's Finitude evokes the absolute scission of a transcendence that punctures the horizon of objectivation, but does so in order to relate Being's determination of beings to Being's determination by *that which is not* in beings. This non-being within beings is the noumenon as intelligible nothing, a thought-entity that is at once substance-less concept and formless thing. But to think this non-entity as the ground of phenomena is to concretise absolute abstraction and acknowledge the differentiating power of the in-different: the Real as indivisible divisor of reality and ideality. This is the dialectical inversion through which the thought of absolute difference, i.e. difference in its non-relation to identity, non-subsumable by the categories, turns into the thought of absolute indifference, the One as absolutely indivisible immanence, which is the operator of absolute, a-categorial differentiation precisely in so far as it is without distinction or differentiation. For Heidegger as for Laruelle, such an outcome is at once too dialectical, because of its assertion of the reversibility between the abstract and the concrete, and too idealist, because of the way in which it affirms the convertibility between transcendence and immanence. Abjuring this dialectical, and hence perniciously philosophical conversion, Laruelle seeks to isolate the moment of scission, the irreversibility of the absolute division between transcendent division and immanent indivision, and to separate it from the reversibility proper to the dialecticisation of scission. Yet is this separation itself not precisely the dialectically necessary acknowledgement of the need to think the absolute abstraction of scission in and for itself, even if this entails insisting on its foreclosure (non-reciprocity) to and for thought? In this regard, Laruelle's attempt to think immanence in and from its absolute separation is the necessary next step in unfolding the logic of absolute abstraction, one that provides an exemplary dialectical absolutisation of abstraction. Laruelle subjects the general dialectic of the One and the Dyad, of Finitude and Difference, to a one-sided splitting (or 'dualysis'), but mistakes his own abstract separation of abstraction for its realisation. He separates the separate and the inseparate – indeed he uncovers the logic of this separation without separation, which he calls 'unilateralisation' – but he misconstrues this startling twist in the dialectic – the dialectic of dialectics and non-dialectics – for a suspension of dialectics, and ergo of philosophy, as such. For what is the One conceived as fulcrum for the articulation of dialectics and non-dialectics but an effect upon philosophy?

Obviously, this is not how Laruelle himself will view the situation. He will insist that, despite Heidegger's 'finitising' reduction of objectivating transcendence, the transcendence of the entity in-itself is not so much given as *posited as given* by both Kant and Heidegger, in a manner that remains a priori, idealising, and hence transcendent (which is to say, objectivating). Countermanding this residual concession to idealism, Laruelle will claim that the One is not a conceptual posit but an experience given independently of all phenomenological objectivation. Unobjectivisable transcendence is the intra-philosophical symptom of an unobjectivisable immanence that is no longer philosophisable because it is of the order of a 'non-thetic experience' that determines conceptual determination, without being conceptually determinable in return. The One is this non-thetic experience, presupposed without being posited, given-without-givenness, etc. Thus Laruelle insists that he has converted the philosophical absolutisation of immanence into a non-philosophical radicalisation that 'unilateralises' and hence marginalises philosophical absolutisation as such, in the name of an experience of immanence – or rather, of a radically immanent experience – whose immediacy is no longer susceptible to dialectical mediation.

But is Laruelle invoking the reality of a concrete experience of immanence, or the concretisation of an absolutely abstract conception of immanence? Here the congenital ambiguity constitutive of the logic of abstraction and concretion persists, and it infects both the transcendence and the immanence attributed to the entity in-itself: Is it the One *qua* indivisible that withdraws (i.e. divides), or is its withdrawal (i.e. division) One *qua* indivision? If the withdrawal of the One is not a thing but rather an absolute 'un-thinging', then the 'un-thing' (*unbedingt*) exerting this power cannot be identified with any individual entity – least of all the human person. Likewise, ambiguity persists in the meaning of 'absolute' transcendence and 'absolute' immanence. Is it possible to separate them? Or is the separation itself the ultimate abstraction? Has Laruelle realised abstraction or abstracted the Real? Or has he identified the Real itself (=One) with abstraction? At this juncture, the problem of dogmatism, and of Laruelle's relation to the critical-transcenden-tal legacy from which he draws inspiration, re-emerges. Laruelle uses philosophical abstraction to define the non-philosophical Real that suspends philosophical abstraction: 'lived experience', 'knowing-without-knowledge', 'Man-in-person', 'One-in-One', etc. Yet he insists these have a non-constitutive, merely occasional, nominative function: they do not constitute what they name or describe. But what do they name or describe? Immanence 'itself', the immanence of the Real 'in flesh and blood', as he likes to put it? Or the abstract reality of an absolute abstraction that positively realises the transcendental negativity of the Kantian noumenon as objectless 'thought-entity'? Laruelle insists on the former, on the grounds that 'we know' ourselves to be this immanent experience; a claim which he of course immediately qualifies with the proviso that we know it without 'knowing', which is to say, without the conceptual mediations involved in reflection, comprehension, understanding, judgement, etc. This is *gnosis* understood as a 'radically immanent' mode of knowing immunised against the all-too-philosophical demand for justification: 'Man-in-person is defined by this idempotent "gnosis", this indissolubly scientific and philosophical lived experience, which is not a being in the world, or a being in philosophy. The genericity of man consists in being knowledge that he himself does not "know", a lived experience that is not reflexive and cumulative.'[26] The problem is that this distinction between immanent gnosis and transcend-ent knowledge already presupposes the separation it is supposed to secure: the separation between the Real-One as that which is already determinate ('without-determination'), and the realm of philosophical ideality as the domain of that which is determined *as* this or that, as subject or object, as immanent or transcendent, as abstract or concrete, etc. Laruelle invokes a self-authenticating experience of the Real in the wake of its conceptual separation in order to prevent what he has separated in an abstraction which he of course immediately disavows – the One as radically immanent experience is 'separate-without-separation', 'abstract-without-abstraction', etc. – from being re-incorporated into the necessarily interminable movement of abstraction. What shores up this pre-emptive blockage of abstraction? Simply Laruelle's identification of the Real-One with the 'human in flesh and blood' qua ultimate determinant of abstraction. But this continues to beg the question: How do I know I am the One 'in-person'? What distinguishes this gnosis from any number of merely doxastic empirical identifications I am able to reel off unreflectingly ('I am François, I am a man, I am French, I am . . . etc.')? Laruelle presumes to be able to discharge himself of the obligation to justify the gnosis that motivates this nomination, yet the case for exemption continues to depend upon a (highly sophisticated) theoretical rationale saturated with the kind of conceptual understanding that gnosis itself is supposed to render redundant. Shorn of this elaborate theoretical alibi, Laruelle's identification of the Real with 'Man' or 'the human-in-person' – a nomination which retains a determinate semantic valence, relying as it does on our understanding of the *meaning* of terms such as 'Man', 'human', and 'in-person' – is as arbitrary, abstract and ultimately as 'decisional' as other possible identifications of that which is pre-eminently Real, whether as Self, Spirit, Life, or Nature. It is important to remember that everything that distinguishes the latter's alleged philosophical transcendence from the former's supposedly non-philosophical immanence is itself abstract, and hence nothing if not conceptual.

Ultimately, Laruelle faces a dilemma: either he regresses to Michel Henry's phenomenological idealisation of radical immanence,[27] or he accepts that the radicalisation of the immanence of the Real necessitates the dissolution not only of intentionality, but also of intuition itself, which is to say, of gnosis. Our knowledge of ourselves certainly comprises a dimension of non-inferential immediacy that endows us with a privileged epistemic access to our own internal states, but only within certain limits, since the immediacy of self-knowledge is itself mediated and cannot be evoked to ratify the appeal to an allegedly intuitive, pre-discursive gnosis of ourselves as 'the Real-in-person'. Only the appearance that immediacy is not the result of a mediating self-relation allows experience to be absolutised. This is, of course, 'the myth of the Given', originally targeted in Hegel's critique of sense-certainty, and more recently dismantled – arguably in a more profound and definitive fashion than it was by Hegel – by Wilfrid Sellars.[28] But the crucial Kantian insight is that we can abjure this myth without succumbing to the lure of absolute idealism, once we realise that the reality of appearances is grounded in the reality of what does not appear; that acknowledging the concrete reality of the phenomenon requires acknowledging the abstract reality of the noumenon; and ultimately, that sensible being is founded upon the intelligibility of *that which is not*. Thus the identification of the Real with 'Man-in-person' is the height of abstraction, for it brusquely identifies the noumenon with the phenomenon, using the divisive power of the former to secure the absolute indivisibility of the latter. The result is a terminal abstraction masquerading as the termination of abstraction. Laruelle has hypostatised an absolute abstraction and subjected it to a premature identification with an empirical instance – the human individual 'in flesh and blood' – in a misguided attempt to stave off its re-idealisation in a transcendence in and of the concept. He successfully conceptualises the separation of the in-itself, but misidentifies it as an experience, refusing to recognise that no residue of experience can withstand determination by mediation. The rejoinder that the One is 'abstract without abstraction' begs the question, for it simply radicalises abstraction in an attempt to neutralise ('unilateralise') the dialectic of mediation and abstraction. The given-without-givenness is certainly a real abstraction, or the Real as abstract, and its absolute separation, or unilaterality, the reality of abstraction. By the same token, Laruelle's struggle with the very possibility of philosophising is undoubtedly more instructive than any complacent *passage à l'acte*. Yet in the final analysis, his attempted suspension of the pretensions of philosophy – epistemological as well as ontological – is more indicative of a frustrated philosophical agenda than of a genuine alternative to the philosophical problematic bequeathed to us by Kant.

Notes

1. François Laruelle, *Les philosophies de la différence. Introduction critique* (Paris: PUF, 1986), translated by Rocco Gangle as *Philosophies of Difference: A Critical Introduction to Non-Philosophy* (London

and New York: Continuum, 2010). Page references will refer to the French edition followed by the English translation.

2. Ibid., p. 57/40 (translation modified).

3. This is a point made by Wilfrid Sellars: see his *Kant and Pre-Kantian Themes* (Atascadero, CA: Ridgeview Publishing Co., 2002), p. 168.

4. See Immanuel Kant, *Critique of Pure Reason*, translated by Paul Guyer and Alan Wood (Cambridge: Cambridge University Press, 1998), A261/B317.

5. Ibid., Bxxvi.

6. Ibid., A252.

7. Ibid., A253.

8. Ibid., A109.

9. See ibid., A253. This is one of the more confusing passages in the First Critique. In the course of explaining why the transcendental object is not the noumenon, Kant writes: 'I cannot think [the transcendental object] through any categories, for these hold of empirical intuition, in order to bring it under a concept of the object in general. To be sure, a pure use of the category is possible, i.e. without contradiction, but it has no objective validity, since it pertains to no intuition that would thereby acquire unity of the object, for the category is a mere function of thinking, through which no object is given to me, but rather only that through which what may be given in intuition is thought' (A253). But the determination of the concept of the transcendental object via the pure category of substance, understood as the relation of inherence and subsistence, does not surreptitiously endow the category with objective validity, since it does not involve conflating the transcendental object with an empirical object.

10. Ibid., A290–2/B347–9.

11. Ibid.

12. See Wilfrid Sellars, *Science and Metaphysics: Variations on Kantian Themes* (London: Routledge and Kegan Paul, 1968), p. 41. See also Sellars, *Kant and Pre-Kantian Themes*, p. 65.

13. Kant, *Critique of Pure Reason*, A255/B311 (my emphasis).

14. We will write 'objectivating' and 'unobjectivisable' rather than the more common 'objectifying' and 'unobjectifiable' in order to emphasise the link with the phenomenological concept of 'objectivation', which Laruelle constantly invokes, and which Rocco Gangle retains in his admirable English translation of *Philosophies of Difference*.

15. These three distinctions are discussed by Heidegger in *Basic Problems of Phenomenology*, translated by Albert Hofstadter (Bloomington and Indianapolis: Indiana University Press, 1988), pp. 88–99. The

context there is a discussion of the scholastic distinction between essence and existence.

16. Laruelle, *Les philosophies de la différence*, p. 63/46 (translation modified).

17. This is one way of understanding ontological transcendence, as when Heidegger describes Being as 'the *transcendens* pure and simple', in Martin Heidegger, *Being and Time*, translated by John Macquarrie and Edward Robinson (Oxford: Blackwell, 1962), p. 62.

18. Laruelle, *Les philosophies de la différence*, p. 56/40 (translation modified).

19. Ibid., pp. 62–3/45–6. Here one could object to Laruelle that neither neo-Kantianism, nor Husserlian phenomenology, nor Habermas' communicative discourse theory, treats the a priori conditions of objectivation as a transcendent (trans-historical) 'fact of reason' in this uncritical sense. On the contrary, all have sought in their different ways to historicise the a priori. But Laruelle's point seems to be that even a historicised a priori is posited as given relative to a set of empirical data. And because of this co-dependence between a priori factum and empirical datum, the former becomes relatively transcendent with regard to an empirical conjuncture. For Laruelle, it is the very relativity of the a priori that perpetuates the metaphysical hypostasis of transcendence as intelligible form or Idea. He views it as the source of the residual dogmatism infecting even the most historicised forms of idealism.

20. Heidegger, *Basic Problems*, p. 98.

21. In this regard, the distinction between Being and the entity-in-itself in Heidegger can be understood as analogous to that between the transcendental object and the noumenon in Kant.

22. This is Richard F. Grabau's interpretation in his unduly neglected paper, 'Kant's Concept of the Thing-in-Itself', *Review of Metaphysics* 16.4 (1963), pp. 770–9. Although Grabau explicitly distances his interpretation from Heidegger's interpretation of Kant, of which he is critical, there is an undeniable affinity between his interpretation of the in-itself in terms of the presence of the phenomenon and Heidegger's characterisation of Being as that which does not show itself within appearances and yet constitutes their 'meaning and ground'. In Heidegger's own words: 'that which remains *hidden* in an egregious sense, or which relapses and gets *covered up* again, or that which shows itself only *"in disguise"*, is not just this entity or that, but rather the *Being* of entities' (Heidegger, *Being and Time*, p. 59).

23. Laruelle, *Les philosophies de la différence*, pp. 79–80/63–4 (translation modified).

24. Thereby revealing the extent to which the impulse for non-philosophy, its conceptual motivations and theoretical rationalisations, still come from philosophy – a point that is too often overlooked in any straightforward affirmation of the discontinuity between philosophy and non-philosophy.

25. Laruelle, *Les philosophies de la différence*, pp. 79–80/63–4 (translation modified).

26. François Laruelle, 'The Generic as Predicate and as Constant: Non-Philosophy and Materialism', translated by Taylor Adkins, in *The Speculative Turn: Continental Materialism and Realism*, edited by Levi Bryant, Graham Harman, Nick Srnicek (Melbourne: re-press, 2011), p. 248 (translation modified).

27. An idealisation he has himself vigorously criticised. See François Laruelle, *Prinçipes de la non-philosophie* (Paris: PUF, 1996), pp. 133–43.

28. See Wilfrid Sellars, *Empiricism and the Philosophy of Mind* (Cambridge, MA: Harvard University Press, 1997).

6

The Science-Thought of Laruelle and its Effects on Epistemology

Anne-Françoise Schmid

Translated by Nicola Rubczak

Laruelle has a conception of science. What are its characteristics? First of all, it is not an epistemology; it is not a philosophy of science. Why not? All of these approaches to science, in one way or another, place science and philosophy in a continuous relationship, with philosophy here positing itself as some sort of philosophical generalisation of the sciences, and epistemology supposing that, by reading fragments of the sciences, it can form an idea of their methods. Laruelle begins by positing or admitting a heterogeneity of science and philosophy. If nothing can persuade us that there are continuities between sciences and philosophies, let us assume that they presuppose postures which are entirely independent from each other. In this case, we can construct much richer interactions between the two, since supposing given continuities actually limits possibilities for interaction. We must see that this separation is not a negation, but, by contrast, the opening of fictions between science and philosophy. It allows for a theory of philosophy; a theory which is not an auto-modelling, but rather a knowledge or a science of philosophy under scientific principles.

Some elements to aid comprehension:

1. There is an opacity of science that has no direct description. The knowledge we have of science depends on the Real, the future, and has the effect of cloning concepts.
2. Science is a guarantee of democracy: It is not science that establishes hierarchies; these are the philosophical projections onto the sciences which give place to the domination of one discipline over the others.
3. Science as a silent witness of a relation to the Real. This

relationship means that each term can be related, in the last instance, to the Real; that two terms can be considered as identical or as radically separate. The practice of science must be able to separate notions and parameters, and not transform them into one another, as in philosophy.

4. There is a sort of seriousness and opacity of all of the terms and ingredients of science, which is their relative autonomy; their non-reduction to a principal term.

5. Philosophy is a theorisation of the relation to the Real in so far as it does not admit that the Real precedes it. This is philosophical sufficiency; the Real is co-determined by it. Wanting to surpass its sufficiency signifies admitting that the Real 'precedes' philosophy. This is to commit to a thinking of unilateral duality; it is no longer a dialectical or a topological relation between philosophy and the Real.

6. But this is neither the end nor the death of philosophy, as is supposed by one of the myths emanating from philosophy. Philosophy always continues, and its concepts and distinctions can be the object of fictions and of non-philosophical extensions. Philosophy offers very rich materials for non-philosophical invention.

7. Non-philosophical invention puts philosophy in touch with its 'exterior' elements: science, ethics, technics, aesthetics, religion, mysticism. Treating them as exterior allows the production of a non-philosophical knowledge of man; to understand him as One and as Real, and not as the mixed product of technologies, sciences and philosophical ideas, or as the philosophical future rendered always 'transhuman'.

8. There is a history of these exteriorities in non-philosophy. It travels through chaos, the fractal,[1] or the 'non-Gödelian'.[2] Recently,[3] it has very much taken shape through the quantum, which facilitates a grouping of principles that allows the positing of a matrix of relations between philosophy and science.

I do not pretend that these hypotheses are the fundamental principles of non-philosophy or of non-standard philosophy (this would entail an explication of Dualysis, determination-in-the-Last Instance [DLI], the non-convertibility or non-commutativity of Being and the One). Rather, from these indications it is possible to show the important transformations that they can produce and induce in thought and the practice of epistemology.

'Words' or First Terms of Science in Laruelle

Firstly, we will extract the terms that we find in Laruelle and in classical epistemology that accompany the word 'science'. These terms are evidently not exhaustive, but they are numerous enough to demonstrate a difference in approach or posture. What is important here will be to understand what engages these differences, and whether they can produce interactions.

Here is a Laruellean list: Science, opacity, virtual, future, cloning effects, generic, matrix, generic experimentation, science of philosophy, superpositional, imaginary number, quartile (geometric interpretation of the imaginary number), non-commutativity, modelling, non-Einsteinian, non-Gödelian, non-Schrödingerian, non-Cohenian, fractal identity, amplitude of futurality, oraxioms.

What is interesting in this set of terms is that they are not those that we find in classical epistemology. Those that we do find here comprise the following series: theory, fact, model, observation, experience, measure, verification, scientific criteria, verificationism (Carnap, Vienna Circle), falsificationism (Popper), research programme (Lakatos) or anarchic dispersion (Feyerabend).

These two series of terms are so different that we may well ask if they characterise the same category or grouping of phenomena. Moreover, geography or geometry do not show these same lines of force. In the epistemological landscape, we do not escape a great tension, one allowing science to be translated into the language of true and false, of what can be verified, be falsified, putting theory in relation with 'facts' through observation or experimentation; allowing the construction of intermediaries between theory and fact (models, measurements). There is an organisation of terms that are the projection of a philosophical logic onto science: that of 'opposites'. Here we are given a complementarity between theory and fact: theory without fact is open, or purely speculative; fact without theory is blind. This and other similar types of opposition are nearly inevitable in classical epistemological discourse. They are partially dissolved in wider approaches such as that of Lakatos who chooses a more comprehensive fundamental notion; that of Feyerabend who shows that all directions are partially independent dimensions in his epistemological anarchism; or more synthetic approaches of 'research programmes'. Nevertheless, the tensions of epistemology are what have guided the widening of its concepts, the works remaining in the margins of them, and as such, dependent on them.

The Laruellean series is not organised by this foundational tension. It 'forgets' certain organisational terms in epistemology – for example that of fact, but also to some extent that of theory, which, in his texts, is more often related to philosophy than to science. His series prefers 'modelling' to model. At first glance, it changes 'the grand order': there comes the virtual, a term that, within the horizon of epistemology, is reserved to the informational and to 'immaterial' knowledges. In Laruelle, the virtual is not reserved to a particular field; by contrast, it is tightly linked to his conception of the future and of futurality. There is a certain 'colour' of science, that of opacity, which is not the colour of philosophy (that is characterised more by Platonic illumination). There are also forms of extending the scientific, which we will see in the usage of 'non', an extensive rather than exclusive negation, as in the classical model of 'non-Euclidean geometry' to which Laruelle occasionally refers. Certain Laruellean terms seem to be directly drawn from the sciences, such as: superposition, idempotence, imaginary number, non-commutativity. Any such 'citation' of directly scientific terms seems naive and arbitrary to classical epistemology.[4] Taken as such, they cannot inscribe themselves in the organisation of classical epistemology; nothing can give place to them in its grand organisational tension. Laruelle undoes this tension and epistemological organisation, accredits a lived experience to science, opacity, its 'relationship' to the Real, sees science as a subject, thinks it through the future and not the past history of sciences upon which epistemology constantly leans, changes its 'grain' (the virtual rather than fact), gives its rules extension, the 'non-'. He uses science in another register than that of a 'meta' or overhanging mode, which gives this effect of an all-too rapid reprisal of scientific terms in the eyes of the philosopher of science, or, by contrast, of arbitrary transformations such as 'oraxiom'. In its relationship to the past, epistemology always has examples; for Laruelle, there is no 'example' of the sciences, even if he makes his own usage of sciences.

Philosophy and Science in Laruelle

If we allow that epistemology organises, in a philosophical way, the meta-concepts that allow it to describe science, the most apparent difference will be that of the relations between philosophy and the sciences. If Laruelle no longer places 'knowledge' over science under this antithetical form it is because he posits the 'relations' between science and philosophy, between sciences and philosophies, elsewhere.

In Laruelle, there is a concern for democracy. We can allow the heterogeneity of science and philosophy. If we admit this heterogeneity, we can show the interrelations, the interlacings of the two.

We know few things of the sciences, not even their opaque relation to the Real (opaque in the sense that science admits the Real, but does not explicate it). This relationship allows the modification of its own concepts, but not of the Real. We have no theory of philosophy since each attempt at theorisation gives place to a new philosophy; it escapes any theory in producing another.

From this double situation, Laruelle draws foundational consequences. The first is that we cannot speak about the sciences or describe them directly; rather, it is always in an indirect manner that we engage them ('indirect' is one of the terms in the glossary of non-standard philosophy). The second is that knowledge of philosophy cannot be an auto-knowledge, but must make use of a heterogeneous element in order to construct its theory. Since Plato, there have been auto-modellings of philosophy, but they do not allow the creation of a theory of philosophy. But why should we create a theory of philosophy? Precisely to undo the spontaneous relations we posit between philosophies and sciences. These spontaneous relations suppose philosophy presiding over the sciences; it classifies them, organises them, constructs their norms, gives them a semblance of 'consciousness'. Yet this 'presiding' is the emptiness itself of all understanding, and as such of theory. Scholars have often understood philosophy as a sort of generalisation at the extremities of science, beyond equations, beyond hypotheses of application, beyond limit conditions; at the same time, though, they use it, because it allows them to speak about sciences while making use of the same words, even though they mistrust philosophy because they know the 'dangerousness' of such generalisations within scientific limits. This is the chiasmic system Laruelle wishes to leave: there is science, there is philosophy, but the continuities and generalisations spontaneously produced in order to comprehend one or the other distort the view of there being two sides. Above all, these generalisations are the manifestation of a sufficiency that masks the relationship that science and philosophy *could* have with relation to the Real. This sufficiency can be marked by the idea that philosophy can directly describe the sciences, from their texts, their accounts, and the observation of their laboratories.

According to Laruelle, we can say almost nothing directly about the sciences. Even if science and philosophy are radically heterogeneous, there will be usages of sciences and usages of philosophy that allow the emergence of a discourse over them. The usage of sciences cannot be a usage of 'positive' sciences, because we cannot transfer, in a directly scientific fashion, 'numerical' and 'experimental'. As such, 'superposition' or 'non-commutativity' would not be the positive repetition of positive notions, and would be reworked through an encounter with philosophy. But superposition, idempotence and non-commutativity would also be, for philosophy, the means of separating it from its sufficiency. Heterogeneity is apparently simple, but the links are subtle. We cannot directly speak of science; we must, therefore, find a way to make use of it. The positivity of science and philosophical sufficiency are thus reworked together. The whole question is to know how to produce a generic knowledge, which is to say, a knowledge that would be at once of science and of philosophy. The generic is not a simple transcription or repetition of philosophical or scientific concepts; the generic demands a transformation through the 'colour' of science, through this relationship without relation to the Real that unglues each concept of its discipline and allows for the possibility of interactions between sciences and philosophies. These do not pass to a macroscopic or unitary level as in classical philosophies (Kantian philosophy with Newtonian mechanics, Badiou's philosophy with the set theory of Zermelo-Fränkel initially and Paul J. Cohen latterly), but to a 'micro' level, 'virtual', where these convergences and interactions cannot be taken under the form of 'facts'. This is no longer the macroscopic *unity* of a system that determines it, but its *identity* – one that is eventually chaotic or fractal, though also always coming back, in the last instance, to the Real; an identity that is not that of synthesis or of combination. The generic is a sort of immanent encounter between philosophy and science, on the condition that this is not with a unitary aim, but just at this level where philosophy can be at once the concept and the means of science, as well as where science can be at once the concept and the means of philosophy. We cannot completely isolate, in the generic, an origin that would be scientific or philosophical: this would be a classically philosophical means of posing these questions.

The question of the Real is a question of method, which entails an order of questions. Science does not precede the Real, philosophy does not precede it, does not co-determine it, according to the rules of reversibility which philosophy has traditionally supposed between Being and the One, as between its 'opposites'. Between the Real and human productions, there is unilateral duality. Science allows this Real in an opacity which is in a way the 'place' of its immanence. Classical philosophy, which in contrast explicates the relations between philosophy and the Real, science and the Real, becomes for Laruelle a 'fiction' of the multiplicity of their possible, future, past and present relationships. Indeed, philosophy is made to continue in this fashion because the critique gives rise to new philosophy (but any 'new' philosophy can be reduced to a 'return' to ancient traditions, this continuity being the very form of its sufficiency).

There is, then, a link between the Real and immanence. Without the Real, immanence would be like any old transcendence; it would be arbitrary. For Laruelle, it is not arbitrary, but it partakes in contingency because it is radical and not absolute, because one can think it as materially as one likes. Immanence is not attached to any specific historical model, even a radical ego. It is identity when it can be 'developed' under the non-algebraic or non-logical form of idempotence whereby identity is not 'A' but 'A*A=A' (* designating an operation). The operation extends the A, as being identical to AA. This is not the arithmetical, but the undulatory extension of A. It is also, for this immanence, the possibility of seeing the manifestation of transcendences, of the fact of the 'operation' * and the multiplication to the N-degree of A. In this way, the undulation is not 'fine'; it 'superposes' undulations resulting in only one entity, it takes on a superposition not of 'layers' or 'levels' or 'archaeology of knowledges' but of oscillation. The wave, the oscillation: it is precisely these that distinguish the macroscopic, corpuscular and delimited concepts of classical epistemology. 'Transcendence', positive science for example, can 'fall into immanence' through its generic transformation. The imaginary number under the form of the quartile allows us to draw together these superpositions, circles, quarter-turns, oscillations, immanence, and transcendence in immanence.

This transformation cannot be the effect of positive science on positive science, nor of sufficiency on sufficiency. There must be a transformation here, a 'dualysis', which makes each term into a non-unitary identity, a science without positivity, a philosophy (or mathematics) without sufficiency.

In the 'Glossaire de la quantique générique' in *Philosophie non-standard* there are two words that are not nouns, or not directly transformable into words, but which can be explicated precisely in terms of 'indirect' and 'under'. These are two means of genericity. I cite each of them in different places in this chapter.

> *Indirect (indirect discipline or interdiscipline).* A generic discipline is indirect if it reaches its object through an inseparable double relation, if its object is part of its means, if its principal means is also an object. A quantum of philosophy makes use of philosophy not only as object but as means. A generic discipline of the quantum makes use of it as a means and not only as an object. Any object of a discipline is also a means of that discipline. The vectorial action of the module does not in general depend on the phase, but invests it with its object all the same. An indirect science is that of means, before being that of simple or rational 'objectivity'.[5]

We can see, then, why 'superposition', 'non-commutativity', etc., can be used without epistemological naiveté: they are generically transformed; they are *means*; they permit the extension of science without an overarching general system, without hierarchies, between notions.

In terms of philosophy, the role of science is the democratisation of philosophy, while the role of philosophy in terms of silenced science is putting science into discourse; each role admits even the most 'crazy' heterogeneities in relation to positive disciplines and doctrinal philosophies. Because 'sufficiency' reduces heterogeneity to homogeny (sometimes through mathematics), sufficiency is conceived as 'universal' by reducing the heterogeneous in the unicity of the same 'language'. If Laruelle chooses physics rather than mathematics to produce an understanding of philosophy, it is precisely with a concern for heterogeneity. Mathematics reduces heterogeneity in physics, so mathematics can be put into a situation of sufficiency, close to, and the twin of, philosophy. If he chooses the quantum, it is because that is the first science whose objects are not explicitly macroscopic or microscopic 'objects' – however we may imagine or perceive them to be – but 'operators' or 'states'. This situation, we will see, will produce a change of 'level' or 'regime' in epistemology.

The positive disciplines, the philosophy-systems, always exist, but this double mediation between philosophy and science causes the relationships between disciplines and systems to be profoundly transformed. Interdisciplinarity no longer consists only in a combination or transfer of the latest positive understandings from one discipline to another, but emerges from a sort of generic sharing that not only allows it to understand complexity, but, moreover, to transform completely the scientific idea of the object (in a non-phenomenological sense). This generic sharing has effects not of simple repetition, but of cloning: the encounter between the generic and philosophies that reproduces identities, concepts, or subjects, can itself be cloned, just as immigrant, clandestine strangers can sometimes be rendered visible on the philosophical horizon.

Science, then, is not taken in its positivity; it is a subject, as in Kant, but there it is as an effect of an afterthought. In Laruelle, science is a subject; it is a dynamic form of immanence, an 'open secret' of pre-priority, not real, not cloning, but in an asymmetrical relationship between the Real and cloning. The idea that science is a subject has two faces: science has a knowledge face, which is the lived human experience and immanence, but also an understanding face that is, in contrast, aimed towards the World and transcendence. Any science has a mystic face without religion, an understanding face without sufficiency. The mystic is a characterisation of immanence, at once intense and open; the understanding face is a 'place' – and not a foundation – for positive disciplines, 'place of an interdiscpline'.[6] It is a limit that allows positivities to build themselves, to construct their practical and conceptual conditions, to render their disciplines inventive and dynamic. Such a place, in order to be shown and explicated, needs a 'generic epistemology'.

In a certain naive and too often 'exaggerated' [reconté] fashion, we could say that Laruelle reinserts man into science. In a very elementary, minimal and generic state, the human and science are identical; they both have this clandestine character, non-discursive, silent. They start to talk within disciplines, within philosophies, as they dispose of limiting and specific principles. By contrast, positive disciplines and philosophical systems speak of the human on occasion, but without knowing it, without really showing it – they render it 'public' and 'authoritative'. So, in the generic, the human produces a sort of 'collective intimacy of science'.[7] This intimacy defends man in science, and thus, in philosophy, undoes philosophy's sufficiency through the rules of rewriting.[8]

Democracy is equally a 'putting-into matrix'. This, in effect, allows the play of heterogeneous elements in equality, with the occurrence of two variables, science and philosophy, each generically transformed and as such, already transformed one into the other, but on a 'virtual' and not a factual level. It allows a combination, not of the latest results, but an immanent combination 'under' a condition. This is not Heisenberg's matrix, which is a 'positive' matrix, but a matrix affected through an 'under'.

Under (under-consistence, under-determination, under-foundation, under-subject). A very indeterminate preposition in its philosophical usages. The general effect of generic forcing (acting of the non-acting) when it proceeds through quantum immanence (superposition) and not through philosophical and dialectical means that combine under- and over-potentialisation/over-empowering. Through relation to philosophical and mathematical sufficiency as double transcendence, it is an effect of de-potentialisation/disempowering and not of de-localisation. We must not confound the formulas 'being without foundation' (which is to say 'in a regime of auto-foundation' like philosophy) that indicates localisation, and 'being under-founded', which, on the contrary, indicates a certain dismemberment of auto-foundation. 'Under quantum' signifies 'in a quantum regime' of re-quantification, but not directly the effect of under-determination of transcendence.[9]

The putting-into immanence of the matrix, which is necessary in order not to recommence philosophical sufficiency, is also to put it 'under' quantum condition. There is a fusion of the quantum and philosophy under the quantum.

This 'under' is very important. Elsewhere we can see that we say 'overdetermination' like 'under-determination'. We can characterise philosophy, for example, as the place of all exterior over-determinations (sciences, technologies, ethics, aesthetics, religions, etc.), but Laruelle sees them as 'under-determinations', as a group of interrelations that never adopt hierarchical positions. We must think the relations between sciences and philosophies under the species of under-determination, and this is what really modifies the practices of interdisciplinarity as truly generic, which is to say, allowing man to re-enter science and to respect heterogeneity without discipline. This is how Laruelle's works are organised;

not only in waves (Philosophy I to V), but also by the under-determinations, by science,[10] technology,[11] ethics,[12] aesthetics,[13] religion,[14] psychoanalysis,[15] the political struggle in philosophy,[16] and philosophies of difference,[17] each time rethought in different thrusts and oscillations.

What Does Laruelle Have Against Epistemology and the Philosophy of Science?

What Laruelle has against the philosophy of science and epistemology is the implicit continuities that they posit between philosophy and the sciences. They suppose that one can only speak of science by effectively admitting such continuities, and as such assuring for philosophy a normative authority over the sciences, and for the sciences an authority of positive understandings. Both are undoubtedly 'true'; we can always think of science as not knowing how to elaborate its own norms – even if in contemporary sciences, programmes and meta-programmes are thoroughly blended – and we can always think of philosophy as lacking positive understandings. But is this distinction pertinent? All we can say is that it renders the possibilities of interactions between philosophies and sciences very strict, because, rather than affirming their radical heterogeneity, it posits an asymmetry resting on a loose consensus of continuity. This asymmetry, which has found its best formulations in literature – 'science without conscience is but the ruin of the soul' (Rabelais) – has greatly harmed the relations between philosophers and scientists, both 'lacking' something essential that the other possesses. This is a bad relation, because the invention of ideas here becomes reactive. If we want to form a theory of the interrelations between philosophy and science, it must widen the field, not 'close down' science and philosophy, and not bequeath unto them a 'bad conscience' or an arrogance of one in relation to the other.

Laruelle, like epistemology, makes a usage of the sciences. But, in fact, the epistemological use is a 'moral' one. Its guiding thought is that philosophy must be able to recognise itself directly in the sciences. And this thought revolves around a moral that is expressed in the idea that one cannot understand mathematics or physics unless one 'gets one's hands dirty', that is, when one knows how to reconstitute a continuity between the details of a text or a discipline within philosophy. Philosophy, in its generality, abandons properly scientific prescriptions, equations, limit conditions, but only has a sense if it has been able to follow the paths of its scientific elaboration. This is where we identify, in a supposedly 'general' language, science and its positive results. This is also to limit the possibilities of interaction. It is undoubtedly necessary to be entirely ignorant, but this only signifies that it is necessary to refigure the interrelations between philosophy and science over morality. It is a question of taking account of knowledge and non-knowledge, art and non-art, for otherwise our understandings will only be fragmentary, separated by disciplinary boundaries, perhaps even 'institutionalised'. We must seriously think about ethics, then.

Notions of epistemology are also too closed, too corpuscular, or 'molar' as Deleuze would say. Such notions can only be pertinent to a certain level of science, where we can repair and recognise them; but as such, they limit scientific analysis to given historical states. We know that the history of epistemology itself repeats the history of the sciences, in the order of mechanical, physical, chemical, biological and human sciences, and that at each stage it has had to widen its criteria. History of science is necessary, epistemology is necessary, but it is not necessary that they be blended in this way, because that limits what we can say about each science, because it leaves one with a determined model. This is undoubtedly why Laruelle speaks more willingly of 'modelling' than of model; this is a way of seeing the importance of models, but without identifying any precise model. The degrees of freedom are thus augmented; the 'unsticking' of notions in relation to their origin becomes possible.

The important issue is to mollify and enrich the relations between science and philosophy, and to diminish sufficiency and arrogance. This is not a moral end, but an end that is at once scientific and philosophical, generic, related to the human (though not extending to the good sentiments by which conscience adds 'consequences' to 'technology'). How can we open problems which are able to find their sense in large waves, and not only in their 'corpuscular' interpretation and in conceptual atomism?

Laruelle gives us a technique for this, which exists in epistemology, though in a local and partial manner: 'fiction'. Chaos, the fractal, the quantum, have never functioned in Laruelle as foundations, that upon which we 'rest' all philosophical representation, but as fictions, allowing the idea of science to be extended

(somewhat in the manner in which we construct algebraic extensions), respecting the 'places' of science, without substituting
the philosophical idea of foundation for them.[18] The philosophy
of science critiques the idea of foundation, but depends on it
structurally.

What is fiction? It is a method of renewing understandings and
knowledge, now with the aid of a preposition (which does not,
however, appear in the 'Glossaire de la quantique generique'). Is it
also a means of rendering our knowledges generic, of multiplying
disciplines and their interrelations? This preposition is 'without',
'with no', though it does not designate a lack. What is a philosophy without sufficiency? Is a philosophy that invents new means
of writing more experimental, and does it allow forms of compatibility with constituted philosophies under other hypotheses?
What is a philosophy without the transcendental? It is a philosophy rethought as a matrix with the sciences, and 'under' them.
The 'without' supposes an exterior addition – other philosophical writings, sciences, technologies, ethics, aesthetics, religions,
political positions in theory, in order to better think philosophy
outside of its auto-modelling. Fiction, then, is at once an extension of thought; it must have an exterior element, an 'imaginary
number', but also an extension of understandings, neutralised
usages (without sufficiency) under the form of materials for non-
philosophical thought. What is extraordinary here is that we can
see this method developing in diverse disciplines and continents, in
Anglo-Saxon philosophies of mathematics (to enrich the concept
of 'mathematics' by asking what a mathematics might be without
object, proof, number, etc.), and also in the theory of conception,
the concept/knowledge theory that treats technical objects not as
objects with a new property, but as an X that, without one of its
properties, distributes its others in unexpected ways amongst the
disciplines, thereby rethinking both the object and its understandings of which we make use. It is astonishing to see such diverse
independent convergences on a question of method; this is a
symptom that shows that neither the idea of foundation nor that
of the ontology of objects can allow us to take account of the idea
of science. Or, if such an ontology exists, it will be under the categories of unknown object and of futurality. These are not foundations, but places where continuities and extensions are regulated
by stops, those of research into new compatibilities.

The Transformations of Epistemology by Thought-Science

What is epistemology? A discipline borne of the illumination and the multiplication of scientific disciplines. The term, appearing in English in the middle of the nineteenth century, at the start of the twentieth century in French, aims to describe scientific methods in a more precise and local manner than the philosophy of science. The necessity of this new discipline came from the appearance of facts irreducible to the principles of mechanics. As such, new criteria for the scientific were needed, as was, undoubtedly, a renewed theory of understanding.

Here are the general implicit hypotheses upon which epistemology developed:

1. A recovery of science by philosophy, a certain conception of 'meta' and of the norm, sometimes in the form of philosophical concepts before 'recovering' those of science. These are the species of 'rationalism'.
2. A passage from the particular case or the historical to the universal. These are the species of hierarchisation and of the recognition of a case under an idea.
3. A morality of relations between sciences and philosophies, where 'dirty hands' are in science, and 'clean' ones are in philosophy. These are the species of a division in culture and not of the unilateral, between the Real and the multiplicity of cultures.

All of these implications are hypotheses of continuity between philosophies and sciences, as we have seen, but also foundations of rationalisms, of orders supposedly between beings, of divisions and of borders, which weaken multiplicities and heterogeneities.

The principles of Laruelle's thought-science and those of epistemology seem so different that it is difficult to imagine any relevance of the former for the latter. Its relevance is, however, multiple: it modifies epistemology by admitting that it does not directly carry over into the sciences; it allows all of the ingredients of the sciences, as such, to be given their autonomy; it allows the rethinking of the scientific object; and finally, it allows interdisciplinarity to be given criteria of scientificity. These transformations exist and are possible, even if epistemology

focuses on positive disciplines. They specifically allow the generalisation of the distinctions of these disciplines in relation to their
historical and particular origins. I will treat all of these points
separately.

1) A non-epistemology does not bear directly upon the sciences
What are the consequences of such a principle? It compels us
to see the interactions between the notions of epistemology,
rather than relating each concept in isolation to a scientific phenomenon. These interactions within epistemology are not rich
enough for the current state of contemporary science. The idea
of the complementarity of the categories of theory and experience has caused the two to be seen as massive referents, for which
we have sought massive connections too; for example, between
hypothetical-deductive structures or logical syntax and theory
(as if theory itself was basically an undifferentiated object). The
notion of the model is not 'stable' in such a conceptual group: it
is divided by the theory/experience opposition – so either it is a
'true interpretation' of theory, which is to say a concretisation,
or it is a generalising extraction of experience or observation (so
it is a process of abstraction). We know the lively battles that this
division has caused in French epistemology.[19] The model oscillates
between contradictory interpretations, and in any case, disappears
as soon as the theory is complete. This is how we have interpreted the model of the intermediary or 'mediator'.[20] The notion
of hypothesis, too, lacks consistency in classical epistemology:
confirmed, it becomes an empirical law; refuted, we abandon it
and it becomes an evanescent substance. Anything that is found in
the 'between two' of theory and experience has a median status,
ready to be reduced to notions taken as fundamental because they
straighten out the great epistemological tension. The issue is to
know whether contemporary sciences – their diversity, their complexity – bear witness, then, to successive widenings of epistemology, and can be taken into account by such a molar and barely
mobile system. Some think that the science of today does not differ
from that of the Enlightenment. But, they are obliged to consider
models, modellings, and simulations as pragmatic extensions of
science that are not really part of it. We leave, then, hypotheses
which begin by excluding in principle those things that do not
resemble classical epistemology, as this is precisely the opposite of
morality. If we wish to understand the sciences without making a

priori exclusions, even within the positive sciences, then we must 'conserve' the distinctions of epistemology, though in a space that delivers them from oppositional structure.

This demands an unsticking ['*décollement*'] of the idea that epistemology bears directly on the sciences. The richness and multiplicity of notions appears when we no longer seek to reconcile epistemological and scientific concepts. We must see that this is a means of destroying or dispersing rationalism, which fundamentally rests on two orders, philosophical and scientific, in parallel. Here, parallelisms are not denied; they are simply particular instances of dispositions of heterogeneous dimensions.

From here, epistemology could enrich notions serving as referential. Why must a theory resemble those from the origins of modern science? We devalorise as such disciplines organised on multiplicities of ends of theories, like biology or the human sciences. It does not suffice to affirm that experience is experience of theory continued in other ways in order to reaffirm the consistency of the notion of theory; it must be 're-quantified' through means other than positive science.

2) Non-epistemology is a formula of autonomy

Non-epistemology will use epistemology as materials. All epistemological distinctions will be taken seriously, as they safeguard a type of stability and anatomy that the classical and philosophical structure of epistemology destroys in intermediary or unstable notions. Every notion has the freedom of the city, and what is important is to make it generic, no longer dependent on 'observation' made by a separate science or a particular 'model'. Every distinction is consistent, multiple and plural. The table of distinctions can always be augmented, which is proof of its pertinence; analysis does not stop, does not trip up on notions considered as permitting the hierarchisation of an order. This situation has value for epistemology in terms of science firstly as a system of proofs and justification. The rules of autonomy allow us to see the sciences in a less monolithic manner, creating 'objects' and 'fictions', creating positive and non-positive oscillations.

Here, too, non-philosophy finds its 'place' in science. It creates an indefinite space where distinctions allowing science to be indirectly qualified can be settled or pushed into immanence.

Non-epistemology allows the reconsideration of notions of model, hypothesis, simulation, etc., and many others – as many as can be found in another way, without ever identifying science with one or other of these notions. Epistemology is just a space of distinction and of non-exclusion allowing philosophy, as non-standard and not sufficient, to show something of the 'scientific'. The invariants will be minimal and generic, not macro- and unitary, leaving a complete freedom of combinations.

3) Non-epistemology shows 'objects' of science in a new way
In classical epistemology, objects are assessed by disciplines ('natural' object), their combinations (modelled object), and their convergences (complex objects). All of these objects are taken as given or partially given, and all can be 'recovered' by science, as if Poincaré's theory of forms recovering a surface could have efficacy within epistemology. But we have seen, with fiction, that we deal with unknown, future, non-positive objects, where there is no longer a face to face or an intention in the phenomenological sense. These are no longer 'manipulable' objects, but objects we could call forms of oscillation and waves of thought-science. The allocations to homogeneous and heterogeneous are no longer classical, and are no longer organised by disciplinary cartographies like Serres' *Northwest Passage*. The transformation of 'objects' consists in taking oscillations into account with the non-phenomenological intention of the researcher – the two are no longer combinatory. They are not only unities of arithmetical, corpuscular, or molar parts; there are links between oscillations and particles, as between immanence and transcendences, as two states upon which operations bear.

We have called these 'integrative objects'.[21] They are the objects that actual science creates, and not just the 'technoscience' of Gilbert Hottois in which one seeks to immerse all of contemporary science, assuming its end (as in Jean-Marc Levi-Leblond), which is once again to believe that epistemology must directly describe this end (and also to transfer the idea of the 'end of philosophy' onto science). If there is science, it is also a creator, and not reduced to a logical system of proofs (between true and false and their intermediaries) that becomes institutional.

We have no 'direct' proof of these new objects. But we know that if we do not take them into account, we are creating exclusions within contemporary science. These questions of pertinence are highly important, but they are also indirect.

4) Non-epistemology is a generic epistemology

Such objects at least allow philosophical, ethical and aesthetic considerations within the sciences. The principal question is no longer that of knowing if this or that scientific proposition is verifiable or refutable. There are all sorts of circumstances where verification and refutation lose their meanings. The question is, rather, if our understandings are indirect, how can we make the piece of knowledge we produce compatible with other knowledges? What forms of compatibility does non-standard philosophy have with standard philosophies? Or non-epistemology with classical epistemologies? This question is very important, as it breaks the continuities extended by sufficiency. The research into compatibility requires much invention; it does not subsume a particular case under a universal, it demands fiction, under-determination, taking exteriorities and heterogeneities into account, openings in the field of epistemology.

The research into the classical criteria of the sciences lacks this aspect of the invention of compatibilities. I know of only one scholar who has developed such an idea in this manner: Henri Poincaré. He does not seek 'scientific criteria' (as we termed them) in his work. His scientific oeuvre has a particularity: he is a mathematician who makes discoveries outside of mathematics – not only within mathematics, but in all domains of physics. His discoveries always have the characteristic of results that make rapid gains from one discipline to another. It is as though, for all possible formulations, he sought formulas of compatibility with other disciplines, from arithmetical groups to the stability of the solar system; from mechanics to algebra, etc. He himself speaks of 'decomposition', whereby a generalisation only has scientific meaning when translated into a mathematical or fundamental physical language. 'Poincaré's criterion' breaks with sufficiency, and is no longer a criterion situated in the space of true and false . . . We could say that there is a mathematical non-sufficiency in Poincaré, in this research of invention through compatibility. This compatibilisation acts as a transcendence that 'falls into immanence'.

One of Laruelle's ideas, which we have cited but not explicated, resonates with the idea of decomposition and of re-quantification: it is that of 'oraxiom', which no longer declines like decomposition in positive science, but as a generic conjugation of axioms under the form of a portmanteau. A final quote from the 'Glossaire de la quantique générique':

Oraxiom: a portmanteau (axiom and oracle) which speaks, under the form of a unique conceptual particle, of the superposition of the mathematical axiom and the philosophical decision. The 'axioms' of non-philosophy or those that declare that Generic Science and in particular Determination-in-the-Last-Instance conjugate two types of decision – one mathematical, opening a formal structured field – the other an arbitrarily philosophical (though regulated) or undecidable decision. The oraxiom is spoken by radical immanence and is under-determined by it. The other nuances of the term – sibylline, enigmatic, abyssal or baseless, delirious – are brought into philo-fiction and must be transformed according to the same rules. Futurality is, *par excellence,* that which is declared or performed by oraxioms.[22]

From this 'decomposition' we can make a 'criterion' – which we call Poincaré's criterion – for all scientific progress, whether it be disciplinary or non-disciplinary. In the treatment of a scientific problem, we can multiply the disciplinary dimensions, provided that we assure compatibilities, at each step. A 'scientific' problem can include an 'ethical' or 'philosophical' parameter, though generic and minimal, without losing its 'scientific' character.

The sociologists of *Social Studies* and the 'relativists' of the 'postmodern' world have shown us that the criteria for scientificity established in the twentieth century can no longer be treated as universal criteria, but only as occasionally pertinent epistemological distinctions. Some have seen in this the death or non-pertinence of epistemology. But that was to rest one's case on classical positions, supposing that science is entirely given in its positivity and that it can be directly described by a science or a knowledge – a blend of philosophy and science that bears upon it. No, as for all the other sciences, we have the right to make hypotheses in order to understand the sciences, or philosophy, or technology, or ethics, without seeing their death in the realisation of one through the other, as postmodernism did. Let us take all of the forces of postmodernism, but reopen the space of a generic epistemology. We hope to have shown that the non-standard philosophy of François Laruelle can contribute to this aim, even if by indirect means. These indirect means allow for the invention of generic concepts, which open new under-determined interactions between science, philosophy and ethics.

Notes

1. François Laruelle, *Théorie des Identités. Fractalité généralisée et philosophie artificielle* (Paris: PUF, 1992).
2. François Laruelle, *Principes de la non-philosophie* (Paris: PUF, 1996).
3. François Laruelle, *Philosophie non-standard. Générique, Quantique, Philo-Fiction* (Paris: Kimé, 2010).
4. On this question, we must avoid a misunderstanding, which would be to believe that Laruelle speaks 'of' quantum mechanics. This is evidently not the case. He draws on the concepts of quantum mechanics to form a certain usage, which he transforms through philosophical means, in order to create a non-automodelisational philosophical understanding, and to provoke the effects of indirect knowledge in epistemology. He does not pretend to intervene in physics, and refuses any 'Sokalian' objection. In any case, his usage of certain concepts from quantum mechanics is in fact akin to that which Muchel Bitbol and his team practised in the recent work *Théorie quantique et sciences humaines* (Paris: CNRS éditions, 2009). Among the concepts used: superposition, intrication, imaginary number, non-commutativity.
5. Laruelle, *Philosophie non-standard*, p. 54.
6. Anne-Françoise Schmid, Muriel Mambrini-Doudet, and Armand Hatchuel, 'Une nouvelle logique de l'interdisciplinarité', *Nouvelles Perspectives en Sciences Sociales* 7.1 (2011), pp. 105–36.
7. Ibid.
8. See François Laruelle, *Philosophie et non-philosophie* (Liege/Bruxelles: Pierre Mardaga, 1989). This rewriting gives rise to experimental texts, sometimes under a poetic form, some of which have been published in *La Décision philosophique*.
9. Laruelle, *Philosophie non-standard*, pp. 60–1.
10. See François Laruelle, *Le Principe de Minorité* (Paris: Aubier, 1981), *Théorie des Identités*, and *Philosophie non-standard*.
11. See François Laruelle, *Une Biographie de l'homme ordinaire. Des autorités et des minorités* (Paris: Aubier, 1985) which is undoubtedly Laruelle's most Spinozist work, at least in the beauty of its theories of the soul.
12. See François Laruelle, *Théorie des Etrangers. Science des hommes, démocratie, non-pyschoanalyse* (Paris: Kimé, 1995), and *Ethique de l'étranger. Du crime contre l'humanité* (Paris: Kimé, 2000), and the forthcoming *Théorie générale des victimes* (Paris: Fayard-Mille et Une Nuits, 2012).

13. See François Laruelle, *Le Concept de non-photographie/The Concept of Non-Photography* (Bilingual Edition), translated by Robin Mackay (Falmouth: Urbanomic, 2011).

14. See François Laruelle, *Future Christ: A Lesson in Heresy*, translated by Anthony Paul Smith (London and New York: Continuum, 2010) and the forthcoming *Christo-fiction*.

15. See Laruelle, *Théorie des étrangers*. This aspect has been developed in a work by Didier Moulinier, *De la psychanalyse à la non-philosophie. Lacan et Laruelle* (Paris: Kimé, 1999).

16. See François Laruelle, *Introduction au non-marxisme* (Paris: PUF, 2000), *L'Ultime Honneur des intellectuels* (Paris: Textuel, 2003), *La Lutte et l'Utopie à la fin des temps philosophiques* (Paris: Kimé, 2004), and *Anti-Badiou. Sur l'introduction du maoïsme dans la philosophie* (Paris: Kimé, 2011).

17. See François Laruelle, *Philosophies of Difference: A Critical Introduction to Non-Philosophy*, translated by Rocco Gangle (London and New York: Continuum, 2010).

18. This point was especially developed at a conference in Bordeaux on 5 July 2011, in collaboration with members of the Russian Academy of Sciences, in a colloquium organised by Marys Dennes, 'Europe as place of an interdiscipline'.

19. See Alain Badiou, *The Concept of Model: An Introduction to the Materialist Epistemology of Mathematics*, edited and translated by Zachary Luke Fraser and Tzuchien Tho (Melbourne: re.press, 2007), originally published in French in 1969, wherein Badiou recognises only theoretical interpretations of the model as scientific, and the responses of biologist Jean-Marie Legay, who escapes this duality by positing that models are not representations.

20. See Mary S. Morgan and Margaret Morrison, *Models as Mediators: Perspectives on Natural and Social Science* (Cambridge: Cambridge University Press, 1999).

21. Schmid et al., 'Une nouvelle logique'.

22. Laruelle, *Philosophie non-standard*, pp. 57–8.

7

1 + 1 = 1: The Non-Consistency of Non-Philosophical Practice (Photo: Quantum: Fractal)

John Mullarkey

Philosophy is to be made, and this is good news. It is not given in its history, its institutions, its texts, its unconscious: it is always other than its past ... *Philosophical invention* has a program: take into account the novelty and energy of the philosophical decision, stop the 'critique'. And it has a maxim: *Invent Philosophy!*[1]

Non-photography is thus neither an extension of photography with some variation, difference or decision; nor its negation. It is a use of photography.[2]

Introduction: Revisions of Thinking

One must remember: Non-philosophy is a practice first and foremost: it is 'performative', Laruelle writes, 'and exhausts itself as an immanent practice rather than as a programme'. Non-philosophy is also described as a *use* of philosophy rather than one more new theory *of* it. Hence, one must ask what non-philosophy *does* with philosophy (or any other field), rather than what it itself is. Its being is its doing, or performativity.[3] This performative practice involves redescriptions (of thought) that are also revisions of it, or as Laruelle puts it, 'the unlimited redescription ... of the vision-in-One itself'.[4] Non-philosophy performs re-descriptions on the raw-material of philosophy, *and, in doing so, it is performative – producing real effects on how the texts are seen.*[5] This raw-material comprises what Laruelle regards as the essence of philosophy, which involves an invariant structure that serves to contaminate the One or the Real with itself – that is, its various conceptual presuppositions or decisions that endeavour to transcend the Real, to represent it. This contamination results in a *'mixte'* of the two. The revisionary descriptions of non-philosophy, on the other hand

– called 'cloning' or 'dualysis' – strive to 'de-*mixte*' or dissociate such philosophical decisions from mediating the Real. It operates in the reverse direction to that of philosophy, therefore, going from the Real to thought (which Laruelle calls a thinking 'according to' or 'alongside' the Real), rather than from thought to the Real (representing the Real).

This reversal or re-orientation can also be seen as a change of regard, or posture, toward the body of philosophical work:

> non-philosophy is not an intensified reduplication of philosophy, a meta-philosophy, but rather its 'simplification'. It does not represent a change in scale with respect to philosophy, as though the latter was maintained for smaller elements. It is the 'same' structure but in a more concentrated, more *focused* form.[6]

A 'more concentrated' form: this is an idea of abstraction as physical concentration rather than higher-order representation. And it is more 'focused': one might even say a better optics or photography. And this optics results in a new democracy of thought. Philosophy does not have the monopoly on (philosophical) thinking. As we know, the 'non-' in non-philosophy is not a negation of philosophy, but a performed expansion, an 'amplification'.[7] This is why Laruelle's is emphatically not a 'philosophy of the no', but an egalitarian affirmation: 'I posit the equivalence of all philosophical decisions.'[8] Furthermore, non-philosophy insists on the identity of *all regions of thought*, be they in art, science, ethics, or technology, but only 'in-the-last-instance'. It postulates their 'identification-in-the-last-instance', which is a *hypothesis* of their real identity (that we will examine later under its other name, 'idempotency').[9] Everything thinks.

So, where metaphilosophy is hierarchical, non-philosophy instead offers a '*unified theory of science and philosophy*' without hierarchy, without pre-conditions.[10] Laruelle is profoundly un-Kantian in that neither the conditions of possibility of thought (for Kant), nor its *real* (virtual) conditions (as for Deleuze) interest him. The 'conditions of possibility' of 'force (of) vision' in non-photography,[11] for example, is not 'our problem' he says.[12] Non-philosophy is unconditioned thought – it is self-standing knowing or 'gnosis'. As the recent *Philosophie non-standard* puts it, gnosticism denotes the 'equality in principle' of all knowledges, and its vision thereby strives to replace the 'struggle' between thoughts with an 'equalising' [*égaliser*].[13] Being without condition means that everything *already* thinks – as we will see in the case of non-photography – though philosophers will never accept this fact so long as they continue to think that there is something singular, or definite, to extant philosophical thought.

Here, then, we arrive at the purpose of this essay. Given that non-philosophy is *already* a practice, *already* performative, we ask: can one also apply it, or is it always already an *applied* thought? Does non-philosophy always already exist, everywhere (in all the 'regions' that are, thereby, no longer regional)? After all, if everything thinks, if thought is *already* democratic, what purpose is there in *commending* it? What purpose is there in extolling as a right, as an aspiration, what is, and must be, already true in fact? This question leads us back to that of conditions, namely the condition for, as a desire, as a need, non-philosophy. Certainly, despite its name, non-philosophy is not only about (or a usage of) philosophy, but opens out into a host of other expansive fields of enquiry (non-photography being the one we will examine here). If it were otherwise, non-philosophy would indeed be led (as has been charged) into the endless narcissism of philosophical auto-commentary,[14] instead of being the liberating force it claims to be that opens up new ways of thinking. Indeed, it is precisely by extracting (dualysing) any spontaneous philosophy *out* of our thinking about photography (as in a *philosophical aesthetics* of photography) that photography's own discoveries come into view. Not more philosophy, but less. But what we are interested in is the idea that non-photography, say, is already non-philosophy without any regional sub-status. That is, as a thinking according to the Real, non-photography is non-philosophy in another name, and its discoveries can be mapped on to those of the other sciences – quantum mechanics and fractal geometry for instance – in such a way as to show that there are no distinctions of regional-versus-fundamental science for Laruelle. As he puts it in his preface to the English translation of *The Concept of Non-Photography*:

These essays aim to disencumber the theory of photography of a whole set of ontological distinctions and aesthetic notions imposed on it by the Humanities, with the help of philosophy, and which celebrate photography as a double of the world. Written around 1992, they contain the entirety of non-philosophy as exposited in *Theorie des identites*

(Paris: PUF, 1992) and make the link with the quantum themes of *Philosophie non-standard* (Paris: Kimé, 2010). It is enough to understand that the term 'identity' – perhaps not the happiest of terms, given its logical associations – assures the passage between the One (the perennial object of our research) and that of quantum 'superposition' our key concept at present. Just a minor change of vocabulary would suffice.[15]

The applied is already the 'pure' theory. The pure is the applied. In this chapter, beginning with the non-philosophical thinking embodied in non-photography, but also glimpsed in quantum mechanics and fractal geometry, we examine the theoretical ramifications that follow from this innocent remark that 'just a minor change of vocabulary would suffice'. It is worth noting that a fractal is an irregular geometrical shape that is generally reproduced (self-similar) at arbitrary scales – coastlines and snowflakes being the most famous examples actually occurring in nature. And fractal thought is just one model Laruelle offers for thinking how non-philosophy operates. But just how self-similar, or fractal, then, are all the different implementations of Laruelle's non-philosophical thought, as we move from quantum, to photo, to philosophy? How 'recursive' do things appear when we are faced with what remains after the distillation of philosophy from all the other fields of thought (in both the sense of an extraction of its contaminating decisions and a simplification of the non-philosophical thought indigenous to those fields)? The identity between them is real: rather than being a logical relation of 'A = A', it is a non-philosophical Real identity of force (of) vision, what he will call 'idempotency' in later works. How does this Real identity differ, though, from a logical identity, such that each practice is allowed some specificity without being reduced to one another or the One or Real? Furthermore, is it judicious of Laruelle to insist, as he so often does, on his views concerning non-philosophy being *consistent* throughout? Indeed, is his insistence on consistency, or rigour, in formal argument a legacy from philosophy that Laruelle cannot do without? Is it possible that there be a non-reductive, expansive conception of consistency at work here too? These are the questions that animate the following discussion. Before we get to that, however, is it worth looking a little at Laruelle's view of science and reduction.

What is Scientific About Science?

Non-philosophy experiments with philosophy scientifically: it tests the hypothesis, 'what effects follow from thinking of philosophy *as belonging to* the Real rather than as about the Real'. It does this by changing the significance of philosophical vocabulary from representing reality to thinking 'alongside' or 'according to' the Real. Wherever there was a circularity of presupposition and conclusion in the original philosophy, this identification installs a relation of 'determination-in-the-last-instance' (by the Real) instead – a real identification.

This hypothesis is scientific for Laruelle because it involves the performative test of a truth, not the truth of statements that purport to correspond with an actual state of affairs. Like Spinoza's, Laruelle's conception of truth is immanent to itself. That means that it is its own *standard* (when it is 'non-standard') – 'the proof of itself' in its own gnostic existence, without trying to represent a pre-given World: as *The Concept of Non-Photography* puts it, 'truth-in-photo is detained in the photograph itself; and the latter, in the photographic posture – force (of) vision or "photography".'[16] Non-philosophy is a *gnosis of itself* – a 'first science', or a 'science of science'. All the same, it emphatically does not regard itself as a *foundational* science for other disciplines: rather, it is a knowing (science) that is auto-foundational.[17] That is why Laruelle's thought purports to have the status of a *discovery*, that of the Real, rather than being one more philosophical decision, one more, always constructive, representation, such as a philosophy *of* a science (like physics or mathematics) that would say why (in 'philosophical' terms) physics or mathematics is the foundation for all knowledge.[18]

And yet, Laruelle's idea of science is conflated all too frequently with a scientism of some ilk.[19] In fact, it is both more and less extreme than that. It is less extreme because it never lays any claim to mathematicism or physicalism or biologism. All knowledges are equal, 'flat', vis-à-vis their discoveries:

> If philosophy has not been able to explore the nature and extent of flat thoughts, let us change our general hypothesis and horizon: science, a new science perhaps, shall be the guiding thread that will allow us to penetrate into the heart of the photographic operation. On condition that we globally re-evaluate and reveal the 'thinking' at work in science.[20]

Hence, photography too, as a theoretical practice, can lay claim to being no less scientific than physics or mathematical geometry: to prioritise one over the other would be a philosophical hierarchisation of knowledge:

> To identify, doubtless, art and theory (for example, fractal theory as scientific), but in a very particular mode of identity that we will call the *One-in-the-last-instance* . . . We shall call it a *unified theory of the photography of fractality*. Far from being their unitary and reductive synthesis, for example in the mode of metaphor and for the greater glory of philosophy, it *poses as an hypothesis to experiment*, test, modify and render fruitful in knowledge, the identification-in-the-last-instance of these two things . . .[21]

Theories (discourses of photography, physics, or mathematics) are unified, not reduced, in order to test a hypothesis that they *are all* part of, or think according to, the Real. But Laruelle's idea of science is also more extreme because it does not

> propose this irreflective thought with reference to any regional model, any experience drawn from a particular scientific discipline. Logic itself is perhaps no more sufficient than any other such discipline. Rather than understanding blind or deaf thoughts on the model of logic, with its formal automatism and 'principle of identity', we must render intelligible their practice of radical adequation through *Identity*, doubtless – but a real Identity, not a logical one.[22]

Photography is 'a technique that simulates science', offering us the same 'flat and deaf thinking, strictly horizontal and without depth, that is the experience of scientific knowledge'. It is a 'purely transcendental science', however, which is why a photo 'feels like one of those flat, a-reflexive, ultra-objective thoughts that are a discovery of scientific modernity'.[23] In fact, it was such flat, 'irreflective thinking' as this that enabled both the 'non-Euclidean' and the 'non-Newtonian' mutations in geometry and physics. Photography, shorn of the philosophical aesthetics to which it so often cleaves, is a science, a non-philosophy, and it makes real discoveries:

> we will cease to make commentaries on them [artists] and to submit them to philosophy so as finally not to 'explain' them but, on the

basis of their discovery taken up as a guiding thread (or, if you like, as cause) to follow the chain of theoretical effects that it sets off in our current knowledge of art . . . To mark its theoretical effects in excess of all knowledge.[24]

Laruelle will even generalise from this research into its effects in knowledge to say that art as such can be what he calls a 'half-science' rather than a 'half-philosophy', the 'half' here meaning something that is not 'poorer than science' but possibly 'more complex'.[25]

So, if photography is a science, or indeed if any other acknowledged science is a science too, it will be on condition that it is not conflated with what Laruelle here calls 'techno-science'.[26] What Laruelle is interested in is the 'scientificity' of science – which operates at a level of 'radical', material abstraction (concentration and simplification) that allows photography to participate as an instance of it.[27] It is not a scientism that reduces everything to one regional science, supposed fundamental.[28] He seeks some '*a priori* photographic content – being-in-photo', that would be a participant in this scientificity of science (as equally as physics might be) simply because it was the most materially abstracted, simplified or condensed aspect, what we could call the 'photographicity' of photography:[29] 'The photo – not in its material support, but in its being-photo of the object – is none other than that which, through force (of) vision, is given immediately as the "in-itself" of the object.'[30] And the photographicity of photography, or being in-photo, is a 'pre-analogical' or 'prepredicative' semblance, one that stems neither from 'iconic manifestation nor from pragmatics or the norms that make of the photo a visual index, but from the photo's non-specular manifestation of Identity'.[31] The question remains as to just how similarly non-philosophical (*qua* Laruellean broadening practice) are the non-philosophies (*qua* noun) such as physics or photography.

Photography Must be Delivered From its Philosophical Interpretations[32]

Certainly, both the (non-)philosophical actuality of photography, as well as its equivalent proclivity to falling into philosophical decisionism, is grasped by Laruelle throughout the text of *The Concept of Non-Photography*: 'the dissolution of ontological

Difference is the great work of photographic *thought* – for photography, when we think it, also thinks; and this is why it does not think like philosophy'.[33] Laruelle's usual task of discerning all the amphibologies, hybrids, correlations or 'empirico-transcendental' doublets infecting philosophical mediations of the Real can also be found in its *mixte* with photography: 'If we wish simply to describe or think the essence of photography, it is from this hybrid of philosophy as transcendental photography that we must deliver ourselves, so as to think the photographical outside every vicious circle, on the basis of a thinking – and perhaps of a "shot" – absolutely and right from the start divested of the spirit of photography.'[34]

By contrast with the circular attempts 'to photograph photography (the philosopher as self-portrait of the photographer)', we are offered this non-philosophical attempt at 'describing it as a thinking'.[35] And it is indeed a *descriptivism* at work here, just as it is throughout Laruelle's more obviously 'intra-philosophical' works: 'non-photography' is 'a new description and conception of the essence of photography and of the practice that arises within it to seek an absolutely non-onto-photo-logical thinking of essence, so as to think correctly, without aporias, circles or infinite metaphors, what photography is and what it can do'. Significantly, a non-onto-photo-logical thought of essence is not *essentialist* at all in terms of actively constructing a philosophical or logical identity: the Real identity to be discovered is founded *passively*: 'it is philosophically sterile: photography takes place in an immanent manner, it has nothing to prove, and it doesn't even necessarily have a will – for example, to critique and to transform the World, the City, History, etc.'[36] Hence, only Laruelle's 'rigorously non-photographic thought' is able to 'describe photography without begging the question'.[37] In other words, the thinking of photography, or in the photo, is not *constructed* by an extension of a philosophical model of thought (in its illustration in photo). Rather, it is native, or immanent to the photo, and is only *discovered* by a non-philosophical *stance* or 'posture' toward it.

This is *objective* science – an 'intrinsically realist knowledge' toward the Real (rather than the World) – that discovers new forms of philosophical thinking, rather than – *pace* our opening quotation from *En tant qu'Un* – *inventing* new forms of it that only ever beg the question through their presuppositions.[38] Or better still, philosophy is continually reinvented via discovery of new forms of thought in non-philosophical realms. And it is the practice of non-philosophy that *sees* this – it is a *seeing* or 'way of looking' – and so connects the two (discovery and [re]invention):[39] 'Photography . . . is an immanent process that traverses and animates this materiality [its technology, optics, or aesthetics], a *thinking* instigated by the artificial simulation of perception.'[40] Or better still, again, it is the *immanent* cause of photography, the embodied 'photographic posture' and force (of) vision, that thinks. Indeed, for Laruelle 'the non-' of 'non-photography' must be grasped through the twin concepts of 'photographic posture' and force (of) vision.[41] These are thought-experiences (*experiments/ hypotheses*) rather than ontologies, ones that are occasioned, in-the-last-instance, by the Real.[42] Whereas philosophers question photography in terms of the 'being of the image', Laruelle wishes to incite a 'new experience of visual representation', with the photographic process understood through its immanent 'cause' in this idea of posture or force (of) vision. To be precise, posture 'is not only the requisite of the reality that every photo needs in order to continue being "received" by the photographer' (there are also social, technological and aesthetic factors facilitating this reception), but it is 'its cause-in-the-last-instance, an intransitive cause, exerted only in the mode of immanence'.[43] In the next section we will look further into why this discovery of photography – of the 'in photo' – *is* a thinking no less than any other.

The Non-Photography of Thought

At one point in *The Concept of Non-Photography* Laruelle writes: 'it is a matter of relieving it of its unthought philosophical residues'.[44] One of these residues is the representationalist fallacy ('thought is *about x*', 'images are *about y*'), shared by photography's own 'spontaneous' philosophy with its academic form: 'For common sense, and still for the philosophical regime, an image is an image-of . . . a photo is a photo-of.'[45] But for non-photography the photo is no longer *of an object*, it is its own Reality, it photographs, or puts 'in-photo', the Real. It does not merely picture the World (though it *can* obviously be seen as only that); rather, in its own being, it identifies the Real, it *is* the thing – 'the affect of identity that a photography gives': 'the distinctions form/ground, horizon/object, being/entity, sense/object, etc., and in general the distinction between the transcendent thing and the transcendence of the thing: they are now strictly identical or indiscernible'.[46] This identity, as we said, is not logical, nor any 'synthesis of ground and form, of horizon and object, of sign and thing, of signifier and signified'. As Real, it is 'fractalising' not 'totalising':[47] it is 'a non-decisional self-identity, that which gives the ground of force (of) vision'.[48] The photo itself communicates the 'affect and the experience of "flat thought"', and this is why Laruelle maintains that the photo is an 'emergent, novel representation, a discovery, and that it precedes photography. . .'.[49]

This is a 'flat' thought, then, that disallows any disparity between fundamental and regional domains, or vertical philosophy. The view we will articulate here therefore – which will be a strong interpretation of non-philosophy that Laruelle's own transcendentalism might retreat from – is that non-philosophy is *not applied within or illustrated by* non-photography, for example, it *is* non-photography (and vice versa). These are all *Really* identified with each other such that the one adds nothing to the other (*as* application, *as* illustration). Non-Philosophy = Non-Photography = Non-Newtonian Physics = Non-Mandelbrotian Fractal Geometry = . . . = . . . = . . . Laruelle calls this 'Idempotency', which has, in mathematics, the formula, $1 + 1 = 1$. *And* in Non-Newtonian Physics it has the quantum mechanical phenomenon of 'superposition' (where *all* the possible states of a physical system coexist, including mutually exclusive ones). *And* in Non-Photography it has the ontological facet of being 'in-photo'.[50] And all of these 'ands' are themselves non-summative, that is, they do not add increasingly to each other but always equal, or equate with, the same real identity, One, or the Real. If they are parts rather than representations (applications, illustrations), if they are related mereologically to the Real rather than representationally, that is, if they are immanent to the Real rather than transcendent, then this is not a matter of any additional quantities but of one identifiable quality, of sharing the same *qualis* (of what kind One is).

A Problematic Consistency

Questions stemming from this position, however, will be thorny: if everything is already the Real, then why, as we asked earlier, does this *fact* need to be commended? Also, we should ask how this notion escapes the philosophical virtues and vices of Michel Henry's auto-affective Life (which has been described as a tautological formula, 'A = A'), or Gilles Deleuze's Univocity of Being.[51] After all, for Laruelle these are both circular philosophical positions. The former has led to charges of vicious circularity, which Laruelle, we will see, would need to by-pass via a differentiating structure wrought through a distinction between pure self-similarity or recursion and a Generalized Fractality, *creative* similarity.[52] But even the creative response to the charge of tautology seems to land Laruelle squarely in the Deleuzian camp of upholding a productive/creative notion of repetition (virtuous similarity), univocity meaning that the one same thing about everything is that everything is different, as held up in the formula 'monism = pluralism', and so on. However, Laruelle is no philosopher of difference, nor even a non-philosopher of difference (this latter being a contraction in terms), so how he can respond to the impression of philosophical univocity – commending the (non-Greek) One, as well as (non-Jewish) creation, but *without* '*Gréco-philosophique*' difference or logical identity – remains to be seen.

One way out may well come by looking closely at Laruelle's own axiological starting points in consistency (there are others, such as 'lived experience' or the 'ordinary', but we will keep to consistency, or 'rigour', here). Is Laruelle being consistently non-philosophical in his constant valuation of consistency? Certainly, consistency is used as a term in the content of what he writes – 'The task of a rigorous thought is rather to found – at least in principle – an abstract theory of photography.'[53] But in the physical *form* of non-philosophy (form here referring to its performative practice), we would ask whether consistency is logically identical throughout his work (which would be a failing in Laruellean terms) or *really* identical, that is, *non*-consistent in the sense of broadening our notion of consistency in *paraconsistent* ways. There is a foreshadowing of this problem in Jacques Derrida that is worth pausing over for a moment here. The post-structuralist turn is often marked by Derrida's interventions of 1966 and 1967 (especially the lecture 'Structure, Sign, and Play in the Discourse of the Human Sciences' in 1966) wherein certain operative terms of structuralism, such as 'law', 'science' and even 'structure' itself, were put under the same differential analysis that structuralism had already applied to its classical objects – authorship, meaning, consciousness, history, and so on. The positive meaning of these terms was lost, and with that, structuralism's claims to authority. When structuralism turns (on) itself (and so mutates into post-structuralism) it does so, however, in an avowedly reflective and reflexive mode of heightened self-awareness. Of course, this metatheoreticism – which identifies the Real with itself by moving from the premise that everything is 'philosophisable' (as Laruelle puts it) to the conclusion that everything then must *already* be philosophy or at least be accessible through philosophy (Being can be thought by philosophy = Being is philosophy) – is *not* amenable to Laruelle because non-philosophy is not a *heightened* reflection, *higher*-order representation, or metaphilosophy (understood in Lacanian terms as second-order logic). Derridian metaphilosophy (even in the mode of theology or literature-as-philosophy) is simply more philosophy (uncreative self-similarity). Non-philosophy must be something more if it is worth commending and needs to be commended.[54]

After all, it is difficult to deny that the ongoing prerequisite for philosophy is its desire to avoid contradiction, to assure consistency. Derrida, it is said, stopped arguing *for* his quasi-concept of *différance* in the 1960s in favour of actually performing it in the 1970s (in works such as *Glas*) *in order to be consistent* with his message regarding the futility of self-present argument (logocentrism). For here is the rub: if *in-consistency* (be it through alterity, *différance*, multiplicity, etc.) is the 'content' of one's philosophy, of one's message or argument, then one must invent new forms of argument, new kinds of consistency, and even new types of thought in order to stay 'true' to it. Yet Laruelle's contention is that *this cannot be done while still being philosophical at all, given his view that philosophy must always totalise what counts as thought under a current (or its current) definition.* Laruelle will not so *define* thought, but leaves it open to (or 'occasionally' caused by) determination-in-the-last-instance. It is a thought unconditioned (by philosophy) because *it* is occasioned by the Real. Yet the 'it' here is not a *new philosophy* but simply all the thoughts (of philosophy, but also of the sciences, arts, politics, and so on) revisioned as material, as *parts* of the Real rather than as *all about* the Real.[55] As Laruelle himself puts it 'I absolutely do not overturn philosophy; were I claiming to overthrow it, it would be a pointless gesture, a zero-sum game. The entire enterprise would then be contradictory.'[56]

Of course, the *philosopher's* perennial reply to all this will be, 'how does he know?' How does Laruelle know that non-philosophy thinks 'alongside the Real'? And his answer will simply be, as it must, *because it is Real*. He replies to an epistemology, a desire for a philosophical account of himself, with a non-philosophical *performance*. In fact, this is what happened in a dialogue with Derrida when he asked Laruelle from where he got his idea of non-philosophy if not from philosophy itself. Laruelle replied: '*I get it from the thing itself*. This is as rigorous an answer I am able to give. Because the criterion for my discourse was a rigorously immanent or transcendental criterion, there is no other answer I can give.'[57] This is the only way that Laruelle can reply without returning to philosophy, that is, to providing a sufficient reason (or commendation) for epistemology (and so re-entering the circular game of 'how do you know that you know. . . ?). As he also says, 'You have to start from the real, otherwise you'll never get to it.'[58] Thought *dissociates from* the Real, rather than being a set of associations reaching the Real. This is not yet to say that thought *is* the Real, but to suggest that it is aligned to the Real in a non-representional way.

Should we give Laruelle the benefit of the doubt, then, to allow him to test this hypothesis (thought as identical to the Real in the last-instance)? The alternative is to charge him with sheer folly, as he himself acknowledges:

> I have to tell you that this is an absolutely standard, normal, common objection; it is always the one people put to me first: 'You use philosophy in order to talk about something which you claim is not philosophical.' Listen ... the objection is so fundamental that it is tantamount to indicting me of a crude, rudimentary self-contradiction. It is entirely obvious that I allow myself the right, the legitimate right, to use philosophical vocabulary non-philosophically.[59]

Yes, Laruelle uses philosophical terms like 'transcendental' non-philosophically (that is, ripped from being transcendent and representational) – but they are performed or enacted to give them a new status or produce a different experience. And doing so also ensures that he does not fall into self-contradiction: 'since I take as indissociably given from the outset a certain use of language, which is not that of the logos, and the One which founds it, I do not contradict myself, I do not relapse into philosophical contradiction'.[60]

Yet, we should note this tell-tale reference to 'philosophical contradiction'. It begs the question (according to the logic of my essay at least) as to what other kind of contradiction might be in play here, and so of what other kinds of consistency. Might there be types of the two such that non-philosophy, *to be itself*, must not and cannot argue along the old lines that invoke (as Laruelle still does even here) 'a requisite degree of internal rigour or consistency' as though these were neutral, one-size fits all, exemplars (that is, philosophically transcendent) rather than highly mutable and open to mutation?[61]

That philosophy adopts a singular consistent approach to consistency is all too evident to Laruelle.[62] It is 'a habit' of philosophers, his *Philosophies of Difference* tells us,

> of somewhat artificially raising problems of doctrinal coherence in order to give oneself the function and the 'benefit' of resolving them. 'There were no contradictions! See how good and clever I am, how I have saved this author!' 'There is an insurmountable contradiction: see how I know the author better than he himself, how I myself am a good author, more Kantian than Kant, more Spinozist than Spinoza!' In order to avoid this Samaritan poison, we will postulate immediately that all these authors are not only systematic but – taken in their totality – coherent up to the point of their sometimes unbridled manner of making Difference play. We will posit their internal rigor in order better to reject them globally.[63]

So if (as I argue) non-philosophy turns around (as it must) to look at its own key-term, consistency, *in a non-philosophical mode*, then it will be to inflate *both* the meaning of consistency and so also the meaning of non-philosophy. In other words, non-philosophy loses any permanent (transcendental) status, or stance, that sets it outside philosophy because it is simply a more 'focused' photograph (of) philosophy – philosophy in-photo (just as being in-photo is non-philosophy). Everything *is* non-philosophisable,[64] but this does not lead to vacuous explanations where all things ooze into each other (to be met with an abject horror of groundless thought): rather, what oozes are new forms of perfectly *identifiable* non-philosophy, or non-standard philosophy, non-photography being only one of them. Non-philosophy is not singular or special, it is not of a higher-order. Rather, its number is legion. It is indeed everywhere, but *hidden* in the background, beneath and behind the philosopher's gaze *at any one time*. Hence, it needs to be commended, to be attended to, or seen in-photo so that it can be brought into visibility. It may even *become* philosophy eventually. If it is a metaphilosophy, it is 'meta' understood physically as 'beyond' our standard 20/20 vision, in the periphery, out of sight, just glimpsed. Non-philosophy is the *transformation* (a processual practice) of what counts as philosophy as seen in the full, centre-field of (our) vision. As such, it is always, from the perspective of philosophy at least, heretical or 'mutant philosophy' ('meta-philosophy' as 'muta-philosophy').

Hence, unlike Laruelle, I see no difference between 'transcendent' and 'transcendental' thought: be they philosophically enunciated or non-philosophically performed, they are both illegitimate forms of hierarchism, the latter basing itself on a putatively disembodied (de-psychologised) logic, a view from nowhere. So I take the 'vision-in-One' as a necessarily situated glimpse, each variant or mutant of which bringing along its own logic. To think otherwise privileges one logic over others, whereas, *performatively*, we should equalise all logics even if we have to embrace regressive self-referential paradox. And to ask, is this latter 'embrace' a logic too? – the answer would have to be yes, but it is a logic of a different type, a type that keeps creating new types, even of 'regressive logic', which is indeed something Laruelle might endorse (as we will see).

Laruelle himself comes close to this situationalism in non-photography with the notion of *posture*:

> what does it mean for the transcendental posture to realise itself as force (of) vision, if not to suspend from the outset or to immediately reduce this transcendence of the World, and all the phenomena of authority that follow from it, and to pose all the real problems of photography as a function of the immanence of force (of) vision?[65]

The transcendental – as science – is realised or embodied as a *posture*, as force (of) vision.[66]

Fractal Consistency Beyond Scalarity (Geometrics and Quantum)

The glimpse that non-photography affords of the Real is complementary, or *creatively* self-similar, to that in Laruelle's work on quantum mechanics and fractal geometry. Within the 'internal drama' of looking at, and being looked at by, a photo, he argues, there is a *new* concept of fractality. Laruelle names it 'non-Mandelbrotian' or 'generalised fractality', thereby showing how broadened both the fractal and being 'in-photo' can be, as both ooze toward each other, without becoming logically identical.[67] The irregular self-similarity here is not tied either to natural fractals (like snowflakes or coastlines) nor even mathematical fractals as defined by Mandelbrot, however:[68]

> a *unified theory* of the fractal and of the philosophical in the form of a *generalised* or *non-Mandelbrotian fractality*. This theory would not be a mere theory in the classical sense of the word, but in its own way a true integration of the fractal and of the philosophical: a fractal practice of philosophy at the same time as a 'de-intuitivation' of the fractal itself; and an ontological or real use of the fractal extended beyond physical or geometrical intuitivity at the same time as a refusal of the metaphorical use to which a 'fractal vision of the World' inevitably leads.[69]

Likewise, the photographic practice of 'multiple-exposure, superposition or stacking of visual givens' is not logically identical with Laruelle's generalised fractality either. Nonetheless, the fractal photograph is no less a facilitator of generalised fractality than is Mandelbrot's fractal geometry itself.[70]

Quantum mechanics also operates 'in-photo' – superpositionary elements being complementary to photographic and quantum phenomena.[71] Indeed, the photo has a 'fractional aspect, irreducible to wholes, to "whole" dimensions or to the classical dimensions of perception and perhaps of *philosophical objects*'.[72] The photo is non-Newtonian too. Through it (and physics) philosophical concepts (objects) are not just rescaled but re-rendered as ondulatory (quantum mechanical waves) and new visualities (in-photo): they can interfere with each other, can be superposed, and have probable (hypothetical) existence *as* (not just *like*) waves – though all in-the-last-instance. Philosophy is a quasi-physics, as *Philosophie non-standard* shows, with 'conceptual particles' created by or as 'vibrations, diffractions, superpositions, interferences'.[73] But it is no less a quasi-photography as well. And physics, like photography, is a quasi-philosophy, or rather, non-philosophy too – just a minor change of vocabulary would suffice.

Fictional Rigour

So, to return to the one question at the centre of this chapter: can a quantum-fractal-photo-oriented thought embody this real identity without falling into the lure of valorising a philosophical (that is, aspirationally monological) notion of consistency, even as it performs a set of ideas that are 'idempotent' ($1 + 1 = 1$), and as it aspires to avoid any (vicious) circularity (a classically philosophical aspiration if ever there was one)? One short-cut out of this dilemma might simply be to say that Laruelle is not really interested in consistency at all, and actually valorises *inconsistency*. The evidence for this comes from his identification of the Real with the One as inconsistent or nonconsistent; it is, he says in one essay,

> devoid of ontological, linguistic, and worldly consistency. It is without-being and without-essence, without-language and without-thought, even though it is said to be thus with the help of being, language, and thought, etc. This non-consistency entails that the One is indifferent to or tolerant of any material, any particular doctrinal position whatsoever.[74]

Even more, his identification of the Real with 'Man-in-person' goes further again, stating it to be 'also foreign to all inconsistency. It is the without-consistency. Man-in-person or identity can be defined . . . as *the separated middle*, which is neither included nor excluded, neither consistent nor inconsistent, etc.'[75] Admittedly, such a 'middle' – neither included or excluded, and so neither consistent or inconsistent with bivalency – muddies the water as regards what the Real is. But it does little to redeem many of the naive statements from Laruelle, cited above, when defending his consistency to philosophers. It is certainly not practised in any way similar to, say, his practice of either culling or expanding the vocabulary of Representation or Reality or World from philosophy's scale of values.

The concept of 'philo-fiction' (also called 'hyper-speculation')[76] might be of more help here, however, for it involves the rigour or consistency of fictional invention (much like Badiou follows the rigour of mathematical conventions, but without suturing it to the one science as Badiou does). As *Philosophie non-standard* explains it, a 'scientific philo-fiction' involves a 'statistical production of quantum and probabalistic fictions', a 'radical fiction', that is also an 'invention by fiction and rigour of philosophical possibles'.[77] So two things, two truths, therefore, may coincide, rather than fixate upon the bivalent truth of either/or. And this has a fictional rigour to it, that is, an invented rigour (the rigour of invention, not convention) akin to the science of the quantum, where things may both exist and not-exist (Schrödinger's cat).[78] After all, the 'Law of Identity' in classical Aristotelian theory, is a *logical identity* (not Real identity) that rests on a consistency, of 'A = A'. But that *type* of consistency (and corresponding inconsistency, as in 'A v ¬A', 'either A or not-A') is also material. Bivalent (either/or) logic is moulded on one specific type of matter and material consistency, the 'classical dimensions of perception and perhaps of philosophical objects', as Laruelle puts it. But there are many consistencies to the material Real that we are a part of, not just the one logic of solids, but also other possible logics of fluids or gases or quantum events. 'Con-sistency' has different meanings, one of which concerns the way in which a substance, like a liquid, 'holds itself together' – its thickness or viscosity. Not all logics have the rigidity that a philosophically 'rigorous or consistent' argument is said to have to follow. Rather than conflate all consistency with one, macro-physical consistency, then, Laruelle exposes the rigour of quantum matter and quantum invention, of new, non-bivalent (am-bivalent) consistencies emerging with new fields of thought. But these inventions are *not* fantastical constructions, but, because they are rigorously invented (that is, they never delude themselves into thinking that they are autonomous, nor that they represent the Real – either directly or by proxy), they think alongside the Real, and so rediscover the Real thereby.

Conclusion: New Types of (Non-)Philosophy

New philosophies emerge from other 'non-philosophical' subjects immanently as a moment within them (usually of crisis or revolting horror).[79] New, mutant philosophy does not stand over them, waiting to be illustrated by them or applied to them. Nor does non-philosophy, in Laruelle's idea of a science of philosophy, stand in that relationship to them. Indeed, it never stands (still) at all – it is a movement, a temporal phenomenon emerging from the (common-sense) idea of a non-philosophical discipline when its normal logic (laws of consistency) breaks down. When new logics emerge, so then the discipline becomes philosophical, now in a (Laruellean) non-philosophical manner. Whether that (non-) philosophical moment solidifies to become a part of the normalised Philosophical Canon (within a philosophy *of* art, *of* physics, *of* mathematics, etc.) will be due to a host of other factors (economic, technological, political as well as intra-philosophical). Nonetheless, at these moments of crisis, or revolt, philosophy expands: that is, the (non-Laruellean) non-philosophical becomes 'philosophy' (as Laruellean non-philosophy views it). Laruelle, however, denies that there is such becoming-philosophy, but only on account of the philosophical baggage in the concept of becoming: it is too Deleuzian, too virtualist, too 'philosophical' for him because it is a *philosophy of* becoming. Understood as mutating-philosophy, however – the becoming (of) philosophy – it could well be another name for non-philosophy as Laruelle thinks of it. As his own essay for this collection points out, what is 'philosophisable' is generated like a 'Theory of Types' applied (*'appliquée'*) to philosophy, to its paradoxes or vicious circles.[80] But perhaps, again, the term 'applied' is unhelpful here: it is the paradoxes and vicious circles generated within seemingly 'pure' philosophy *no less than* those generated in supposedly non-philosophical disciplines (when their logic or consistency enters into crisis or 'goes critical') that generate new, mutant types of logic, consistency, thought and philosophy – and this generation precisely is *their* non-philosophical moment.[81]

Against this view, as we would expect, Laruelle would argue that, in terms of being a *mixte*, photography is *not like* philosophy: it is instead a mix of 'an experience of immanence that is this time radical (the posture of force (of) vision that is not of the World or hybridised) along with, once again, the experience of the hybrid of the World'.[82] This is because, for Laruelle, philosophy is the original contaminant, the pure contaminant that mixes with all other fields to create philosophies of them and so alienate them from the Real. It is the paradigmatic representational, decisional, thought. This purity of philosophy (as pure mixer, pure impurifier) reflects his dichotomous thinking as regards the philosophy–non-philosophy dyad (the former having the *invariant* structure of a decision), which we contested earlier by putting it in play, by making the gap between the two *only a momentary one – a thing of the moment*: it is a temporal gap that *also* loosens the hobgoblin power of absolute 'consistency' over the mind, the power which supposedly renders non-philosophy *transcendental*. All the same, though photography, or quantum mechanics, or fractal geometry may not be like philosophy, this still does not offset the possibility that Laruelle's *non*-philosophy *is creatively* self-similar with *non*-photography, at least *in-the-last-instance*.[83] They are all sciences, for they all articulate new discoveries and new types of logic. As such, they pursue the programme that Laruelle is always at pains to commend – '*Invent Philosophy!*'

Notes

1. François Laruelle, *En tant qu'Un: La non-philosophie éxpliquée au philosophes* (Paris: Aubier 1991), p. 4.
2. François Laruelle, *Le Concept de non-photographie/The Concept of Non-Photography* (Bilingual Edition), translated by Robin Mackay (Falmouth: Urbanomic, 2011), pp. 4–5.
3. François Laruelle, *The Non-Philosophy Project: Essays by François Laruelle*, edited by Gabriel Alkon and Boris Gunjevic (New York: Telos Press Publishing, 2012), p. 205.
4. François Laruelle, *Philo sophie et non-philosophie* (Liege/Bruxelles: Pierre Mardaga, 1989), p. 170. For a definition of 'vision-in-One' see François Laruelle et al., *Dictionnaire de la non-philosophie* (Paris: Kimé 1998), pp. 85–6: 'In any case, the vision-in-One "gives" the One and it alone; it is "the" given entirely, the given as the identity of the given, as the given-without-givenness, unfolding or doublet of the given and givenness. It is thus radical phenomenon, without the background phenomenological world in its vastest sense: without Being behind the phenomenon or related to it. But if it does not give the One and if it neither exceeds it nor is alien to it, it also gives the Thought-World, but it still gives it in-One or in the form of given-without-givenness.'
5. See Laruelle, *En tant qu'Un*, p. 40.
6. Laruelle, *Non-Philosophy Project*, p. 220 (my emphasis).
7. See François Laruelle, *Philosophie non-standard. Générique, quantique, philo-fiction* (Paris: Kimé, 2010), pp. 15–44.
8. Laruelle, *Non-Philosophy Project*, p. 83.
9. François Laruelle, *Principes de la non-philosophie* (Paris: PUF, 1996), p. 22; Laruelle, *Non-Philosophy Project*, p. 38.
10. Laruelle, *Principes*, pp. v, 11, 12; on metaphilosophy, see Laruelle, *Dictionnaire*, p. 95; Erik del Bufalo, *Deleuze et Laruelle. De la schizo-analyse à la non-philosophie* (Paris: Kimé, 2003), p. 47.

11. Though *force (de) vision* in *The Concept of Non-Photography* is translated into the English throughout as 'vision-force', we prefer to keep to 'force (of) vision', which is the norm in English translations of Laruelle.

12. Laruelle, *Non-Photography*, pp. 41–2. At Laruelle, *Principes*, pp. 326–8 he speaks instead of a 'non-Copernican mutation in truth', which would be such an amplification of Kantianism as to render its critique utterly blunted.

13. Laruelle, *Philosophie non-standard*, pp. 500, 502.

14. See Graham Harman, 'Review of *Philosophies of Difference*', *Notre Dame Philosophical Reviews*, 8 August 2011. Available at <http://ndpr.nd.edu/news/25437-philosophies-of-difference-a-critical-introduction-to-non-philosophy/> (accessed 13 February 2012).

15. Laruelle, *Non-Photography*, p. viii.

16. Ibid., p. 56, translation amended. We have also amended the English translation of *posture* to 'posture', in place of the extant 'stance'.

17. del Bufalo, p. 42: It is a '*science première*' because, estranged from philosophy, it is 'the essence (of) the science of science'.

18. See Laruelle, *Non-Photography*, p. 86: 'What I describe with the term "essence of science" are the structures of any science whatsoever. Once these transcendental structures have been elaborated, or rather once these already existing structures have been described (it is not my description which creates them), it then becomes possible to envisage a specific science *for* philosophy and to extend, so to speak, scientificity as I understand it to the study of philosophy itself.'

19. See, for example, John Roberts, 'The Flat-Lining of Metaphysics: François Laruelle's "Science-Fictive" Theory of Non-Photography', *Philosophy of Photography* 2.1 (2011), p. 138: 'Fractality, irregularity-force, "stranger-thought", unilateriality, idempotency and the generic, are all frustratingly without objectifiable outcome. At no point do we learn in *The Concept of Non-Photography*, for instance, how General Fractality works as an engagement with extant photographs.' This accusation misses the point that a non-philosophical revision of a photograph would *not* involve an *application* of a specific scientific concept like fractality to it (this would be scientism, a science of *x* explaining *x*): rather, General Fractality (a concept, but a non-philosophical one, that is, a (non-)photographic one) emerges directly from the revision of being 'in photo' itself. The *concept* of non-photography is merely the hypothesis, offered by Laruelle, on the *basis of a discovery by photography*, of its identity with the Real.

So *non-photography* itself, qua thinking, offers its own revisions that also have knowledge effects beyond its domain (hence its generalisation, or uni-versalisation), according to this hypothesis. Roberts' call for an 'engagement' remains a philosopher's call, not only for a verbal account, but one based on an extant (representationalist) usage of 'philosophical' vocabulary. He neglects Laruelle's claim that he is *not* trying to 'submit' artists (and their work) to philosophy so as finally 'to "explain" them but, *on the basis of their discovery* taken up as a guiding thread . . . [t]o mark its theoretical effects in excess of all knowledge' (*Non-Photography*, p. 71, my emphasis).

20. Laruelle, *Non-Photography*, p. 30.
21. Ibid., pp. 72–3 (my emphasis).
22. Ibid., pp. 30–1.
23. Ibid., pp. 11, 36, 38, 94.
24. Ibid., p. 71. See also p. 86: 'One should not think, however, that the work of artists is for us a mere occasional cause, that it is secondary. It is rather that it is the symptom or the indication of a theoretical discovery that has not yet produced all its effects in art itself and above all in its theory.'
25. Ibid., p. 143.
26. Ibid., p. 32.
27. Ibid., p. 86. Yet this is an abstraction, or abstract, without the act of abstraction, which would be philosophical (and circular, as Berkeley noted): 'I lay claim to the abstract – the Real or One – rather than to abstraction. The One is an abstract-without-an operation-of-abstraction' (Laruelle, *Non-Philosophy Project*, p. 157). 'Identity is not found by abstraction, it is not a symbol, though it and its effects are articulated in a "play of symbols." It is abstract without an operation of abstraction' (p. 201).
28. Laruelle, *Non-Photography*, pp. 8, 31.
29. Ibid., p. 57 (my emphasis).
30. Ibid., p. 21 (translation modified).
31. Ibid., pp. 112–13.
32. Ibid., p. 17.
33. Ibid., p. 102.
34. Ibid., p. 4; see also pp. 13, 28, 36, 42, 43.
35. Ibid., p. 27.
36. Ibid., p. 24.
37. Ibid., p. 4.
38. Ibid., p. 10. See also p. 8 for more on this classic distinction in Laruelle: 'The realist illusion proper to philosophy (even, and above

all, when it is idealist) – its auto-factualization – impregnates the theory of photography with its fetishism, giving it, across apparently contradictory aesthetics, one and the same figurative (so to speak) conception'; and pp. 21–2: 'By in-itself, we designate what is most objective or exterior, but also what is most stable in that which is capable of being given to vision: objectivity and stability no longer as attributes or properties of the perceived object, but as they might be given and lived in their turn on the basis of immanent vision alone.'

39. Ibid., p. 15.

40. Ibid., p. 39. As regards being in-photo losing any essential relation to its material conditions, he goes further, though perhaps too far: 'without being constrained to reduce it to its conditions of existence, whether perceptual, optical, semiotic, technological, unconscious, aesthetic, political. All of these certainly exist, but will be demoted to the status of effective conditions of existence specifying and modelizing photographic thought, but playing no essential role, and powerless to explain the emergence of photography as a new relation to the real' (ibid., p. 34). The question that arises here is whether at least some of these 'conditions' might themselves warrant non-philosophical analysis that would so broaden their meaning as to make them indiscernible from (and so not the condition for the Identical either) being in-photo. Preeminent amongst these, I would argue, are the perceptual-optical.

41. Ibid., p. 6 (translation modified).

42. See ibid., p. 74: 'A unified theory must be able to do as philosophy does, that is to say, to include the problem of essence – for example that of the being-in-photo and the fractal-being of photographic objects or fractal figures – but to treat them by *hypothesis*, deduction and experimental testing' (my emphasis).

43. Ibid., pp. 57, 41 (translation modified).

44. Ibid., p. 43.

45. Ibid., p. 46. Laruelle continues 'one does not photograph the object or the "subject" that one sees - but rather, on condition of suspend- ing (as we have said) the intentionality of photography, one photo- graphs Identity – which one does not see – through the medium of the "subject"' (p. 47). 'It is the congenital automatism of the photo itself, of semblance, that creates the impression of an "objective" resemblance and subsequently of a magical causality of the object over its representation that "emanates" from *it*' (p. 115).

46. Ibid., p. 51.

47. Ibid., p. 103.

48. Ibid., p. 52 (translation modified).
49. Ibid., pp. 119, 120.
50. *And* a 'non-cinema' has the feature of 'montage-thought' (itself a kind of non-summative addition) (as I argue in John Mullarkey, *Philosophy and the Moving Image: Refractions of Reality* [Basingstoke: Palgrave Macmillan, 2010]).
51. Laruelle would avow the influence of Michel Henry on his thought, though the phenomenological appearance of his work has been on the wane from its very start, and even more so since 1992. Yet in *The Concept of Non-Photography*, we still have very Henry-like statements such as that 'Photographic appearing is itself the immanent *that-which-appears*. The givenness is the thing itself in-its-image, rather than the image-of-the-thing' (p. 95).
52. Ironically, it is because Real identity is stronger than self-similarity that it avoids circularity. See Laruelle, *Non-Photography*, p. 82: 'It [identity or One-in-the-last-instance] is thus far stronger than mere "self-similarity", which we know to be an identity that is weak, variable and an effect of resemblance.'
53. Ibid., p. 8.
54. Clearly, even in a seemingly tangential field like photography, Laruelle insists that a Derridian approach to art will not suffice: 'No philosophical interpretation escapes this illusion, not even those that deconstruct this convertibility of the image and the real' (ibid., p. 65).
55. The term 'part' here is both material and partial in sense, though, as we'll see, it would be best to think of this part not as a fragment of a closed whole but as a fractal.
56. Laruelle, *Non-Philosophical Project*, p. 83.
57. Ibid., p. 87
58. Ibid., p. 92.
59. Laruelle, *Non-Photography*, p. 88. For more on this non-philosophical use of philosophical vocabulary, see Laruelle, *Principes*, pp. 262–8.
60. Laruelle, *Non-Philosophy Project*, p. 89.
61. Ibid., p. 90. See also p. 93: 'I content myself with being consistent, which is to say that I try to develop a rigorous science.'
62. Though one suspects that, upon closer inspection, inconsistencies might appear, at least to certain points of view.
63. François Laruelle, *Philosophies of Difference: A Critical Introduction to Non-Philosophy*, translated by Rocco Gangle (London and New York: Continuum, 2010), p. xv.

64. This remark is a corollary of the 'good news' Laruelle announces in *En tant qu'Un*, p. 246, where he says that 'not everything is philosophisable'.

65. Laruelle, *Non-Photography*, p. 19 (translation modified).

66. Laruelle, *Non-Philosophy Project*, p. 93: Non-philosophy is 'realized [in] the "stance" proper to science'.

67. Laruelle, *Non-Photography*, p. 78.

68. See ibid., pp. 125–6: Laruelle's meditation on Edward Berko's art adds another set of fractals 'to the most well-known fractal objects – the sea, its waves, its storms, its turbulence, its "Brittany coasts"....'. In art, we would add Da Vinci's flexuous line-drawings to this list, at least as they are discussed by Félix Ravaisson in Laruelle's analysis, *Phénomène et différence: Essai sur Ravaisson* (Paris: Klincksieck, 1971). For a discussion of the self-similarity between the properties of the flexuous line and non-philosophy, see John Mullarkey, *Post-Continental Philosophy: An Outline* (London and New York: Continuum, 2006), pp. 153–6.

69. Laruelle, *Non-Photography*, pp. 139–40.

70. Ibid., p. 86.

71. See ibid., p. 81: 'it becomes possible to understand, or to *explain why*, for example, in Hautem's work, an animal skin *is* a cloud as much as a wave, and does not *become*, or *pass into* one or the other, does not metamorphose into something else but acquires from the start its *identity* or is *manifested* in itself rather than *in* another thing.' We would add that, through the vision-in-One of these works and others, 'it becomes possible to understand' how a particle can be a wave and vice versa.

72. Ibid., p. 75, my italics.

73. Laruelle, *Philosophie non-standard*, p. 497; see also pp. 488. For philosophy as 'quasi-science' see also Laruelle, *Philosophie et non-philosophie*, pp. 11–12.

74. Laruelle, *Non-Philosophy Project*, pp. 30–1.

75. Ibid., p. 199.

76. See Laruelle, *Philosophie et non-philosophie*, pp. 242–4; p. 40.

77. Laruelle, *Philosophie non-standard*, pp. 492, 489. See also Laruelle, *Non-Photography*, p. 24: 'Photography has its own "intention" – it is that quasi-field of pure photographic apparition, of the *universal photographic Appearance or Fiction* (that of the vision-stance).'

78. See Laruelle, *Philosophie non-standard*, pp. 181–4 for a formulation of the Copenhagen interpretation of quantum mechanics according to a 'non-Schrödingerian cat'.

79. For more on this connection between philosophy, non-philosophy and horror see John Mullarkey, 'Animal Spirits: Philosomorphism and the Background Revolts of Cinema' in *Angelaki*, special edition on *The Animality Revolutions to-come: Between Techne and Animality*, edited by Ron Broglio and Frederick Young; and John Mullarkey, 'Spirits in the Materialist World: Revisionist Metaphysics and the Horrors of Philosophy' in *Angelaki*, special edition on *Immanent Materialisms: Speculation and Critique*, edited by Charlie Blake and Patrice Haynes (both forthcoming 2012).

80. See Laruelle's essay 'Is Thinking Democratic?' below p. 233: 'The philosophisable is not the philosophical, but is derived through the determination of the Whole by the individual. Relatively speaking, it plays an identical role to that of the theory of types but applied to philosophy, to its vicious circles or paradoxes.'

81. For more on the Theory of Types applied to philosophy, see John Mullarkey, *Bergson and Philosophy* (Edinburgh: Edinburgh University Press, 1999), pp. 181–5.

82. Laruelle, *Non-Photography*, p. 142 (translation modified).

83. One might again ask here why this does not leave non-philosophy as a Deleuzian philosophy of creation (of productive repetition). However, it may not be important that Laruelle is not Deleuzian, *in the aspect of creative, and generic, self-similarity*, but simply that non-philosophy does not take creativity as an all-encompassing and self-sufficient axiom as Deleuze does in his valorisation of Life. My thanks to Anthony Paul Smith for pointing this out.

8

Transcendental Arguments, Axiomatic Truth, and the Difficulty of Overcoming Idealism

Michael J. Olson

The object of this chapter will be Laruelle's axiomatic materialism. In order to bring this position into focus and produce a point of critical contact with Laruelle's sprawling and conceptually demanding work, the chapter will proceed in two parts. The first part will focus on a traditional but exemplary transcendental argument against Idealism – Kant's Refutation of Idealism – and the insufficiency of such arguments by the lights of Laruelle's analysis of what he claims is the invariant and structurally idealising structure of philosophical thought as such. With Kant's transcendental and Laruelle's axiomatic rebuttals of the dominant philosophical idealisms of their times placed side by side, we will see, first, the reflexive structure Laruelle identifies as the heart of philosophical reasoning and, second, the motivation for a philosophically unjustifiable axiomatic intervention in, or perhaps better, subtraction from, the process of philosophy's reflexive self-justification. Together, these two points will show what the basic structure and remit of Laruelle's axiomatic materialism are.

The second part of the chapter will investigate the epistemic credentials of the Laruellean axiomatic. Laruelle's argumentation appeals, on the one hand, to dense conceptual articulations of fundamental philosophical structures and their blind spots in order to expose the necessary foreclosure of the radical immanence of the Real and, on the other hand, to the immediacy of a transcendental experience of the One as immanent Real. This tension in Laruelle's writing restages an early dispute in the modern mathematical development of the axiomatic method. The tension – that between formal or structural guarantees of an axiomatic's ability to produce truths and the grounding of a logical system in the immediacy of an experience of the Real – is very well captured in the debate between Gottlob Frege and David Hilbert regarding the relationship between axioms and the truth that they represent or produce. In light of Frege and Hilbert's correspondence on this issue, the decided success of Hilbert's understanding of the axiomatic method borne out in the history of twentieth-century mathematics, and recent critical appraisals of Laruelle's project from Ray Brassier and Quentin Meillassoux, I will argue finally that in so far as Laruelle's axiomatic thinking of the foreclosure of the Real as radical immanence relies on the immediacy of an experience of the Real in the form of a *veritas transcendentalis* it remains, as Meillassoux charges, a position that asserts the foreclosure of the Real while simultaneously attempting to obscure this assertion through the lofty language of axiomatisation. The limitations of Laruelle's intuitive axiomatic should not, however, obscure the power of his criticisms of the idealising power of the mechanisms of philosophical grounding. In so far as Laruelle's axiomatic indication of the indifference of the Real to its philosophical capture is the product of a structural analysis of the necessary but largely unrecognised commitments of philosophical reflection itself, it provides a helpful diagnosis of the fundamental, and so philosophically unjustifiable, principles of philosophical reflection and the consequences of those principles for the project, currently underway in many forms, of articulating a fully materialist metaphysics.[1] The goal of this essay will finally be, then, to gauge the success of Laruelle's materialist attempt to grasp the necessary idealism of philosophy as such on the basis of an axiomatic assertion of the radical immanence of the unity of the Real.

The Struggle Against Idealism: Transcendental and Axiomatic

Although the tension between idealism and materialism runs throughout nearly the whole of the history of philosophy, this struggle becomes considerably more interesting, I would argue, after the emergence of Kantian transcendental philosophy. For most of this history, the dispute between idealism and materialism focused, in one way or another, on the sufficiency of materiality to account for a range of phenomena (necessity, intelligibility, etc.). Rarely, though, was there much confusion about whether a given position asserted the primacy of non-material substance. In the early days of transcendental philosophy, however, whether a position was idealist or materialist was by no means so clear.

Kant's position, for example, was assailed in the rather famous and certainly contentious Göttingen Review as a resuscitation of Berkeleyan idealism. Similarly, Jacobi decried Fichte and others as crypto-materialists and atheists during the so-called *Pantheismusstreit*. Since at least the end of the eighteenth century, then, we argue not only about the truth or falsity of idealism and materialism, but also, and often more heatedly, about which positions are in fact idealist and which materialist. It is within this context, and in particular in relation to the question of the idealism of Kant's transcendental philosophy, that I will turn to Laruelle.

The philosophical value of transcendental thought within the current general intellectual consensus in favour of some species of materialism, naturalism, or at least anti-idealism has been a subject of energetic research in the recent histories of both analytic and continental philosophy.[2] Laruelle offers what is without a doubt the most powerful and sustained analysis of transcendental philosophy, which he takes to be constitutive of philosophy as such, in continental philosophy since Hegel. Transcendental philosophy, he claims, is structurally idealising to a degree that bars it – and so philosophy as a whole – from accessing the Real. Transcendental philosophy has since its early Kantian articulation, however, rejected the claim, for example, that transcendental idealism is tantamount to either empirical or metaphysical idealism. What is more, there are explicit transcendental arguments against the claim that it amounts to an idealism. In order to render the debate concerning the idealism of transcendental thought more concrete, I will turn now to an early though remarkably representative argument against the idealism of transcendental philosophy and then address Laruelle's analysis of the idealism of the philosophical decision.

The most obvious site of Kant's resistance to the charge of idealism is the Refutation of Idealism, a section of the text that was added to the 1787 edition of the *Critique of Pure Reason*. This argument, like many important passages in the *Prolegomena* before it, responds to the criticisms of the Göttingen Review by explicitly rejecting what Kant refers to as material idealism. In contrast to his own transcendental or critical idealism, which is, the claim goes, the only possible empirical realism, material idealism asserts the ideality of the content or matter of knowledge and not merely the ideality of its form. Kant identifies two species of material idealism: dogmatic idealism, which denies the existence of material objects in space, and problematic idealism, which holds that the existence of material objects in space can only be cautiously inferred from the immediate certainty of the existence of the self. Berkeley represents the former position and Descartes the latter. In order to argue against these positions and to exorcise any fear that his own transcendental idealism amounts to a genuine, metaphysical idealism Kant frames his refutation of idealism around spatiality rather than more directly around materiality.[3] After fairly quickly dismissing Berkeley's dogmatic idealism by referring to the results of the Transcendental Aesthetic, Kant affirms the critical attitude exhibited in Descartes' sceptical or problematic idealism, which, he writes, 'is, in so far as it allows of no decisive judgment until sufficient proof has been found, reasonable and in accordance with a thorough and philosophical mode of thought'.[4] Rather than flippantly rejecting problematic idealism as he does dogmatic idealism, Kant attempts to overcome Cartesian idealism's claims concerning the priority of self-consciousness by supplying what is perhaps the first explicitly transcendental argument.[5]

The aim of this argument is to establish the existence of external things in space and, so, to establish that spatial intuition of the material world is in principle epistemically reliable. The argument works, as all transcendental arguments do, by showing that the disputed conclusion, in this case, the indubitable existence of spatio-material objects, is in fact a necessary condition for an undisputed phenomenon, in this case the temporality of self-consciousness.[6] One's certainty of the reality of spatial intuition and the existence of external things is not, the argument goes, the result of an always dubious inference from the indubitable existence of the self. The certainty of one's own existence in time is instead possible only on the basis of the existence of external things, which ground the veracity of external sense. Empirical self-consciousness, in other words, is no more and no less certain than consciousness of the existence of external things. Kant's argument proceeds in three steps: first, he notes that we are conscious of our own existence in time; second, he explains that the determination of any existence in time requires the existence of something permanent in perception against which the specific temporal location and determination can be measured; and, third, that this permanent element of perception must itself exist independently of my representations. Taken together, then, the argument intends to show that self-

consciousness, which the problematic idealist accepts as indubitable, is conditioned by the existence of spatial things, and so that
spatial intuition is not illusory. Kant summarises: 'the mere, but
empirically determined, consciousness of my own existence proves
the existence of objects in space outside me'.[7] I will now provide a
slightly more detailed exegesis of the three steps of the argument
before examining how Laruelle's account of the philosophical
decision reveals a deeper idealism at work in Kant's Refutation.

The first step in Kant's argument against problematic idealism
explains that self-consciousness, the bedrock of all knowledge
according to problematic idealism,[8] is an instance of empirical
knowledge like any other. The importance of the empirical character of self-consciousness is laid out in Note 1 of the Refutation.
Following the results of the Deductions and their clarification in
the Paralogisms, Kant notes that self-consciousness is not reducible to the transcendental necessity that 'I' exist as the subject of
the unity of thought. Self-consciousness is importantly a kind of
knowledge and not only a thought. 'Certainly, the representation
"I am," which expresses the consciousness that can accompany
all thought,' Kant writes, 'immediately includes in itself the existence of a subject; but it does not so include any *knowledge* of
that subject, and therefore also no empirical knowledge, that is,
no experience of it.'[9] If the knowledge of one's own existence is,
according to the problematic idealist, the lone datum of immediately certain knowledge, then certainly that knowledge must be
the consequence of the immediate experience of one's own existence (as a thinking thing, for example) and not only a recognition
of the necessary logical unity of thought. All experience, as Kant
argued in the Deductions, requires intuition, and since time is the
form of inner intuition, even if self-consciousness does not require
the spatiality of outer intuition, it must at least be determined with
respect to time. Self-consciousness, Kant concludes, is really a consciousness of one's own existence in time.

The second step analyses the conditions necessary for tempo-
rally determined self-consciousness. Here Kant reminds us of the
importance of the temporal permanence of substance, which he
described in the First Analogy of Experience. We are, he writes,
'unable to perceive any determination of time save through
change in outer relations (motion) relatively to the permanent in
space (for instance, the motion of the sun relatively to the objects
on the earth)'.[10] Any knowledge of the endurance of my own

consciousness, of the fleeting or persistent existence of my own thoughts, and the recognition of my own temporal finitude can only be empirically determined relative to an instance of permanence against which the impermanence of my own representations can be measured. This necessary instance of permanence can be neither an empirical representation of the permanent in space, since the reliability of outer sense and the certainty of the existence of external objects is precisely what is at stake here, nor the transcendental necessity of the 'I think', since, as we have already noted, the unity of transcendental perception is a logical condition of thought and not a real object of experience.

The third and final step of Kant's argument is the heart of the Refutation of Idealism. After arguing for the necessity of something permanent in perception Kant distinguishes between 'something *permanent* in existence' and 'permanent representation'.[11] A representation can only be determined to be permanent or fleeting, Kant says, on the condition of the availability of some real permanence that is irreducible to my representations. Or, in the preferred language of Kant's late corrections to the second edition:

> this permanent cannot be an intuition in me. For all grounds of determination of my existence which are to be met with in me are representations; and as representations themselves require a permanent distinct from them, in relation to which their change, and so my existence in the time wherein they change, may be determined.[12]

The permanence accessible to perception, then, must be genuinely external – and not merely intuited as external – to my representations. When combined with the previous steps of the Refutation, this amounts, Kant's argues, to a refutation of the Cartesian's scepticism regarding the external world. Empirical self-consciousness is possible only on the basis of an implicit metaphysical realism, and so the problematic idealist must concede that inner sense is no more certain or immediate than outer sense.

Real objects outside of thought considered in themselves, independent of their phenomenal appearance, are of course beyond the scope of any possible knowledge according to Kant. It can be known as absolutely as we know our own existence in time, however, that objects of outer sense, though always known through my representations of them, are irreducible to those representations. As thin as the realism represented by this claim might be, Kant thinks it enough to rebut any suggestion that his critical idealism is really an idealism.[13] Given the relative weakness of Kant's anti-idealist credentials, we should perhaps be surprised at the similarity between his Refutation and the recent glut of philosophies of embodiment that largely pass as materialist by explaining that consciousness can never be finally separated from material, bodily existence. Either Kant was a materialist, or philosophies of embodiment need to say considerably more to qualify as materialist themselves. Laruelle's analyses of the necessarily idealising structure of the philosophical decision provides the resources for determining that Kant's Refutation of Idealism, and by extension any isomorphic argument for embodied consciousness, is insufficient to overcome idealism, even if its idealism is no longer paradigmatically Cartesian. I will now offer a brief recapitulation of Laruelle's account of what he calls the philosophical decision and how it, on his account, leads to the necessity of an axiomatic intervention that at once shatters the circularity of philosophical reasoning and makes possible a genuinely materialist thought.

The whole of the history of philosophy according to Laruelle is characterised by an invariant structure of reflexive, self-grounding thought.[14] This structure is described as the philosophical decision. Philosophy has been captured, Laruelle argues, by the classical metaphysical problem of identifying and comprehending the ultimate unity of the diversity of empirical manifestations or phenomena. The highest philosophical concepts, then, have been the Idea, the One, God, the subject, Spirit, Being, matter, etc. Philosophy is even a thinking of the One when it thinks the One as difference.[15] The intended unity of these philosophical objects is always compromised, however.

Philosophy is constitutively incapable of thinking the unity of the Real as a genuine unity, Laruelle writes, because 'the One has always been experienced in the last instance [by philosophy] not in its essence but in the mode of scission in general and therefore inevitably in the mode of one of two contraries or differends that it unites'.[16] Philosophy thinks the One, that is, only in so far as the One, which outstrips or surpasses any empirical experience, both conditions and is realised in a multiplicity of empirical beings. The unity of the One can only be thought philosophically by being divided against itself. The unity of the Real multiplicity of the world is both One, in so far as it surpasses and unites all merely empirical differences, and multiple, in so far as it is both One and the multiplicity that it unifies. This failed attempt to think the unity of the Real as One cannot simply be corrected, however, by, for example, immediately thinking the unity of the One. The philosophical demand for reflexive self-validation requires that One as Real be split into two, such that immediate access to the diversity of the Real guarantees the validity of the philosophical postulation of the Unity of the Real, which retroactively renders intelligible the multiplicity on which its postulation depends.[17] Philosophy's critical aversion to dogmatic assertion demands that it verify its cognition of the Real, and in the process prevents itself from thinking the unity of the Real as a genuine, undivided unity.

Not only is philosophy prevented from thinking the Real as One because of the One's division or scission at the hands of the philosophical demand for reflexive self-validation, but in the process of failing to think the unity of the Real which provides its initial motivation the reflexive operation verifying its own cognition of the Real convinces the philosopher that she has in fact succeeded. The reflexivity of the philosophical decision, that is, guarantees both that philosophy will fail to think the One as One and that philosophy will have, by its own reflexive lights, have succeeded in thinking the Real. This double effect of the critical demand for epistemic validation results in what Laruelle names the principle of sufficient philosophy, which 'articulates the idealist pretension of philosophy as that which is able to at least co-determine that Real which is most radical'.[18] In its attempts to think the Real unity of the world, philosophy covers over its failure to do so with an autistic account of its own epistemic sufficiency that ultimately refers only to itself and leaves the unity of the One untouched. The self-validation of the idealisation of the unity of the Real, then, masquerades as knowledge of the reality of the One.

Kant's Refutation of Idealism nicely exhibits the failure of philosophy to think the Real precisely at the moment when it is most urgently demanded. The One Kant here attempts to think in order to stave off the appearance of idealism is the undivided permanence in perception, which, Kant adds, has no real conceptual name 'save only matter'.[19] Transcendental idealism is not a real idealism, he argues, because, regardless of the emphasis on the determining functions of subjectivity, it must be admitted that self-consciousness is conditioned by the existence of external, spatio-material objects. In the Refutation of Idealism, self-consciousness is presupposed as a datum that is conditioned by and so requires that we posit the a priori factum of the existence of the Real as permanent and external to consciousness. The external permanence of the Real as condition is reciprocally presupposed, however, as already given as the condition of the self-consciousness whose possibility it posits. This circularity, the mutual presupposition and positing of real condition and ideal conditioned, cleans up any loose ends that would threaten to reduce philosophy to mere dogmatism, and so Kant's transcendental argument for metaphysical realism satisfies the demand for epistemic validity. It does so, however, only by dividing the externality of the Real against itself. The permanent in perception, which is the condition of the determination of self-consciousness in time, is both external to any representation and posited precisely through the representations, as their necessary condition. The permanence of external reality is only external, in other words, to the extent that it is both presupposed and posited by that consciousness to which it is supposedly external. The Real, then, is only external or anterior to self-consciousness to the degree that self-consciousness constitutes the Real as external permanence as one of its own necessary conditions. Rather than eliminating any suspicion of his idealism, then, Kant's Refutation buttresses that idealism by transforming the autonomy of the Real into the co-constitution of the real and the ideal such that the philosophical-critical demands of the ideal guarantee the existence of the now only supposedly autonomous Real. This, like all transcendental accounts of the Real, matter and the One, is structurally doomed to failure, according to Laruelle. The only option available for thinking the real autonomy of the One must break decisively with the reflexive self-validation and consequent idealisation characteristic of the philosophical decision.

Laruelle introduces the axiomatic method of non-philosophy as a means to interrupt the reflexivity that both secures the credentials of philosophy and prevents it from thinking the immanent unity of the One. In the face of the philosophical impossibility of knowing the Real as radically immanent, identical, always already given without givenness, etc., Laruelle asserts these axiomatically. The radical immanence of the One cannot be grasped through philosophy, since its inaugural decision requires the splitting of the ultimate unity of its object in order to secure the legitimacy of its access to that object. If it is the critical care of philosophical self-validation that prevents it from accessing the unity of the Real, Laruelle wagers, then the unjustified and unjustifiable power of the axiom might provide precisely the supplement necessary to think the Real.

When Laruelle introduces a series of real axioms he does not pretend thereby to comprehend the Real, but to rigorously grasp the constitutive idealism of the structure of philosophy and the concomitant foreclosure of the Real. The axioms of non-philosophy cannot found a formal science of the Real without falling into the brashest form of dogmatism. The axiomatisation of the radical immanence of the One, then, belongs to a thinking, not of the Real, but of the relation between philosophy and the Real. Laruelle's analysis of the philosophical decision exposes a series of axiomatic truths that underpin but remain invisible to the reflexivity of philosophical reasoning. Underlying an analysis of the structural idealism of the reflexivity of philosophy is a 'transcendental experience' of the immanent unity of the Real. Laruelle writes:

> That the One would be the object of a transcendental experience that is non-thetic (of) itself, absolute and without remainder, this would signify that it is given immediately (to) itself as what it is. Indivision is given (to) itself in the mode of indivision: it is 'non-reflexive' or immediate. This is why a thinking of the immediate givens of the One . . . is opposed to the philosophies like those of Difference which posit, after Hegel, after the entire tradition, that is, philosophical decision, that the One or the absolute is given *through* and also *with* scission, given in loss and in the mode of nothingness.[20]

Philosophy can only think the One in so far as it is divided against itself, but we nonetheless sense the immediate, undivided unity of the Real and its indifference to our conceptual distinctions, and so formalise a critique of philosophical reasoning on the basis of assertions concerning the radical immanence of the One despite the fact that such assertions are formally unjustifiable within the confines of philosophical reasoning itself. The axioms of the immanence of the Real as One are implicitly operative, then, within philosophical reflection despite their philosophical inadmissibility.

Where philosophy constitutively fails to think the immanence of the Real in its indifference to its philosophical conceptualisation, Laruelle attempts to supplement this philosophical failure with his own non-philosophical thinking *according* to the Real. Laruelle's non-philosophy comprehends the idealism of philosophy, that is, on the basis of an axiomatic assertion of the foreclosure of the Real to philosophical thought. Without asserting the axioms of the Real, Laruelle could not identify the idealising function of philosophy or the crucial difference between the genuine unity of the Real, the One-in-One, and the differentiated one of the philosophical Real, the One-in-dyad. Laruelle's materialist rejoinder to the structural idealism of philosophical reasoning then rests finally on our peculiar sense of truth of the axiomatics of the immanence of the One.

If Laruelle's axioms of the Real immanence of the One can successfully correct the principle of sufficient philosophy and the hallucinatory reference to the Real in the idealising self-legitimation of the philosophical decision, however, these axioms cannot draw their theoretical power from the sufficiency of thought itself. It might appear, though, that Laruelle has replaced philosophy's fastidious concern with establishing the legitimacy of its own primary distinctions with a wanton abandonment of such concern in the name of bare axiomatic assertion. Of course this could only exacerbate the idealism Laruelle has so carefully diagnosed in the structure of the philosophical decision: whereas the philosophical decision validates its distinctions by recovering their ultimate unity, axiomatisation, if it turns out that axiomatisation is in the end reducible to mere assertion, seeks no justification for its claims outside the simple fact that it asserts them. If thought posits the radical immanence of the Real, it would seem that it could only do so through the resources of thought itself. Any materialism, then, even Laruelle's axiomatic, non-reflexive materialism might, in the end be possible only on the basis of a central operation of thought, and so turn out to be a very weak materialism indeed. This is the thrust of Quentin Meillassoux's criticism of Laruelle's attempts to dispense with what Meillassoux calls the correlationist circle. After reviewing Laruelle's position, Meillassoux concludes:

> Laruelle gets this first position just by force, just by a *coup de force*. The Real is *posited* as indifferent and as non-related to thought. After that, Laruelle reflects on the possibility of his own theory by claiming the relative autonomy of thought; but it seems, on the contrary, that his thought is able to posit the Real itself and its relation to the Real ... For the Real is now linked more than ever to his concepts, more dependent on more and more intricate elaborations aiming at the exhibition of its independence.[21]

If Laruelle's axiomatic interventions are to prove useful in resisting the idealising tendencies of philosophical reflection, if axiomatisation is to undercut the reflexive foreclosure of the Real to the structure of traditional philosophical thought, then we must more carefully examine the nature of axiomatic thinking. To this end I will now turn to seminal debate concerning the use of the axiomatic method in geometry and the relation between axiomatic systems and truth.

The Source of Axiomatic Truth: Frege, Hilbert, Laruelle

The short-lived and occasionally heated correspondence between Gottlob Frege and David Hilbert revolved around Hilbert's attempt to formally axiomatise Euclidean geometry in the *Grundlagen der Geometrie*, first published in 1899. Although their correspondence, which is comprised of six letters and three postcards over the course of nine years, contains in germ a whole series of important debates in mathematics and logic,[22] I would like to focus on a single aspect of the dispute: the relations between axiomatic systems, truth or provability, and existence. One finds in Laruelle's own thinking about the extra-mathematical employment of the axiomatic method a tension that very nearly parallels that which emerges in Frege and Hilbert's correspondence. After reviewing the terms of their divergent understandings of the relation between axiomatic provability or truth and existence, I will return to the question of the epistemic grounds of Laruelle's axiomatic materialism.

The crux of Frege and Hilbert's disagreement concerns the order of priority between an axiomatic system's consistency and the truth of its results and existence of its objects. Frege argues that the axioms of Euclidian geometry are consistent because their truth is independently verified by a rather Kantian conception of spatial intuition. Hilbert, on the other hand, maintains that truth, provability and existence are results of the non-contradictory nature of the ensemble of axioms themselves. In what is introduced as a confusion concerning Hilbert's distinction between definitions and axioms Frege presents his own understanding of the proper role of the axiom. Although definitions and axioms both stand beyond any possible proof, a definition, Frege explains, 'does not assert anything but lays down something',[23] which is to say that a definition establishes the characteristic mark used to determine whether a given object does or does not possess the quality in question. Axioms, on the other hand, assert something, namely the 'fundamental facts of intuition'.[24] Definitions, then, establish fixed references for mathematical propositions such that they can possess determinate truth-values. 'I call axioms', Frege continues, 'propositions that are true but are not proved because our knowledge of them flows from a source very different from the logical source, a source which might be called spatial intuition.'[25] Failing rigorously to maintain the distinction between definitions and axioms, Frege warns, threatens to expose Hilbert's *Grundlagen* to the mathematical charge of unnecessarily treating a proposition as an axiom because of the difficulty of its proof. The truth of geometrical axioms, and more importantly the truth of the theorems deduced from them, is secured by the immediacy of spatial intuition itself, and this can be their only legitimate source. It is ultimately because of their independent truth, Frege explains, that geometrical axioms do not contradict each other. The method of Hilbert's *Grundlagen*, however, takes the logical priority of consistency and truth in axiomatic systems to be precisely the opposite.

After expressing doubts about the ultimate separability of definitions and axioms and explaining how his axioms fulfil the traditional role of definitions, Hilbert explains that he has, for some time now, been writing and lecturing on the relation between the absence of contradictions among a set of axioms and their truth, and that he has come to precisely the opposite conclusion to Frege. 'If arbitrarily given axioms do not contradict one another with all their consequences, then they are true and the things defined by the axioms exist. This is for me the criterion of truth and existence',[26] he writes. Although Hilbert is perhaps overstating his position here, it is clear that his understanding of the role of mathematical axioms does not depend on their independent verification through any kind of intuition, whether intellectual or spatial. Axioms are true and their objects can be meaningfully said to exist as long as the deductive consequences of the collection of axioms do not produce any contradictions. By way of example Hilbert writes, 'The proposition "Every equation has a root" is true, and the existence of a root is proven, as soon as the axiom "Every equation has a root" can be added to the other arithmetical axioms, without raising the possibility of a contradiction, no matter what conclusions are drawn.'[27] The truth and existence Hilbert has in mind, then, are not modelled on correspondence and external physical reality. Truth and existence are formal or structural.[28] The significance of this kind of formal truth is lost, however, on Frege, for whom axioms must express the truth of a thought and not only the consequences of a system of principles.

Frege's response to Hilbert exhibits two concerns. He is first, rightly, taken aback by the suggestion that any 'arbitrarily given axioms' that do not contradict each other can ground truth claims and establish the existence of their objects. In order to lay bare what he takes to be the absurdity of Hilbert's method, Frege suggests the following case:

> Suppose that we know that the propositions
> 1) A is an intelligent being
> 2) A is omnipresent
> 3) A is omnipotent
> together with all their consequences did not contradict one another; could we infer from this that there was an omnipresent, omnipotent, intelligent being?[29]

Surely the independent truth of a series of axioms must be significant, Frege objects, or else one could bootstrap oneself into basically whatever statements one is willing to state as axioms. Paraphrasing a worry Frege expressed in an earlier letter, this conception of axiomatic truth would seem to work according to the highly dubious rule: If you can't prove a proposition, Then treat it as an axiom.[30] Hilbert's method can only be either false or based on such a thin understanding of truth and existence that it is entirely trivial, Frege concludes.

In addition to this objection, which is due largely to the differing conceptions of truth and existence that underpin Frege and Hilbert's axiomatic methods, Frege expresses some confusion about how the non-contradictory nature of a collection of axioms could be proved. The productive promise of axioms lies in the theorems whose proofs they found, but the truth of these theorems is only secured, on Hilbert's model, once all possible theorems deducible from the axioms are shown to be non-contradictory. This circularity leaves Frege confused about the method Hilbert proposes for verifying the non-contradiction of a set of axioms. Recalling his earlier tongue in cheek proof for the existence of

God, Frege continues, 'Is there some other means of demonstrating lack of contradiction besides pointing out an object that has all the properties? But if we are given such an object, then there is no need to demonstrate in a roundabout way that there is such an object by first demonstrating lack of contradiction.'[31] If Hilbert's only means of verifying the truth of a set of axioms rests on identifying the absence of any contradiction among their consequences, then Hilbert's axiomatic truths encounter the Rumsfeldian difficulty of discerning the absence of evidence from the evidence of absence. Failure to do so will, in Frege's mind, condemn axiomatisation to error and illusion.

Hilbert's reply to these objections follows after three years and remains quite curt. The problem lies not with his own conception of truth and existence, Hilbert avers, but with Frege's insistence on a correspondence theory of propositional truth and a generally representationalist conception of mathematical formalisms. Hilbert writes:

> As I see it, the most important gap in the traditional structure of logic is the assumption made by all logicians and mathematicians up to now that a concept is already there if one can state of any object whether or not it falls under it. This does not seem adequate to me. What is decisive is the recognition that the axioms that define the concept are free from contradiction.[32]

Hilbert and Frege remained mutually unconvinced of the significance of the other's objections and their correspondence ended. From our perspective, apparently as well as theirs, their positions are irreconcilable, and no amount of correspondence or terminological compromise could smooth over their sharp differences.

Without dwelling on the mathematical legacies of Frege and Hilbert's understandings of the axiomatic method, I would like to mark the considerable difference between their accounts of the source of truth in axiomatic systems. For Frege, the perspicuity of the logical organisation of geometry according to established definitions and clearly articulated axioms is a means of clarifying a truth that is fundamentally human. The source of the truth of the axioms of geometry is, as I noted above, spatial intuition. The truth of the axioms of geometry, and so the truth of all the theorems that follow from them, rests, not on the nature of space, but on the way we intuit space. It would be wrong to say that Frege's conception of geometry and the role of axiomatisation rest on a doctrine of intellectual intuition. It is undeniable, however, that Frege relies on human intuition as the source of truth in an axiomatic system.[33] Hilbert's account of the truths of an axiomatic system, on the contrary, does not at all refer to or rely on human thought as a source of legitimation or truth. An axiom is true and its objects exist as long as that axiom and its consequences in the broader system do not prove contradictory. The truth of an axiom is entirely structural, then, according to Hilbert, and importantly intuitive according to Frege.

The history of mathematics gives us every reason to accept Hilbert's account of mathematical axiomatisation over Frege's. Just like Kant's synthetic a priori account of mathematics before it, Frege's insistence on the independent verifiability of the intuitive truths of mathematical axioms has been surpassed by mathematical practices far less concerned with the ultimate grounds of its formalisms.[34] Moreover, there are good philosophical reasons to prefer Hilbert's account of the structural source of truth in axiomatic systems. If truth, and mathematical truth in particular, is, as has been the conviction for much of the history of western philosophy, genuinely universal, then it should not rest either on the idiosyncrasies of intuition or indeed on the existence of humanity at all.[35] It is precisely on this issue of its rejection of the importance of intuition and the necessity of the correlation between human thought and the world that Ray Brassier praises Laruelle's project.[36] If Laruelle's own axiomatic thought is to surmount Meillassoux's criticism, then, we should expect it to be by marshalling the resource of Hilbert's structural rather than Frege's logical-intuitive understanding of axiomatic systems. What we find in Laruelle's axiomatic is, however, not so straightforward.

The axiomatic immanence of the Real is not the result, Laruelle insists, of the logical formalisation of philosophy. As I have already shown, Laruelle's identification of the idealising operation of the philosophical decision depends on the irrecuperable presupposition of the radical immanence of the One, and so, as he writes, 'It is no longer a question of a logico-formal, scientific axiomatisation of philosophy.'[37] The axiomatic foreclosure of the Real is necessary for his non-philosophical comprehension of philosophy according to the Real, but these axioms are not themselves sufficient to think either the Real or its philosophical foreclosure. The immanent indifference of the Real does not produce or authorise philosophy's conceptual distinctions, but it does determine their final materialist inadequacy. Laruelle's axiomatic materialism is bound, then, to both philosophy (hence the terminological derivation of non-philosophy from philosophy itself) and the 'transcendental experience' of the radical immanence of the Real that is foreclosed to philosophical reflection. These twin sources lead Laruelle's position in turn to depend on elements of both Frege and Hilbert's understandings of the sources of axiomatic truth.

On the one hand, the truth of the axiomatic foreclosure of the Real is a consequence of the lack of contradiction that results from appending non-philosophical axioms to the reflexive operations of philosophy as such. The insufficiency of the axioms of non-philosophy to determine the Real means that they are essentially connected to the logical axioms of philosophical thought as a kind of non-philosophical supplement. So, for example, Laruelle describes the movement to his non-philosophical axioms from out of the system of philosophical reflection itself:

> to think the One 'itself', as independent of Being and the Other, as un-convertible with them, as non-determinable by thought and language ('foreclosed' to thought); to think *according* to the One rather than trying to think the One. But to think this non-relation to thought using the traditional means of thought; this displacement *vis à vis* philosophy with the help of philosophy; to think by means of philosophy that which is no longer commensurate with the compass of philosophy, that which escapes its authority and its sufficiency.[38]

The truth of his axiomatic rejoinder to the idealism of philosophy, then, stems from the coherence of the non-philosophical union of logical and real axioms and their consequences concerning the intelligibility of the Real as such. The truth of Laruelle's axiomatic materialism is in this way secured by Hilbert's conception of the structural or formal nature of this ensemble of philosophical decision and its non-philosophical supplement.

Laruelle's axioms are, on the other hand, simultaneously motivated by an experience independent of the structural organisation of philosophical thought. His diagnosis of the idealism of the philosophical decision, as we have seen, depends on a rather mysterious sense for the immanent indifference of the Real. In so far as his axiomatic materialism relies on a 'gnostic' intuition of the nature of the Real, it follows a considerably more Fregean path. Such an approach is easily identifiable in the following passage:

> Just as there is a 'matter' beyond the Idea and beyond the *hyle*, there is likewise – insofar as we are beyond the distinction between knowing and the real – a knowing beyond ideal essence. No rational, ratiocinative or merely logical argument will be able to overcome the resistance proper to this kind of knowing (should we write *gnosis*?) – a knowing identical to those immediate data belonging to a transcendental experience of the One – through which we know that even the light of the Idea is still relative, relative to this *gnosis* as to an absolute knowing.[39]

Just as Frege appeals to a non-logical source of the independent truth of his axioms before setting them to work within a logical system, Laruelle here appeals to a robustly super-logical guarantor of the truth of the axioms of the immanence of the Real.

Rather than unambiguously adopting either a Fregean or an Hilbertian axiomatic practice, then, Laruelle rather uncomfortably combines the two. Without his rather Fregean reliance on the super-logical source of the axiomatisation of the One on the basis of a sense for a certain *veritas transcendentalis*, the theory of the idealism of the philosophical decision remains unmotivated and the necessity of an axiomatic supplement in order to think the failure of philosophy according to the indifference of the Real remains impossible. Without the structural, Hilbertian grounding of those axioms within the sterile consistency of philosophy as such, however, the axiomatic assertion of the foreclosure of the Real remains blindly dogmatic. Even without adopting a doctrinaire insistence on what has, at least since Gödel, been a problematic if extraordinarily productive conception of the axiomatic method within mathematics and taking Laruelle to task for abandoning the structural rigour of an Hilbertian programme in favour of the intuitive grounding of Fregean axiomatics, we can for good philosophical reasons call the results of his axiomatic materialism into question for their reliance on the weakness of an intuition, supposed to be at once individually compelling and universally available, of the immanence of the unity of the Real. In so far as Laruelle's axiomatic contact with the Real relies on this ultimately Fregean intellectualised intuition, it has not yet led us beyond the idealism of its Fichtean forbearers.

Despite the limits of Laruelle's intuitive axiomatic thinking of the foreclosure of the Real, it should be clear that his diagnosis of the idealising consequences of the philosophical decision renders the relationship between transcendental philosophy and materialism or naturalism extremely problematic. Laruelle identifies what is at least a possible site of a latent philosophical idealism at precisely the strongest point of Kant's advance beyond the solipsistic or sceptical idealism of the Cartesian tradition. The mutual reinforcement of the structures of material existence and self-consciousness, which Kant identifies as the key to overcoming idealism, is convincingly shown by Laruelle to be an exemplary moment of thought's tendency to mistake its own self-sufficiency for a guarantee of the sufficiency of its own structures to the Real they purport to comprehend. Philosophical idealism is not overcome by establishing the imbrication of thought in the material world, and so Laruelle is correct that some means of thinking the anteriority of the Real to thought must be determined. In so far as this new thought turns on a formal intuition of the Real as One, however, the Real remains bound to thought and the project of thinking the Real without reference to its grounding in the correlation of thought and being remains incomplete.

Notes

1. Among the works identifiably engaging in such a project (even if not under the same heading), we would find Quentin Meillassoux, *After Finitude: An Essay on the Necessity of Contingency*, translated by Ray Brassier (New York and London: Continuum, 2010), Alain Badiou, *Being and Event*, translated by Oliver Feltham (New York and London: Continuum, 2007) and *Logics of Worlds*, translated by Alberto Toscano (New York and London: Continuum, 2009), Adrian Johnston, *Žižek's Ontology* (Evanston: Northwestern University Press, 2008) and *Alain Badiou and the Outcome of Contemporary French Philosophy* (forthcoming) and *A Weak Nature Alone* (forthcoming), and Ray Brassier in *Nihil Unbound: Enlightenment and Extinction* (New York: Palgrave Macmillan, 2007).

2. In addition to the specific projects of the Meillassoux, Badiou, Johnston and Brassier texts cited above, a more general engagement with this issue was the focus of the Transcendental Philosophy and Naturalism working group directed by Mark Sacks at Essex. For a general survey of the contemporary state of naturalism, materialism and realism, see, for example, *Naturalism in Question*, edited by

Mario de Caro and David Macarthur (Cambridge, MA: Harvard University Press, 2008), *Naturalism and Normativity*, edited by Mario de Caro and David Macarthur (New York: Columbia University Press, 2010), and *The Speculative Turn: Continental Materialism and Realism*, edited by Levi Bryant et al. (Melbourne: re.press, 2011).

3. Against the backdrop of Descartes' definition of matter as extension, Berkeley's vehement rejection of the experience of spatial distance, and Kant's own definition of matter as the movable in space, the substitution of spatial exteriority for material existence is more intuitive.

4. Kant, *Critique of Pure Reason*, trans. Norman Kemp Smith (Boston: Bedford/St. Martin's, 1965), p. 244. All further citations of this text will refer to the traditional A (1781) and B (1787) edition paginations.

5. A transcendental analysis is different than a transcendental argument in so far as the former lays out the conditions of the possibility of experience (or some similar structure) in order to determine its proper limits whereas the latter aims to reach a positive conclusion in the face of scepticism. Robert Stern provides perhaps the most thorough, if in the end deflationary, explanation and defence of the general philosophical utility of transcendental arguments in his *Transcendental Arguments and Scepticism: Answering the Question of Justification* (Oxford: Clarendon Press, 2000).

6. Stern provides the following description of the general form of transcendental arguments: 'We may therefore settle on a fairly broad characterization of a transcendental argument as involving a transcendental claim of the form "X is a necessary condition for the possibility of experience, language, thought, etc.", where the *rationes cognoscenti* of this claim is non-empirical, and the *rationes essendi* is not that it is analytically true or true by virtue of the laws of nature' (ibid., p. 10).

7. Kant, *Critique of Pure Reason*, B275.

8. See, in the context of the Cartesian example, René Descartes, *The Philosophical Writings of Descartes*, vol. 2, translated by John Cottingham et al. (Cambridge: Cambridge University Press, 1984), p. 22.

9. Kant, *Critique of Pure Reason*, B277.

10. Ibid., B277.

11. Ibid., Bxli.

12. Ibid., Bxl.

13. Kant is by no means interested in defending a materialism against

accusations of idealism. His conception of mechanically deterministic materialism is fundamentally antagonistic to what he sees as the practical vocation of transcendental philosophy. In opposition to both idealism and materialism Kant champions his own doublet: transcendental idealism and empirical realism.

14. Brassier convincingly recasts Laruelle's purportedly transhistorical and genuinely universal analysis of the philosophical decision as specific to the post-Kantian transcendental (or correlationist to use Meillassoux's language) philosophical tradition (Brassier, *Nihil Unbound*, p. 134). I will continue to use Laruelle's language of universal philosophical invariance with the qualification that we should not apply Laruelle's critique beyond the philosophical structures he actually analyses, namely, generally transcendental ones.

15. This is the argument of Laruelle's most prolonged critical engagement with the details of concrete philosophical systems, *Philosophies of Difference*, translated by Rocco Gangle (New York and London: Continuum, 2010).

16. Ibid., p. 187.

17. Rather than dwelling on the structure of the philosophical decision here I will refer the reader to Ray Brassier's excellent analysis, 'Axiomatic Heresy: The non-philosophy of François Laruelle', *Radical Philosophy* 121 (September/October 2003), pp. 24–35 (see esp. pp. 25–7).

18. François Laruelle, 'A Summary of Non-Philosophy', trans. Ray Brassier, *Pli: Warwick Journal of Philosophy* 8 (1999), p. 139.

19. Kant, *Critique of Pure Reason*, B278.

20. Laruelle, *Philosophies of Difference*, pp. 153–4.

21. Ray Brassier et al., 'Speculative Realism', *Collapse* 3 (2007), p. 420.

22. For a more complete account of the stakes of the so-called Frege-Hilbert Controversy, see Michael Hallett, 'Frege and Hilbert', in *The Cambridge Companion to Frege*, edited by Michael Potter and Tom Ricketts (Cambridge: Cambridge University Press, 2010), pp. 413–64; and Michael David Resnick, 'The Frege-Hilbert Controversy', *Philosophy and Phenomenological Research* 34.3 (March 1974), pp. 386–403.

23. Gottlob Frege, *Philosophical and Mathematical Correspondence*, edited by Gottfried Gabriel et al., translated by Hans Kaal (Chicago: University of Chicago Press, 1980), p. 36.

24. Ibid., p. 35.

25. Ibid., p. 37.

26. Ibid., pp. 39–40.

27. Ibid., p. 40.
28. It is this formal aspect of Hilbert's understanding of truth and existence that gives birth to modern problems in model theory, which focuses on the relation between formal systems and their real or empirical models. For an introduction to these issues, see Maria Manzano, *Model Theory* (Oxford: Oxford University Press, 1999). Also of interest might be Alain Badiou, *The Concept of Model: An Introduction to the Materialist Epistemology of Mathematics*, translated by Zachary Luke Fraser and Tzuchien Tho (Melbourne: re.press, 2007).
29. Frege, *Correspondence*, p. 47.
30. Cf. ibid., p. 36: 'If you can't prove a proposition, Then treat is as a definition.'
31. Ibid., p. 47.
32. Ibid., pp. 51–2.
33. The ultimate source of the truth of logical axioms is a matter of considerably more obscurity in Frege's writing. Far from abandoning the importance of intuition, however, it seems to move closer to a doctrine of intellectual intuition. We should not, then, be overly concerned about sliding from specifically geometrical axiomatics to a more general consideration of the axiomatic method on this point.
34. See, for example, Hallett, 'Frege and Hilbert', pp. 454–9. Gödel's incompleteness theorems undoubtedly affected the aspirations of Hilbert's axiomatic method, but did not inaugurate a return to the Fregean axiomatics after the 1930s.
35. This is, of course, the familiar rallying cry of Meillassoux's *After Finitude*, and I wholeheartedly endorse the necessity of this position.
36. Brassier, *Nihil Unbound*, p. 134.
37. François Laruelle, *Dictionary of Non-Philosophy*, edited by Nick Srnicek and Ben Woodard, translated by Taylor Adkins, p. 78. Available at <http://nsrnicek.googlepages.com/DictionaryNon Philosophy.pdf> (accessed 13 February 2012).
38. Laruelle, 'A Summary of Non-Philosophy', p. 138.
39. François Laruelle, 'The Decline of Materialism in the Name of Matter', translated by Ray Brassier in *Pli: Warwick Journal of Philosophy* 12 (2001), pp. 33–40 (p. 39). This short essay is a translation of §27 of François Laruelle, *Le principe de Minorité* (Paris: Aubier Montaigne, 1981).

9

Laruelle, Anti-Capitalist

Alexander R. Galloway

Don't look at Part I, put it aside. Or so goes Louis Althusser's warning to first time readers of Marx's *Capital*. It is important to skip Part I of the treatise, Althusser advised, at least on the first couple of reads. Only when the truth of *Capital* is fully internalised, its scientific intervention into the 'new continent' of history, may one 'begin to read Part I (Commodities and Money) with infinite caution, knowing that it will always be extremely difficult to understand, even after several readings of the other Parts, without the help of a certain number of deeper explanations'.[1] After all, the same political division between social classes, Althusser argued, was mirrored within the text as an epistemological division. Part I contains something close to philosophical idealism, followed by the scientific materialism of the rest of the book. Althusser's advice was thus both practical and political: Part I is not only difficult reading for the young and the uninitiated – Althusser admitted that the proletariat would have no problem reading the book because their 'class instinct' was already attuned to the quotidian experience of capitalist exploitation – it also risks derailing the reader into dangerously Hegelian and philosophical diversions. 'This advice is more than advice', he whispered. It is 'an *imperative*'.[2]

Did he know it? Did Louis Althusser see the colossus issuing forth in the wake of such advice, advice written in March 1969 at such a profound historical conjuncture in France and indeed the world? Was he aware that this would solidify the agenda for the next few decades of Marxian or otherwise progressive philosophy and theory? *The colossus of exchange.*

By focusing on surplus-value instead of, say, the commodity, by insisting that *Capital* and *Capital* alone be the text by which Marx is judged, therefore sidelining the crypto-Hegelian 'young Marx' of species-being and alienation, Althusser placed the emphasis squarely on the scientific structures of exchange: the spheres of production and circulation, the factory floor and the marketplace, the passage from small-scale industry to imperialism. Such an emphasis would continue to dominate theory for decades, both in France and through the adoption of French theory in the English-speaking world. Stemming from his reinterpretation in the 1960s and 1970s, Marx would be rethought primarily as a theorist of exchange. Mating Marx with Freud, theorists like Jean-Joseph Goux would begin to speak in terms of 'symbolic economies' evident across all spheres of life, be they psycho-analytic, numis-matic, or semiotic. Indeed, life would be understood exclusively in terms of relations of exchange. Even deviations from capitalist exchange, as in the many meditations on 'the gift', or even, in a very different way, Deleuze and Guattari's writings on desir-ing machines, would conserve exchange as the ultimate medium of relation. The gift economies of the Haida or Salish potlatch might not be capitalist, but they remain economies nonetheless. Desiring machines might find fuel for their aleatory vectors from beyond the factory walls, but they remain beholden to the swap-ping of energies, the pathways of flight lines, and the interrelation of forces of intensification and dissipation. Althusser had merely identified a general paradigm, *that systems of relation exist, and that they are prime constituting factors for all the other elements of the world, from objects to societies.* As a general philosophi-cal paradigm it would thus forge common currency with other existing schools, chief among them being phenomenology, which must assent to a fundamental relation between self and world, or even to the tradition of metaphysics in general, which assumes a baseline expressive model from Being to being, from essence to instance, or from God to man.

All of this is contained in what Fredric Jameson has called the *second* fundamental riddle in *Capital*, the riddle contained in the equation $M - M'$ (from money to 'money prime' or money with a surplus added). Such is the riddle of exchange: how does money of one value transform into money of a greater value? To answer the question Marx had to 'descend into the hidden abode of pro-duction', revealing the intricacies of the labour process and the working day, in order ultimately to show the origins of surplus-value, what Althusser (and indeed Marx himself) considered the 'illuminating heart' of *Capital*.

But exchange is still just the second riddle in Marx. *Capital* is propelled by another riddle, one which finds its voice in that elusive Part I, the part that Althusser warned his readers to avoid. 'The mystery of an equivalence between two radically different qualitative things' – this is the first riddle, according to Jameson. 'How can one object be the equivalent of another one?'[3] In other words, the riddle is the riddle of $A = B$. The real things constituting A and B themselves, as for example 20 yards of linen (as A) and 1 coat (as B), contribute nothing to the riddle. Rather the mystery derives from the unexplainable, and indeed violent, possibility of inserting an equals sign between them. The riddle is the riddle of the equation; the violence of capital is the violence of the equals sign. Or as Jameson puts it, 'it seems possible to read all of Part One [of *Capital*] as an immense critique of the equation as such'.[4]

The multi-decade legacy of Althusser, who put the final period at the end of the sentence of exchange, has come to an end with François Laruelle. Everything that has thus far been described under the banner of exchange is not simply *a* philosophical paradigm for Laruelle, but *the* philosophical paradigm. There is no philosophy that is not too a philosophy of exchange. There is no metaphysical arrangement that is not too a concourse of convertibility. There is no structure of thought that is not too a structure of relation. There is no phenomenology that is not too an orientation within a world.

Against all these things stands Laruelle, not a philosopher but still a Marxist, who aims to describe not so much Marx's 'rational kernel in the mystical shell' but rather something like an immanent kernel itself for Marx (and capitalism too). Such a real kernel would be devoid of all rationality, all shells, all mystifications, and all chance to interrelate kernels and shells in the first place.[5]

Such is the irony of Laruelle. He deploys Althusserian Marxist language ('determination in the last instance'), he deploys Althusserian Marxist methodology (that science deviates from philosophy and must exist 'in' or 'on' it), yet nevertheless he rejects, in spirit at least, much of what comes after Part 1 of *Capital* and indeed many of the very pillars of Marxism itself.[6] Although, as I hope to show, these pillars are pillars of *Capital* and thus subtend the structure of capitalism, not the Marxian critique levied against it, and therefore not so much Marx himself. Thus, in Laruelle's profound deviation from the Marxian tradition, he ironically remains a Marxist, and in so doing produces one of the most profound critiques of capitalism hitherto known. My proposal here is therefore a simple one, that we must understand Laruelle as both a post-Althusserian Marxist and as someone who brashly ignores Althusser's advice. In the end Laruelle produces an unexpected version of Marx, unexpected not because it supplements Marx in new ways or propels Marx into the future – endeavours impugned by non-philosophy – but because Laruelle ends up endorsing all the old dunderheaded ideas, long ago purged from so-called serious Marxist theory: vulgar determinism, the qualitative purity of use-value, the irrelevance of ideology and 'epistemological breaks'.

Published in 2000, after the collapse of the Soviet Union and the failure of many actually existing Marxist states, Laruelle's book *Introduction au non-marxisme* (*Introduction to Non-Marxism*) is one of the more provocative entries in the decades-long discourses of Marxist theory and constitutes Laruelle's most extended engagement with Marx, although not necessarily with the political as such.[7] True to form, Laruelle refuses to report whether Marxism did or did not fail. He refuses to try to amend or deconstruct Marxism in any way, as that would simply constitute further philosophy.[8] Instead, in the book Laruelle seeks to 'philosophically impoverish' Marxism, with the goal of 'universalising' it through a 'scientific mode of universalisation'.[9] (Was not Althusser's project, 30 years prior, nearly the same?)

Although Laruelle does not often affect an overtly anti-capitalist stance in his work, I want to show here that Laruelle's *ontology*, if not so much his political theory, provides a foundation for one of the most aggressively anti-capitalist critiques since Marx himself, since the Frankfurt School, and since the 'scientific Marxism' of Althusser and post-Second World War France or the autonomist movements in 1970s Italy. Laruelle accomplishes this by militantly denying one of the essential preconditions of any kind of commerce: exchange. Unlike Keynesian economists, or Third-Way liberals, Laruelle does not advocate a mollification of exchange; he does not allow for something like 'capitalism with a friendly face'. Unlike post-structuralists, Laruelle does not acknowledge a system of mutual co-construction between self and other. Instead, he develops an ontological platform that, while leaving room for certain kinds of causality and relation, radically denies exchange in any form whatsoever.

Deviating too from 'process philosophers' like Deleuze, who must necessarily endorse exchange at some level, Laruelle advocates a mode of expression that is irreversible. He does this through a number of interconnected concepts, the most important of which being 'determination-in-the-last-instance' (DLI). Having kidnapped the term from its Althusserian Marxist home, Laruelle uses DLI to show how there can exist causality that is not reciprocal, how a 'relation' can exist that is not at the same time a 'relation of exchange', indeed how a universe might look if it was not already forged implicitly from the mould of a market economy. Herein lies Laruelle's extreme anti-capitalism, an anti-capitalism rooted not in the critique of social relations at the level of politics, but in the prohibition of exchange at the level of ontology.

In order to demonstrate this aspect of Laruelle's thinking, let us consider four interlocking concepts and claims: *science, the infrastructure, the irreversibility of expression*, and *incommensurability*.

The first topic, *science*, is central to Laruelle's conception of non-philosophy as a whole, and central too for Althusser, who viewed science as the only proper response to philosophy. For Althusser science often bears the moniker of practical philosophy, Marxist philosophy, or indeed simply Marxist science. For Laruelle science is synonymous with non-philosophy. Or, to be more correct, 'primary' science, what he also calls 'unified theory', would unify and subtend the common philosophies and the common sciences of the world.[10] As Laruelle puts it, non-philosophical science would be 'primary' vis-à-vis science and philosophy, but would also carry a 'primacy-without-priority' and thus not issue forth or synthesise itself through science and philosophy as their guiding spirit. One must disperse the various encyclopaedias of scientific and philosophical knowledge into 'a chaos of identities', in order to unify such knowledge into a 'democracy' of thought, not by virtue of a common set of axioms or dogmatic truths but by virtue of the generic identity of unified thinking.

So perhaps Marx's eleventh thesis on Feuerbach, which Althusser held up as the most emblematic moment of Marx's intervention into philosophy, is also a fine description for Laruelle's project. The eleventh thesis, Marx's famous maxim that philosophers ought to change the world not simply interpret it, indicates, in the most general sense, that the correct response to interpretation (philosophy) is *not* more interpretation (not more philosophy). Rather, the correct response, if one follows Althusser's gloss of Marx, is to replace philosophical interpretation with a new kind of science, a Marxian science. Such is the elemental discovery of

Marx, a discovery that Althusser suggests was best revealed after the fact by way of Lenin's *Materialism and Empirio-criticism*. But is this not also Laruelle's most essential claim, that the best response to philosophy is not more philosophy? Is it not possible to telescope all of non-philosophy within Marx's eleventh thesis on Feuerbach? *Philosophers have hitherto only interpreted the world in various ways; the point is to articulate a rigorous and immanent scientific non-philosophy of it.*

Like Althusser, Laruelle shuns the lingering abstractions that permeate Marx's work, particularly that of the young Marx. Yet Laruelle reminds us that

> Marxism remains abstract through a lack of universality, a lack of reality, of radicality, not through being poorly adapted to the various avatars of societies and the becomings of history. It is not made abstract by a bad philosophy that would remove it from history, but by an excess of philosophy that plunges it into history.[11]

The problem is thus not a bad philosophy – in this case the bad Hegel, a philosophy pleading to be corrected or 'put back on its feet' – but an excess of philosophy. All this prompts Laruelle to unify philosophy and capitalism together as a single term, 'Thought-World'. Just as philosophy follows a Principle of Sufficient Philosophy (the principle that anything whatsoever is available for solicitation by philosophical reflection) Laruelle writes that capitalism marches to the same tune, via a Principle of Sufficient Economy (the principle that anything whatsoever is available for reproduction and exchange, that capitalism is sufficient to 'englobe', in Laruelle's language, the entire world). So the Principle of Sufficient Economy is a 'universal capitalism', and this means not simply the imperialist extension of capitalism into all corners of the globe, but moreover a perversion of both thinking and being themselves that renders all fixity as permeable and reversible exchange.[12] As Laruelle puts it, even capitalism is incontinent to itself: 'the essence of capitalism is *and/or* is not, in a way that is ultimately reversible, capital'.[13] This is the key to understanding today's trend toward *mondialisation* (literally 'worldisation', but typically translated as 'globalisation'). Only by fusing together philosophy, as Principle of Sufficient Philosophy, and capitalism, as Principle of Sufficient Economy, is it possible to see a single object or a process of 'englobing'. Laruelle means this in quite direct terms: the worlds that populate phenomenology are a question of 'globalisation' as the self englobes its world via orientation and solicitation of attention; but so too the world, or globe, of capitalist globalisation is quite literally the planet itself, the ultimate terrain of the Real. This is why Laruelle is so quick to make philosophy and capitalism coterminous; the two are, quite simply, the same thing for him. Both philosophy and capitalism subject the world to the intercourse of reversibility and exchange, both express things in terms of their opposites, and both destroy (or at least ignore to their own detriment) the ultimate immanence of nature, which for Laruelle is the One and for Marx the real base. So just as science was Marx's response to capitalism, so too is it Laruelle's response to philosophy. And on this last point Althusser would not disagree, for in his estimation Marx's indictment of capitalism was always already an indictment of philosophy. The difference lies more in the composition of the indictment: Laruelle's indictment is made on the grounds of a venomous reversible convertibility; Althusser's indictment on the ground of an odious bourgeois idealism.

This brings us to the second question, that of *infrastructure*. Laruelle finds inspiration not simply in Marx's intuitive understanding of the relation between science and philosophy, but also in what Laruelle views as the immovable, transhistorical, and yes fully immanent material base. Matter or materialism is not simply the topic of Marxism, nor either simply its conceptual core. Matter is quite literally the material of Marxism. Marxism is matter itself; dialects does indeed break bricks. What Laruelle means by this is that Marxism alone posits a pure immanent material base, one that is determinate, immovable and immanent to itself unsupplemented by any idealist scaffold. As he puts it, non-Marxism's goal is 'to universalise matter in an immanent way, without pretending to amend or correct it with any kind of philosophy'.[14] In other words the mere existence of Marxism is evidence of an irresistible One, the material base. This is why Marxism is a politics (and not simply an 'interpretation'), because it saddles itself over the vector of determinacy constructed between infrastructure and superstructure. And this vector is nothing but the determinacy of the One itself. In short, Marxism does not simply describe a relation (between worker and boss or between base and superstructure), it directly embodies this relation and thus, following the Laruellean ontology, must be synonymous with real matter itself.

The non-philosophical term Laruelle assigns to such a situation is 'given-without-givenness', but the Marxian term is 'infrastructure'.[15] The relationship between infrastructure and superstructure, which for many subsequent critics betrayed in Marx a pernicious and somewhat naive determinism, is for Laruelle absolutely crucial, even beneficial. The more naive the better; the more determinist the better.

In *The Eighteenth Brumaire of Louis Bonaparte*, Marx described the 'material conditions of existence, [or the] two different kinds of property', that made up the Party of Order, formed from the alliance of two factions of the ruling class, the Legitimists, the large land owners who were a legacy of the 1814–30 Bourbon restoration period, and the Orleanists, the financiers and large-scale industrialists who were a legacy of the July Monarchy of 1830–48:

> Upon the different forms of property, upon the social conditions of existence, rises an entire superstructure of distinct and peculiarly formed sentiments, illusions, modes of thought and views of life. The entire class creates and forms them out of its material foundations and out of the corresponding social relations.[16]

Later, in a 1859 text that would become a prototype for *Capital*, the 'Preface (to *A Contribution to the Critique of Political Economy*)', Marx also addressed the superstructure and its 'real foundation':

> In the social production of their existence, men inevitably enter into definite relations, which are independent of their will, namely relations of production appropriate to a given stage in the development of their material forces of production. The totality of these relations of production constitutes the economic structure of society, the real foundation, on which arises a legal and political superstructure and to which correspond definite forms of social consciousness.[17]

These passages have been discussed extensively within Marxist discourse, particularly after the Cultural Turn of the mid twentieth century. Yet the use that Laruelle makes of them is unique. His intervention turns on the conceptual shift from 'relate' to 'arise'. Laruelle, who admittedly treats relation with scorn and scepticism, acknowledges the existence of 'definite relations' within the material base of society. These relations constitute the world and thus the world as it is constructed via capitalism and indeed via philosophy. Yet 'in' or 'on' these relations arises a secondary thing, the superstructure. The nature of this superstructure does not matter so much, nor do its qualities and affordances, nor even its ability to reciprocate in a mutually determining way toward the base (these being some of the concerns of the cultural Marxists). Rather what interests Laruelle is the pure and rigorous radicality of such a unilateral and unidirectional causality. To underscore the force of this causal determinacy, let us continue the previous passage from Marx where it left off, revealing one of the most cited passages in his entire body of work: 'The mode of production of material life conditions the general process of social, political and intellectual life. It is not the consciousness of men that determines their existence, but their social existence that determines their consciousness.'[18]

For Laruelle, the words 'conditions' and 'determines' are not sources of anxiety, as they were for many of the cultural Marxists from Althusser to Raymond Williams and beyond. For Laruelle these words must be taken very literally, even accentuated and made more extreme, more radical. The infrastructure of the material base is a given-without-givenness because and only because of its ability to condition and determine – unidirectionally, irreversibly and 'in the last instance' – whatever it might condition and determine, in this case the superstructure. Thus the infrastructure stands as 'given' while still never partaking in 'givenness', neither as a thing having appeared as a result of a previous givenness, nor a present givenness engendering the offspring of subsequent givens. Again, any mollification of Marx's determinism would not simply miss the point for Laruelle, it would undo the entire Marxist project. If Marxism has any force at all, it gains such force by virtue of an immanent material base, synthetic to nothing but determinate in all. Not simply labour-power or 'force of labour' – the French term *force de travail* being so similar to the important Laruellean term *force (de) pensée* (force (of) thought) – but *force of infrastructure*.[19]

If this brief discussion of infrastructure illuminates anything, it is that Laruelle is a vulgar determinist and unapologetically so. So now to the third theme, related closely to the second, which is the way in which determinism leads to an *irreversibility of expression*. In Laruellean language, undeniably infused here with an Althusserian additive, this is known as 'determination-in-the-last-instance' (DLI). Althusser focused on the 'last instance' as a way to soften Marx's determinism, to forge a compromise between the material base and the relative autonomy of the superstructural realm. But for Laruelle the 'last instance' means precisely the opposite. It is not a bone tossed to the socio-cultural sphere, but a trump card slammed down with definitive force. 'In the last instance' does not mean that the One must pander to the world, including it in all its many deliberations. On the contrary, it means that the One remains ultimately 'last', oblivious in its position of causal determinacy. DLI, therefore, which Laruelle admits was 'invented by Marx-Engels for Historical Materialism', describes a specific logic of causality 'which is uni-lateral against all the philosophical phantasms of reciprocity and convertibility'.[20] The real base is not merely one flank that can be brought into relation with another flank, such as the superstructure. The base, as determinate-in-the-last-instance, is a 'final' cause, not a primary one. Thus to make DLI the general axiomatic form of Laruelle's 'non-ontological causality' allows for 'a lifting of philosophical sufficiency by way of the theoretical reduction of philosophy to the radical immanence of its real base'.[21]

Laruelle discusses DLI in a number of places, but in the non-Marxism book it is summarised by way of three distinctive traits. First, DLI is a causality that is unique but calls or supposes an other, as if it is the sole causality but also somehow insufficient. Hence the One supposes the Two (although without necessarily producing or metaphysically expressing itself through the Two). Next, these *secondary* causalities, those of the Two or the clone, are introduced back into the One during the *final* calculus. In other words, the secondary causalities are always already structurally 'in debt' to the infrastructure. Last, DLI operates in the 'final instance' as a quasi invariant or constant, 'in opposition to the variations of nature or region, to the variability of secondary causality'.[22]

What this means is that DLI, if it is expressive, is expressive only in one direction. It is thus properly labelled irreversible. In the structure of ontological expression, DLI exerts an absolute dominance over the world. Would it be too hyperbolic, then, to speak of Laruelle's determinism as a kind of *sadism* of the One, and of DLI as a kind of 'sado-cause'? This is not to slander Laruelle's universe as unfeeling, violent, or even proto-fascist, but simply to underscore the radical hierarchy of force established between the One and its clones. Like the sadist encounter, force flows one way and one way only. Recall that there is a 'force of thought' in Laruelle, but never a 'force of reflection' that would allow for exchange of forces.[23]

Perhaps a useful way to understand Laruelle's notion of the irreversibility of expression is by way of the so-called failure of actually existing Marxism. It does not matter so much which dates are assigned to this failure – be they 1871 in Paris, 1919 in Berlin, or 1991 in the Soviet Union. And it does not matter so much that Marxism be understood as a burrowing mole (or striking snake) able to return from periods of suppression to rise up and blossom again in a new form, as someone like Alain Badiou has recently described with such elegance.[24] In fact Laruelle is careful *not* to reject the failure of Marxism. He considers failure to be an asset of Marxism, not a liability. Laruelle is careful to avoid the 'vicious circle' of so many theorists, those who attempt a Marxism of Marx, which for Laruelle would be just as philosophical as a Kantianism of Marx or a structuralism of Marx. To revel in the failure of Marxism is to revel in the proof that Marxism *can* lapse back to an immanence with the One, that Marxism does not need to be productive in any way (like capitalism must constantly be). So for Laruelle failure is good because it indicates that Marxism is not trying to go outside of itself to affect other things. Thus, ironically, the recession of Marxism is the first step toward considering its radical universality, since via recession it is all that much closer to its own true immanence with itself. Any failure of Marxism, or if you like communism, in for example the historical conjuncture of 1871 when soldiers descended from Versailles in wholesale slaughter of the Parisian communards, cannot be explained *internally* by Marxism itself. 'In this way a Marxist concept of the conjuncture can not *explain* the failure of Marxism, but only offer a specular doubling of it.'[25] In other words, Marxism can never 'truly' be understood in its universality if it is read simply as a corrective or reactionary force vis-à-vis the historical gains of capitalism. So if Jean Baudrillard told us to 'forget Foucault' in order better to understand the totality of power, here we must 'forget capitalism' in order to arrive at a universal Marxism, unfettered by any synthesis or rebirth forged through failure.

Unidirectional and irreversible determination, for Laruelle, is necessary for a truly and radically immanent ontology. But, he cautions, this is not a Marxian immanence, since axiomatically all immanence is immanence in the Real (equivalent to immanence in the One). 'It is the immanence (of) the Real as cause', writes Laruelle, 'and thus an immanence non immanent *to Marxism*.'[26] This brings us to our fourth theme, *incommensurability*. Herein is contained Laruelle's ultimate incompatibility with Althusser. For if Althusser warned his readers to begin after Part I of *Capital* – *Don't look at Part I, put it aside* – it is only *within* Part I that Marx offers his best description of incommensurability. Recall again Jameson's first riddle of *Capital*, which revolves around the seeming impossibility of equating two qualitatively different things. The key to incommensurability is therefore *use-value*. Use-value, Marx instructs, is the 'substance' of value, the 'usefulness' of something. Use-value is understood in terms of physical bodies that are qualitatively different and hence, since they share no scale of measurement in common, are absolutely incommensurable with each other. In this way, use-value in Marx reveals a rudimentary theory of immanence, as objects are defined strictly by way of an identity with themselves, never forced to go outside themselves into the form of something else. The consummation of a use-value, in for example the eating of an apple, constitutes a 'relation without relation': I may eat the apple and have a 'relation' to it as I chew it up and digest it, but its qualities, even as they are consumed by me, act unidirectionally and irreversibly on me, on my tongue, in my stomach and digestive system, and indeed on my health and state of mind. For Laruelle there is no common measure between the One and its clones. As a unilateral duality, they constitute a relation without a relation.

If, previously, DLI revealed a brute ontological sadism, incommensurability reveals what might be called Laruelle's *autism*. Non-philosophy is unable to form real relationships, except those mediated by a more scientific posture. The absolute radiance of the One leaves its clones (entities, worlds, persons) as generically ordinary but also solitary. Laruelle's entities are near-sighted, myopic, shut in. Like the autistic child (at least stereotypically) they are unable to form relations of mediation via the normal channels. But so too are they locked out of immediate communion with the One, immediacy being in Laruelle's estimation simply a perverted form of mediation. Recall that Laruelle's goal is never to make thought and being immediate to each other, but rather to maintain the duality of the two as an identity.

But have I just insulted non-philosophy a second time, first calling it sadistic and now autistic? That is not the intention. The aim of these two epithets is to underscore the 'immedia' evident in Laruelle, his rigorous nullification of any form of mediation. It is only here that Laruelle is able to be understood as an anti-capitalist, indeed one of the most aggressive anti-capitalists in the history of thought. It is not so much that Laruelle comes out against capitalism with this or that political strategy, with this or that economic policy. Rather, Laruelle's anti-capitalism is rooted not in a critique of the mode of production, but in the discovery that the material base is itself ontologically incompatible with exchange.

The ultimate issue, which even Althusser could not see or at least would not accept, is that in order to remove Hegel from Marx it is necessary to go to the limit. One must not simply remove the 'more philosophical' parts, the youthful Marx, the metaphysical even sometimes idealist Marx. In order to fix the Hegelian roots within Marx, one must not simply replace a bourgeois philosophy with a more rigorous dialectical science. The solution is not more dialectics, but less. In order to remove Hegel from Marx, one must *remove the dialectic entirely*. Such is Laruelle's essential aim, a Marxism without dialectics. But is this not the ultimate contradiction of Marxism itself: how to foment to the brink of revolution a certain kind of proletarian history that will obviate the need for any future history? For example, Lenin's concern is not simply how to make revolution but how to make it last, not simply the end of the tsar's dictatorship but the forging of a new dictatorship, this time of the proletariat. Althusser's concern is not simply the supersession of idealist philosophy, but its supersession at the hands of a new higher orthodoxy, what he called the science of 'pure thought' itself or the dialectic as 'Logic'.[27] So, is the ultimate form of Marxism still dialectical, or the indication of an absolute absence of the dialectic? One might return to an earlier moment, to the German Marxist theorist Karl Korsch (rejected by Kautsky and Stalin alike), and recall his assertion, essentially incompatible with Althusserianism and many other varieties of Marxism, that 'Marxian theory constitutes neither a positive materialistic philosophy nor a positive science.'[28] Korsch's suggestion is that one must be permanently critical, and hence vigilant against the ossification of Marxian or party orthodoxy as a newfound dogma. Marxism is critical not positive, wrote Korsch. It is specific not general. Such a modest and provisional view of Marxian science is perhaps a bit closer to the Laruellean method than that of Althusser. Yet whatever the answer for others, Laruelle's position is clear. He seeks an immediacy without mediation. He seeks a finite determinacy without abstraction. He seeks a 'last philosophy' not a return to 'first philosophy'. In short, he seeks a Marx without dialectical synthesis.

According to Laruelle the question for Marx is not 'how to break with Hegel?' but 'how to break with *philosophy* itself'.[29] For Marx, Hegel was merely philosophy's most recent and dazzling avatar. Marx's reticence toward Hegel is, for Laruelle, indication of a non-philosophical instinct *already implicit* in Marx. The eleventh thesis on Feuerbach is only the most obvious and pithy evidence of this. In other words Marx himself was seeking non-philosophy, whether he called it by that name or not, by breaking with philosophy and shifting toward the practical science of political economy.

But the question for Laruelle is not the same. The issue for him is not how to break with what came before, to break with Marx or Marxism. Such a break would only proliferate new philosophical discourses, and as such would fall out of the purview of non-philosophy entirely. 'Not to recognise Marxism but to know it' is Laruelle's intuition. 'To discover it rather than to rediscover it.'[30] To 'recognise' or 'rediscover' Marx would be to reflect on him. But a properly rigorous and immanent science of the Marxian infrastructure would do no such thing. It would withdraw from the decision to reflect, and discover the immanent destiny of nature, perhaps for the first time.

Notes

1. Louis Althusser, *Lenin and Philosophy: And Other Essays*, translated by Ben Brewster (New York: Monthly Review Press, 2001), p. 57.
2. Ibid., p. 52.
3. Fredric Jameson, *Representing* Capital: *A Reading of Volume One* (New York: Verso, 2011), pp. 47, 23.
4. Ibid., p. 22.
5. At a revealing moment, Laruelle stresses that his kernel is 'real' or 'symptomatic' but never 'rational', framing everything against an Althusserian backdrop. 'Althusser's "error"', he writes, 'is to have searched in Marx for the rational (and thus philosophical and idealist) kernel of the Hegelian dialectic; whereas, in all philosophers, one

must first identify the real symptomatic kernel' (François Laruelle, *Introduction au non-marxisme* [Paris: PUF, 2000)], p. 46, this and subsequent uncredited translations are mine). In the following passage Laruelle also evokes Marx's famous kernel metaphor, and, as he often does, uses the analogy of non-Euclidean geometry to outline the position of non-philosophy vis-à-vis philosophy, or in this case non-Marxism vis-à-vis Marxism: 'Such a project, in the spirit of a "non-Euclidean" Marxism, consists in producing, on the bases of this certain ingredient = X [i.e. the non-philosophical ingredient in Marxism], the universal non-Marxist kernel not *of Marxism* but *for it and starting from it* simultaneously as symptom and model, in general as "material"' (ibid., p. 6). In this way Laruelle's Marxism book finally fleshes out the larger claim, commonly heard in non-philosophy, that philosophy must stand as 'material' for non-philosophy. With this book it is clearer what exactly Laruelle means by 'material'; he means the material infrastructure, and further he means materialism as a bridge joining philosophy with scientific non-philosophy.

6. In a surprising turn of phrase, Althusser expresses a Laruellean impulse *avant la lettre* when in a 1976 lecture he writes that 'to support our argument by comparison with the revolutionary State, which ought to be a State that is a "non-State" – that is, a State tending to its own dissolution, to be replaced by forms of free association – one might equally say that the philosophy which obsessed Marx, Lenin and Gramsci ought to be a 'non-philosophy' – that is, one which ceases to be produced in the form of a philosophy, whose function of theoretical hegemony will disappear in order to make way for new forms of philosophical existence' (Louis Althusser, 'The Transformation of Philosophy', translated by Thomas Lewis, in *Philosophy and the Spontaneous Philosophy of the Scientists, and Other Essays* [London: Verso 1990], p. 264). But even earlier, in February 1968, he had already called for a 'non-philosophy' during his explanation of the syntax of the title 'Lenin *and* Philosophy': 'Not Lenin's philosophy, but Lenin *on* philosophy. In fact, I believe that what we own to Lenin, something which is perhaps not completely unprecedented, but certainly invaluable, is the beginnings of the ability to talk a kind of discourse which anticipates what will one day perhaps be a non-philosophical theory of philosophy' (Althusser, *Lenin and Philosophy*, p. 14). Or a few lines earlier when Althusser anticipates Laruelle's emblematic preference for the preposition 'in' instead of the preposition 'of', indeed not just a preference

but an absolute mandate: Althusser tells the audience assembled at the Société Française de Philosophie that his talk 'will be a talk *in* philosophy. But this talk in philosophy will not quite be a talk *of* philosophy. It will be, or rather will try to be, a talk *on* philosophy' (ibid., p. 13). Had he been present, Laruelle would most certainly have agreed with such an elevation of *on* over *of*.

7. Although the political import of Laruelle's work is distributed in a complex fashion across his entire body of work, two books, *Le principe de minorité* (Paris: Aubier, 1981) and *Une biographie de l'homme ordinaire. Des Autorités et des Minorité* (Paris: Aubier, 1985), are notable for their description of dispersive or 'minoritarian' multiplicities and the minority individuation or minoritarian thought of the 'ordinary man' as he exists in a determinative relation to states, authorities and worlds.

   In the non-Marxism book, Laruelle speaks of these categories of subjecthood in terms of a 'subject-in-struggle'. This subject would be a 'non-proletarian' or 'universal stranger' summoned not from the call for 'workers of the world to unite!' but rather from a call to remain 'unified' in immanent identity. See Laruelle, *Introduction au non-marxisme*, p. 118, as well as all of Chapter 6 (pp. 109–39).

   An additional, shorter text is relevant here too, Laruelle's 'précis' of non-Marxism, 'Pour un marxisme clandestin' (manuscript, undated), which reiterates and amplifies the issues first broached in the 2000 book.

8. Innumerable are the ways in which philosophers have tried to normalise materialism in order to make it more palatable, writes Laruelle. He lists several of the guilty parties: normalisation 'by existentialism (Sartre), by structure (Althusser), by the transcendental phenomenology of auto-affecting life (Henry), by the transindividual as a synthesis of the collective and the individual (Balibar), by deconstruction of its "spectres" (Derrida), by contractuality and metastructure (Bidet)' (Laruelle, *Introduction au non-marxisme*, p. 33).

9. Ibid., p. 5, emphasis removed.

10. For an extensive discussion of science and philosophy see Chapter 2, titled 'Primary Science as the Unified Theory of Science and Philosophy, or the Democracy within Thought', in François Laruelle, *Principes de la non-philosophie* (Paris: PUF, 1996). Likewise in his non-Marxism book, Laruelle attacks Althusser directly, devoting a number of pages to how the Althusserian concepts of 'problematic' and 'epistemological break' should be superseded by 'unified theory'. See Laruelle, *Introduction au non-marxisme*, pp. 78–83.

11. Laruelle, *Introduction au non-marxisme*, p. 22.
12. To help explain this sense of 'universal capitalism', Laruelle writes that 'the real universal object of non-Marxism will be capitalism *plus* the entire set of its philosophical conditions structured in their "essence", which is to say "universal" capitalism in the radical sense of the term, the synthesis of capitalism and the essence of philosophy under the auspices, the one and the other, of "World"' (Laruelle, *Introduction au non-marxisme*, p. 8). In other words, one can not simply examine capitalism itself, one must look at the 'World' produced from the grand collaboration between capitalism and philosophy. Laruelle admits, then, that the subject of his non-Marxism book is, in the most general sense, 'philosophically universal capitalism' (ibid., p. 9).
13. Ibid., p. 145.
14. Ibid., p. 10.
15. Ibid., p. 42.
16. Karl Marx, *The Eighteenth Brumaire of Louis Bonaparte* (New York: International Publishers, 1963), p. 47.
17. Karl Marx, *Early Writings*, translated by Rodney Livingstone and Gregor Benton (London: Penguin, 1974), p. 425.
18. Ibid.
19. Laruelle discusses *force de travail* and *force (de) pensée* together in *Introduction au non-marxisme*, pp. 111–15.
20. Ibid., p. 39.
21. Ibid., p. 27.
22. Ibid., p. 40.
23. The DLI logic in Laruelle is indeed unique. Heidegger's being-unto-death is perhaps another instance of this unusual logic, to the extent that being-unto-death requires the construction of a relation with an event, one's death, from which it is impossible to achieve a reciprocated relation in return. See in particular the second half of Martin Heidegger, *Being and Time*, translated by John Macquarrie and Edward Robinson (New York: Harper and Row, 1962). Heidegger writes that death is non-relational and yet nevertheless still 'mine': 'Death is the possibility of the absolute impossibility of Dasein' (p. 294).
24. See in particular Alain Badiou's discussion of the communist hypothesis in *The Meaning of Sarkozy*, translated by David Fernbach (London: Verso, 2008) and in *The Communist Hypothesis*, translated by David Macey and Steve Corcoran (London: Verso, 2010). According to Badiou the communist hypothesis existed already,

under modernity at least, during two historical periods, 1792–1871 from the French Revolution to the Paris Commune and 1917–76 from the Russian Revolution to the end of the Cultural Revolution in China, and which, according to Badiou, is on the verge of appearing again in a third historical phase.

Marx's 'mole', originally from a passage in *The Eighteenth Brumaire of Louis Napoleon* – 'the revolution is thoroughgoing . . . It does its work methodically . . . when it has done this second half of its preliminary work, Europe will leap from its seat and exultantly exclaim: Well grubbed, old mole!' (Marx, *The Eighteenth Brumaire of Louis Napoleon*, p. 121; Marx was paraphrasing from *Hamlet*: 'Well said, old mole! canst work i' the earth so fast?' [Act 1, Scene V]) – has been revived most recently in Michael Hardt and Antonio Negri, *Empire* (Cambridge, MA: Harvard University Press, 2000), pp. 57–8. In contrast to the old mole of the nineteenth and early twentieth century, Hardt and Negri propose a new metaphor of the snake, suggesting that today's political events, with their 'infinite undulations' (p. 57) can strike like a snake at any time and from any place against the very core of Empire.

25. Laruelle, *Introduction au non-marxisme*, p. 17.
26. Ibid., p. 7.
27. Althusser, *Lenin and Philosophy*, p. 36. The Hegelian undertones here – a science of logic as pure thought – are ironic given Althusser's antipathy for Hegel.
28. Karl Korsch, *Three Essays on Marxism* (New York: Monthly Review Press, 1972), p. 65, emphasis removed.
29. Laruelle, *Introduction au non-marxisme*, p. 38.
30. Ibid., p. 37.

10

Theories of the Immanent Rebellion: Non-Marxism and Non-Christianity

Katerina Kolozova

In his 2000 work, *Introduction au non-marxisme*, François Laruelle lays out the principles of his non-philosophical political project of establishing 'thought in terms of radical concepts'. The concerns of this project are chiefly epistemological; or rather, they represent another significant contribution to the development of his more general project – that of establishing a 'science of humans' (*science des hommes*)[1] which, he argues, should come in the stead of philosophy.[2] 'Thought in terms of radical concepts' – which is what non-Marxism in its last instance ought to be – aims to radicalise Marxism by ridding it of its transcendental constructions, fixed and unmovable as its unalienable 'essence'. Laruelle argues that 'Dialectical Materialism' or 'Historical Materialism' is not merely a thesis, hypothesis, axiom, or mere presupposition that can be seen as an individual, isolated claim. Rather, it is a complex 'cosmology', a transcendental structure that represents a system of answers to what are radically rudimentary and fundamentally theoretical questions. It forms a complex, inert and virtually indisputable (by those who adhere to Marxism) transcendental universe creating a closed narrative of answers to questions which are in fact 'affected by the immanence' of the Real which every Human in the last instance is. The questions Marxism asks are phrased in what Laruelle calls radical terms.[3] Nonetheless, the proposed answers are products of philosophical autoreferentiality representing self-sufficient transcendental edifices.

All theoretical questions in their radical form, i.e., at the instance when they hold the status of a 'transcendental minimum', clone the Real rather than the Transcendental – they are posed by the 'Human-in-Human', not the Philosopher. Such are the questions that inspire scientific inquiry. Such are the questions posed by the Gnostics and the Marxists, explains Laruelle.[4] Such are the questions of the Human-in-Human we all are in the last instance. And such are the questions of the Heretics of Christianity and of Marxism.

Philosophy in the technical sense of the word does not recognise heresy,[5] says Laruelle. Still, according to non-philosophy, the 'World' and 'Philosophy' are synonyms – they are one and the same thing.[6]

Philosophy in this sense of the word is scarred by heresy, which is inherently present in it, and stained by the wounds of its persecuted heretics. 'The World' could be explained through an analogy to, say, Foucault's 'Discourse' or Lacan's 'Symbolic Order' and that is why it equals to 'Philosophy' – it is the totality of sense we assign to the mute immanence of the 'Lived' (or the Real) we all are. It is not only that alienated and alienating 'Essence' that weighs on us, it is also the norm, the normality and the discipline the 'World' dictates. Thus it is a 'materialised transcendence', it implies living one's life according to a certain Universe-of-Meaning and it lays the foundations of Right and Wrong – of that which the 'World' praises and of that which it punishes. It is the Orthodoxy in the total sense and, therefore, it too has its heresies and persecuted heretics.

In *Future Christ*, first published in French in 2002 and in English translation in 2010, Laruelle attributes the capacity of 'immanent struggle' to the figure of Christ understood in a way which is, as he puts it himself, 'evidently not very "Christian"', in a way which is heretical.[7] Rebellion (*rebéllion*)[8] or struggle (*lutte*) is the essence of the Subject, maintains Laruelle, and it is so 'because there is a Real cause of struggle that is not itself in struggle'.[9] That cause is the radically insufficient Human-in-Human. Laruelle's Human-in-Human is the instance of the Real behind the subject and – quite similarly to the Lacanian concept of the Real – it is passive. Therefore, it is fundamentally vulnerable. Thus, it necessitates the 'Subject' (or the 'Stranger', as termed in Laruelle's *Théorie des Etrangers* first published in 1995) whose function is to struggle with and for the World.

Laruelle expressly links the heretical understanding of the Christian subject, as one modelled according to the figure of Christ, with the Marxian idea of struggle: in his attempt to explain the 'immanence of struggle without goal',[10] he declares he will rely on Christianity, Gnosis and Marxism.[11] Here, we shall seek to explore how and why Laruelle chooses to explicate the 'subject of immanent rebellion' precisely by virtue of combining Christianity and Marxism and according to the procedures of his non-standard philosophy. It is precisely these non-standard procedures of working with the philosophical or, for that matter, with any transcendental material, which make non-philosophy itself heretical – its abandonment of the authority of the Doctrine (any doctrine), i.e., of the authority of Philosophy itself.

The Status of Heresy in Philosophy

Speaking of philosophy in *Future Christ*, Laruelle says the following: 'The metaphysical forgetting of heresy is its second aspect of significance. *What is there in the essence of heresy such that it still has not penetrated philosophy, never acquired the status of a true concept, even a negative or polemical one?*'[12] 'Metaphysical forgetting of heresy' refers to the fact that, speaking from the standpoint of non-philosophy, heresies do not exist in philosophy – such a possibility is a priori cancelled. As soon as an idea emerges as a 'heretical' re-appropriation of a doctrine, of a system of thought, it unavoidably becomes the foundation of a new philosophical orthodoxy. Such course of development is inevitable by virtue of philosophy's intrinsic tendency to create 'cosmologies' (universes of meaning), systems (even when they claim to be unsystematic or anti-systematic) – its founding principle being that of 'auto-reflection'.[13] Any 'aberration' in the pursuit of truth is susceptible to normalisation. Whatever forms a 'coherent teaching' – a final and enclosed universe (a 'cosmology') of meaning – offering the sense of controlling the Real by way of reflecting it through Thought is part of Philosophy. In other words, whatever constitutes a certain orthodoxy is, in fact, philosophy.

According to Laruelle, by its determination in the last instance, Philosophy deals with itself – not the Real.[14] It has duplicated the Real into the concept of 'Essence' and 'Being', says Laruelle, and its history consists in thinking the endless variations of these two products of its own. The history of philosophy is a history of philosophy thinking itself. Concepts usurp the place of the Real – by suppressing it entirely – and form endless chains of systemic configurations which pretend to be the reflections of reality. Thus the transhistorical philosophical debate has never been about the Real. Rather, it has always been a ceaseless, perennial dispute of different configurations of the auto-referential Transcendental. François

Laruelle argues that even when the 'linguistic' or 'Wittgensteinian' turn in philosophy forwards the claim that the Real is inaccessible,[15] it still has the pretension to *re-present* the reality, simply because it claims there is no reality but the transcendental one we cognitively construct. Thus, the constructed reality has claimed the status of (the only possible) reality. This is in fact the absolute or total completion of the act of philosophy folding into itself and over itself (*se repliant*), i.e., of its duplication or what Meillassoux calls 'correlationism'.[16]

The only possible heresy in philosophy would be that of non-philosophy. Of a stance which is outside philosophy, outside its self-content self-circumscription, which operates with its 'transcendental material' in an irreverent way which dismisses any authority of philosophy over reality or any superiority whatsoever over the scientific (or, for that matter, the poetic). It is a *non-philosophical* posture of thought, one which heretically renders philosophy to mere *chôra* (a mess of unorganised 'transcendental material') with which it operates when theorising while succumbing to the ultimate authority of the Real.

The heretical stance is inherently rebellious. The heretic-subject is of the immanent struggle. Laruelle claims that there is a 'transcendental universe' issuing from philosophy which is irreverently heretical with respect to its origin and founded upon 'radical concepts' – the theoretical universe of Marxism.[17] Marxism is already in its origin a heretical posture of thought that has stepped out of the cycle of philosophy's auto-mirroring. But not entirely, according to Laruelle. It is still subject to the essentially philosophical constraints imposed by the doctrine of Marxism. Orthodox reverence of *transcendental constructs* such as 'dialectical materialism' and the inability to reduce them to *chôra* – mere transcendental material instead of finished conceptual wholes – is what disables the completion of the project of stepping out of philosophy which Marxism initially set for itself (in the *Theses on Feuerbach*).

In order to radicalise its position, argues Laruelle, and place itself outside philosophy, Marxism has to take a step outside itself by virtue of admitting its own transcendental, i.e., philosophical character. It has to adopt the stance of the 'non-' that is situated in the Real that clones itself through concepts. In order to preserve its grain of 'thinking affected by immanence',[18] Marxism ought to become non-Marxism, argues Laruelle. It is only to Marxism and psychoanalysis that Laruelle ascribes the status of theories that are based on 'radical concepts' and have, therefore, accomplished a significant although not complete *Ausgang* from Philosophy.

> The 'real' solution to the problem of the DLI [determination-in-the-last-instance] as the object and cause of its own theory should avoid Hegelian idealism better than it has been done by the materialism. Neither a cause in exteriority nor a dialectical identity of contraries, the Real is the cause by virtue of immanence and determines cognition of its own syntax, of its own causality, through a process that one would call 'cloning' . . . Suppose there is an object X to be cognised. Provided it is affected by immanence or susceptible to DLI, that is seen-in-One, it also can clone 'itself' from the material that is its transcendence.[19]

What remains to be done in order to fully realise the act of exiting the circular entrapment of the Transcendental (that is, of Philosophy) is to adopt the 'Syntax of the Real' in the use of language whose most rudimentary element and defining component is – the thinking in terms of 'radical concepts'. This position of radicalising Thought, bringing it closer to the Real (in the form of it being 'affected by immanence'), is accomplished through the adopting of the heretical posture of thought – a position of immanent, infinite rebellion. To the forms of thought endowed with the potential of radical thought – one that is always already attuned to the Real – i.e., to psychoanalysis and Marxism, Laruelle adds gnosis in so far as it is further radicalised by way of abandoning its philosophical constitution and preserving its 'Gnostic essence', i.e., the immanent *hairesis* of the 'Human-in-Human'.

In order to establish the most radical possible stance of heresy, i.e., heresy in the last instance, one adopts the immanently rebellious position vis-à-vis 'the World', i.e., vis-à-vis Philosophy. Therefore, non-philosophy as a form of heretical situating with respect to the discipline of philosophy is further radicalised through the adopting of the heretical stance informed by Gnosticism and non-Christianity. This positioning of the subject is heretical in the last instance – it is the Human-in-Human in its immanently rebellious situatedness as the 'non-Christian Christ' or the 'Messiah' (terms which do not refer to the historical or doctrinal Christ but rather to the radical idea of it, to the transcendental minimum of the notion of 'Christ').

Marxism and Non-Marxism: Cloning the Real into the Transcendental *Chôra* of Marxism

Laruelle's *Introduction au non-marxisme* represents an endeavour to establish the non-philosophical principles – or rather, the non-Marxist principles – for Marxian theory and practice in a way that will bring forth its 'source of immanence' and 'power (of) thought'.[20] Non-Marxism is a re-appropriation of Marxism which takes place by way of transforming it into a thought of 'the immanent mode' [*de la manière immanente*],[21] which is only possible if it is dismantled as a consummate doctrine or a 'cosmology' – a transcendental structure which, in spite of its potential for various reconfigurations, remains an unchangeable structural minimum. The abandonment of the 'cosmological' foreclosure of Thought leads to its rendering into conceptual *chôra*, the chaos of the unorganised transcendental material.[22] As the result of Thought's succumbing to the authority of the Real, it is affected by the immanence (that the Real is) which produces the cloning of the Real into the Transcendental.

Laruelle argues that in order to arrive at the source of immanence for Marxism, and, in that way, clone the *identity-in-the-last-instance* of Marxian political vision, one has to first evacuate not only Dialectics but also Materialism, and undertake afresh the elucidation of Marxism's Determination-in-the-last-instance (or *la Détermination-en-dernière-instance*, hereafter referred to as DLI).[23] Both Dialectics and Materialism are circumscribed conceptual constructions, closed systems of belief. In other words, they are not subjected to radical criticism which might issue in complete abandonment of both the dialectical and the materialist thesis. This is due to the conviction that if one rids Marxism of these two 'cosmologies', what remains is hardly Marxism. Laruelle's claim is quite the opposite: radical concepts, among which the One which is its 'identity in the last instance', are what defines Marxism, not the finished doctrinal compounds. Radical concepts are always produced according to the syntax of the Real: they are not the result of purely philosophical disputes – although they are engaged inside philosophy and its history – but rather, of the 'transcendental being affected by immanence'. Radical concepts are products of the encounter of Thought with the (indifferent) Real which results in Thought 'cloning' ('describing') the Real by minimum use of transcendental material. The Transcendental 'mimes' the Real. This process is enabled by the Real's status of the Lived. The Real the non-philosophy attempts to correlate with is never the inaccessible In-Itself – it is, rather, the Lived that has not been reduced to concepts, ideas, interpretation according to any worldview or philosophy.

In *Théorie des Étrangers*, Laruelle elaborates the concept of the Lived (*le vécu*) in terms of the non-philosophical appropriation of Lacanian psychoanalysis. The Lived is also termed 'le joui' (the enjoyed) of the 'jouissance' (enjoyment).[24] The latter is always of the 'World' whereas the former represents the sheer experience (preceding Language) of – let us resort to Lacanian terminology – the thrust of *Tuché* (or the Real) into the *Automaton* (Language), i.e., into the 'World' and its instance called the 'Stranger' (the alienated Self or the Subject). By an analogy to Lacanian psychoanalysis, we can explain the Lived as the trauma caused by an intervention of the Real ('le joui' which is the purely experiential derivative of 'jouissance' – that which is plainly *lived*, beyond the dichotomy of the corporal and the intellectual). The Lived is the product of the plasticity (in Catherine Malabou's sense) of the Real. We are resorting to the term 'plasticity' in order to describe the capacity of the lived to form a posture which enables the syntactic configuration of the Real which is then cloned into the Transcendental. It is in this sense that the radical concept 'clones the Real'. It is not the reflection of the Real. The latter continues to remain indifferent to Thought's actions and pretensions. In itself, the Real remains inaccessible to Thought. One of the central goals of Laruelle's non-philosophical project is precisely to rid Thought of its pretension to reflect the Real, to rid Philosophy's determination in the last instance as *relative* to the Real by way of affirming its *unilateral* correlation with it.[25]

The DLI is the core of the 'radical concept' – it is dictated by and necessarily correlates with the source of immanence. The radical concept is the immediate transcendental extension of – or it can also be synonymous with – the *determination-in-the-last-instance* which necessarily succumbs to the authority of the Real albeit generated by the Transcendental. The non-philosophical Real is without ontology – 'Being' is an inherently philosophical notion and non-operative in the context of non-philosophy.[26] Laruelle warns that it should in no way be understood as 'the-Being'. The latter is a purely transcendental product of philosophical auto-reflexivity – in its last instance, the concept of 'the-Being' is unaffected by the Real. Its origin is purely philosophical. In the last instance, explains Laruelle, it is determined by the Greco-Judean history of Thought/Philosophy.[27]

The Real is quite simply a number or a 'number' – it is 'the One'. However, it is an instance which is beyond the dichotomy of Matter and 'Idea', beyond the dichotomy of the Body and the Mind. It is also an instance beyond the traditional philosophical concept of the Number. The One of non-philosophy is not a numerical category in the conventional mathematical (or philosophical-mathematical) sense of the word, since it remains to be the impenetrable In-Itself – the Real which evades any pretention of Thought to reflect it (without a remainder). It is the Real which is indifferent to Thought, one that can never be reduced to a concept.

It is a grammatical category in some way: the Real is that 'one thing', that 'certain something' we are attempting to think, mediate via Language – render it 'meaningful'. It is also a formal category of the non-philosophical thought which prescribes it as the only mode of 'theorising' – *theoria en heni*[28] – that can bring about accuracy (that is to say, a thought attuned to the Real). It is also endowed with *political potential* since it represents the basis for the creation of radical concepts which correlate with the immediate Real the 'Human-in-Human' is. 'The Real' is the 'Lived' of the 'Human-in-Human'.[29] The three terms can function as synonyms or as metonymic renditions of the 'One'. According to non-analysis (the non-philosophical version of Lacanian psychoanalysis), the Real is the Lived prior to its alienation through representation.[30] *The Lived shapes the syntax of the non-philosophical political stance, of the revolutionary (or immanently rebellious) thought and practice of non-Marxism but also of the heretic-subject of non-Christianity.* Laruelle frequently refers to the notion of the 'Lived' as indeed the Real that every Human in the last instance is.

Non-Marxism is grounded in its DLI which describes the Lived and is the product of the non-philosophical vision-in-One.[31] The operation which produces it is the aforementioned 'cloning' of the Real. The latter is a unilateral gesture which renders the DLI essentially non-dualistic or 'unmixed', that is, not constituted by the amphiboly of Thought and (the idea of) the Real it produces, i.e., of what usurps the position of the Real.[32] The DLI is the product of the pure Dyad, a binary whose two components (the

Thought and the Real) are viewed in their unilaterality. The split between the Real and the Thought is insurmountable – thus the Dyad is pure. The Transcendental is defined as that transcending trajectory, that gesture of correlating with the Real which is a mere vector (the opening of *epekeina*) which does not make a circular turn in an attempt to envelop the Real as Philosophy does. In this way, non-philosophy – and, for that matter, non-Marxism as well – escapes the philosophical trap of creating the limitrophy of the Transcendental and the Real which results in a transcendental grounded in the constitutive split (between Thought and the Real). This is what makes all philosophical thinking essentially dualistic. The dualism in question is always embedded in a form of *unity* the two components of the binary inevitably create. The only way out of the 'unitary thought' (and its dualistic foundation) is via the unilateral stance and the thought of the 'pure dyad' it generates.[33]

So, radically different from the *philosophical dyad* where immanence is duplicated by way of creating its re-presentation in the 'transcendental immanence' (by presupposing that a priori the Transcendental ought to participate in the immanence),[34] in the non-philosophical *pure dyad* the immanence remains obstinately mute. By way of affirming its radically different status (that of transcendence as tenaciously irreducible to immanence) Thought only strives to describe the immanence rather than 'express' it.

The 'immanent way' of re-reading Marxism (or its non-Marxist re-appropriation) consists in the search for the cause-in-the-last-instance of Marxism by way of using its transcendental material in accordance with a principle of isolating the radical concepts.[35] As the result of such a procedure of *demontage* of the construction of Marxian orthodoxy we can see the possible obsoleteness of the dichotomy materialism/idealism (and, consequently, the constructs of dialectical materialism or historical materialism). It will also enable us to identify that which really corresponds with the 'Lived' and, thus, to establish a symptomatology of the Real present in the text.

> If it [non-Marxism] would seem to go back there [to Marxism], it would be more to its problems rather than to its texts, and to problems whose solution implies treating the texts as symptoms, by way of suspension of the philosophical authority . . . It is impossible, even in Freud and in Marx, and even more so within a philosophy, to find radical concepts of the Real and the uni-versal – solely the unconscious

and the productive forces, desire and labour. As soon as one arrives to this discovery, psychoanalysis and Marxism gain one utterly new sense – a transformation of their theories into simple material . . . These sorts of disciplines require more than just a simple theoretical transformation – a discovery from in 'non-' that would be the effect (of) the Real or its action.[36]

According to Laruelle, the most radical concept the Marxist corpus of knowledge provides is 'productive forces' or 'labour'. It is the result of 'cloning' the Real into the Transcendental since it comes directly from the *lived* of the exploitation of labour, in a form which is not philosophically conditioned, defined and produced. It is a rudimentary description (of the Lived or the Real) generated as a unique conceptualisation which is heedless to the possible history of philosophical elaborations of a similar concept. The Lived is the *joui* which can follow from the *jouissance* but in fact 'precedes' it – or rather, it is beyond the historic temporality. The *Lived*, the Real of the Human-in-Human, is (in) the *radical past*.[37] Its 'time is without temporality'.[38] Or as Laruelle says, 'The immanent or inecstatic past is inexistent and inconsistent but precisely as capable of determining memory and the present as material for the future.'[39]

The experience of labour and of exploitation of labour takes place *always already* – it happens prior to and after any form of political conceptualisation (which could be any process of transcendental transposition including the non-philosophical 'cloning'). And it is to *the lived of the exploited labour force* that the determination in the last instance of non-Marxism should succumb.

The Source of Ceaseless Rebellion: The Heretic

Laruelle establishes analogous couplings of Gnosis to Christianity and of Marxism to Philosophy claiming that what links Gnosis and Marxism – and, in that respect, what makes them fundamentally different from Christianity and Philosophy – is that they have both tried to respond to the question 'what is the real cause of human struggle'. Not only are their respective determinations in the last instance affected by immanence – i.e., they mainly rely on radical concepts cloning the Real – but they also succumb to the Real of the human struggle (or the immanent rebellion). However,

Laruelle insists, they have both also retained much from philosophy remaining entrapped in the circular arguments engendered by the 'amphibological' transcendental.

In spite of the radical grain they are based on, they are still, in the last instance, part of philosophy and the 'World'. In order to further radicalise their potential – bringing them to the (pure) Transcendental which would unilaterally correlate with the Real and would be determined by radical concepts – Laruelle proposes their transformation into *transcendental chôra*. The produce of this process would be Gnosis transforming into non-Christianity and Marxism turned into non-Marxism. Both the subject of non-Christianity and the subject of non-Marxism are defined by a single trait in common – the Heretical Subjectivity and the immanent struggle it executes.

> We are pursuing an initial goal, indeed if we have one other than that of the immanence-without-goal of the struggle. It is solving the Gnostic problem of rebellion as priority of struggle over war and over every other determination of a theological nature. However, this solution continuously relies on Christianity, gnosis and more distantly on Marxism, but refuses the Greek confusion of struggle with the agonistic that still marks rebellion.[40]

Agonism implies dialectics. It implies a philosophical project and certain eschatology. The immanent struggle, on the other hand, one which defines the Gnostic and/or non-Marxist subject, the heretic or the 'future Christ', is one which originates from the Real, the struggle of the unlearned with the World and its Authority.

The heretic-subject is the subject of ceaseless, immanent struggle. What defines it is its continuous rebellion against the World (against Philosophy, against the Church and Christianity, against all forms of *ortho-doxy*): 'to struggle in an immanent way with the World, this is the theorem of the Future Christ. In the beginning was the struggle, and the struggle was *with* the World and the World did not know it . . . That is rebellion, its reasons and cause.'[41] The rebellion that never ceases is affected by the immanence of the struggle which precedes any political project. It is 'given without givenness' to the Lived since it is only through struggle that it establishes its relation to and within the World. The anteriority of struggle to a political project which is possible only by virtue of being in and of the World is not defined in terms of temporal succession. It is embedded in a form of 'a-temporal temporality', or rather, it dwells in the *tempus* which is constituted by the Lived itself – that of the 'radical past'.

> It makes a clean cut at once with the contents of the past and of the present as well as with their sufficiency, in the name of a radical past and that which does not pass in being-in-the-Past. This is the human immanence of a time-without-consistency, and it makes a clean break from their only sufficiency in the name of the future . . .[42]

The radical past of the Real and, therefore, of the immanent struggle, is pregnant with the potentiality of the immanent and infinite struggle – a struggle to come. Radical future is nesting in the radical past of the Human-in-Human – the real cause of immanent struggle and of the heretic subjectivity. This is an idea which reminds us of Deleuze's reading of Nietzsche's concept of the 'eternal return' as the past of the constant becoming. In spite of the fact that the Deleuzian-Nietzschean 'radical past' does operate as the Real, the Void, the Hole of negativity carved into the World of words, the World of images and sounds, it is still one which remains faithful to the Transcendental or to History. This is so because, in the last instance, it succumbs to the authority of the Transcendental rather than the Real – to the ever Returning Narrative of the Eternal Return and of the eschatological vision of Humanity at the centre of it, coinciding with the 'fissure in time' but only in its aspect of the historic occasion of a 'murder of God or the father'.[43]

Unlike the epic historicity which defines the 'eternal return' and its past ripe with future, the *radical past* of the Lived or the Human-in-Human non-philosophy speaks of is a-historical, or rather, it has no 'historic intentionality' – it is not of the World, it neither uses its means nor does it have the competence to make use of them (the Transcendental of the World) and therefore lacks hegemonic conceptualisation which would be essentially historic.

The Lived (*le vécu*) of the radical past is that which *always already* – or repetitively – becomes the Subject of the World or the Subject of *Life*. The latter, unlike the *Lived*, is made of the Transcendental – and this is what constitutes the 'future Christ'.[44] Subjectivity is of and for the World and so is that of the future Christ, of the non-philosophical Gnostic or of the immanent Heretic – it is made of Language. What makes it essentially heretical is that it is affected by immanence, by the Lived, and follows the dictate of the Syntax of the Real.

The Lived is the radically solitary stance of 'human insufficiency' and prior to the 'intervention of the World' taking place via 'subjectivation' – it is an instance of radical vulnerability. The Heretic Subject remains to be 'affected by immanence' – by the Real or the Lived. It is essentially unprotected, essentially exposed – radically vulnerable, in the precariousness which constitutes the reality of the human animal facing the spectral structure of sheer authority that the World is: '"I (am) in-Life, therefore I am in it for-the-World", is the new cogito in which the Future Christ performs, that is to say every man or every Lived thing [*Vécu*] that becomes a subject.'[45] The heretic's vulnerable opening toward the World exposes the solitary Human-in-Human, immanently incessantly suffering because the *Lived* is sheer suffering (beyond the distinction of pleasure and pain). The protection that can be provided through the instance of the Subject – by mediation of the Stranger (*l'Etranger*) – is fatally porous since the Heretic Subject is affected by the radically vulnerable Lived: 'Because man is without-consistency, he is on principle, in contrast to other beings, able to be murdered, he is even the Murdered as first term for heretical thought and for the struggle that it performs.'[46]

Unlike the other animals which can also be killed by the World, the human animal, the 'Murdered one', as 'the first term of the heretic thought', is not only murdered by but also for the World. The directedness toward the World, this vector or arch (one-way trajectory of a pure opening) of exposed vulnerability toward the World is what the rebellious subject substantially consists of. Hence, the radical vulnerability or the possibility of being murdered is the origin of the immanently rebellious nature of the Heretic Subject or the Future Christ. The Gnostic or the Marxian subject is one defined as a subject-in-struggle and if further radicalised as heretic in the last instance, it becomes the Future Christ the non-philosophy invokes. 'We gain in this way from the most innovative practical part of Gnostic rebellion as well as from class struggle in order to gather with faith as so many simple *aspects* in the figure of Future Christ as subject in-struggle.'[47] The immanence of heretical struggle stems from the fact that the Lived is radically isolated, solitary and in so far as it is simply the instance of the Real indifferent to Thought and its pretension to express or reflect it – it is marked by the struggle to 'translate' itself in/to the

World, by way of estranging itself from itself through the instance of *l'Etranger*.[48]

The opening the Stranger (*l'Etranger*) constitutes exposes the vulnerable Lived to the *lived effects* caused by the World. The *vulnerable Lived* by which the Heretic Subject is always immanently affected generates immanent struggle with the World as the determination in the last instance of the Non-Christian and Non-Marxist Future Christ. The World prescribes the Subject, while the Lived mediated through the Stranger struggles against the inhibiting effects of heightened alienation. The World has the immanent tendency to re-produce estrangement, to frame the Lived as Philosophy, to introduce the constraints of the Transcendental. The Lived is endowed with the tendency of immanence and, thus, of opposing and rebelling against the spectral authority of the Transcendental. All transcendental systems are necessarily authoritarian; the Heretic-subject, the agent of immanent struggle constitutes the inexhaustible source of unending rebellion against the all-encompassing Orthodoxy – the World.

Notes

1. François Laruelle, *Théorie des Etrangers: Science des hommes, démocratie et non-psychanalyse* (Paris: Éditions Kimé, 1995).
2. François Laruelle, *Théorie des identités* (Paris: PUF, 1992), pp. 57–63.
3. François Laruelle, *Introduction au non-marxisme* (Paris: PUF, 2000), p. 21.
4. François Laruelle, *Future Christ: A Lesson in Heresy*, translated by Anthony Paul Smith (New York and London: Continuum, 2010), p. 2.
5. Ibid., pp. 36–7.
6. François Laruelle *Philosophie et non-philosophie* (Liège/Bruxelles: Pierre Mardaga 1989), pp. 42–4; Laruelle, *Théorie des Etrangers*, p. 76; Katerina Kolozova, *The Real and 'I': On the Limit and the Self* (Skopje: Euro-Balkan Press, 2006), pp. 103–7.
7. Laruelle, *Future Christ*, p. 2.
8. The terms 'rebellion' (*rébellion*), 'revolt' (*révolte*) and 'struggle' (*lutte*) are interchangeable in Laruelle's *Future Christ*; consider the following quote from the French original: 'Pour élucider l'enjeu et les limites de la rébellion, posons le problème hors des errements philosophiques. La philosophie est toujours indifférente à l'homme ou, ce

n'est pas très différent, trop vite compatissante. Il y a des souffrances et des aliénations, et l'on conclut du mal, et souvent des maux, à la nécessité de se révolter. Les révoltes ne sont "logiques" que dans ce sens-là. Admirable cercle vicieux de l'incertitude et de la contingence d'une rébellion désirée à la quelle personne ne croit' (François Laruelle, *Le Christ future: Une leçon d'hérésie* [Paris: Exils, 2002], p. 20). Translated as: 'In order to clarify the stakes and the limits of rebellion we pose the problem outside of philosophical bad habits. Philosophy is always indifferent to man or, though this isn't very different, too quickly compassionate. Sufferings and alienation exist in the necessity of revolt and one concludes from this that there is evil, and often evils, there too. Revolts are only "logical" in this way – admirable vicious circle of uncertainty and the contingency of a desired rebellion in which no one believes' (Laruelle, *Future Christ*, pp. 5–6).

9. Laruelle, *Future Christ*, p. 2.

10. Ibid.

11. Ibid., pp. 2, 5, 9.

12. Ibid., p. 36.

13. Laruelle, *Philosophie et non-philosophie*, p. 17.

14. Ibid., pp. 11–17, 26–8.

15. Ibid., pp. 193–5.

16. Laruelle, let us note, uses the term 'correlation' in a different sense – it is a relation which is not 'relationist', one that remains in the One, one that merely correlates with the Real without mirroring it, within the gesture of relative constitution of the both terms. So Meillassoux's 'correlationism' corresponds to the non-philosophical notion of the relative mutual constitution of the Real and the Transcendental, i.e., of Philosophy's Unity (of the Two) or auto-reflectivity.

17. Laruelle, *Future Christ*, p. 5.

18. Laruelle, *Introduction au non-marxisme*, p. 48.

19. Ibid., p. 47.

20. Ibid., p. 48.

21. Ibid., p. 10.

22. Laruelle, *Philosophie et non-philosophie*, p. 18.

23. Laruelle, *Introduction au non-marxisme*, p. 48.

24. See Laruelle, *Théorie des Étrangers*, pp. 221–34, the sections: 'Le Réel ou le Joui-sans-Jouissance' and 'La jouissance : 1) comme organon du Réel' of Chapter III ('Principes de la non-psychanalyse').

25. Laruelle, *Philosophie et non-philosophie*, pp. 54–63.

26. Ibid., p. 7.

27. Laruelle maintains that philosophy as such is the product of the Western civilisation, it is determined by its Greek origin and 'Judaic' appropriations: 'freeing the one from the other, the real as much as representation; drawing them from this aporetic situation where the Greeks, under the name of "philosophy", abandoned them and committed them to preventing each other' (Laruelle, *Philosophie et non-philosophie*, p. 14). He also often refers to the Judaic Other (ibid.) or the Judaic notion of the 'Messiah' (in *Future Christ, passim*). In these ways, it is implied that Philosophy is inherently a Greek or Greco-Judaic civilisational creation or the civilisation itself. [Translations are by Nicola Rubczak unless otherwise noted.]

28. Laruelle, *Philosophie et non-philosophie*, pp. 69–74.

29. Laruelle, *Théorie des Etrangers*, p. 183 ff.

30. 'The identity of the Real is lived, experienced and consumed by remaining in itself without the need to alienate itself representationally' (Laruelle, *Philosophie et non-philosophie*, p. 57).

31. Laruelle, *Introduction au non-marxisme*, p. 37 ff.

32. 'The problem of philosophy in general originates in its not thinking terms in their specificities, but rather as opposites, in their relations or moreover in their borders and neighbourhoods. The *concept* of fiction, then, designates, as any other concept, an amphibological reality, a limitrophe of the real, whether it be beyond the real, below it, or the border between the two. From classical rationalism to contemporary deconstructions, fiction has always been taken as this relation of mixture, which is to say, unitary. Excluded by the real, interiorised within it, and with this interiorisation in turn claiming to co-determine it in every way, never has fiction escaped this play of inter-inhibition of philosophy with itself, and as such fiction can be no more than one pawn among others for a history which claims to exceed it' (Laruelle, *Philosophie et non-philosophie*, p. 232).

33. 'On the one hand, from its real foundation or its essence, this would be nothing but an Identity; it would be rigorously identical to the real without undergoing a division or a Dyad; and on the other hand, it would be a pure Dyad, a radical duality which is moreover not obtained through division, and not re-hybridised with Identity' (Laruelle, *Philosophie et non-philosophie*, p. 56).

34. See Ray Brassier, *Nihil Unbound: Enlightenment and Extinction* (Palgrave Macmillan, 2007), p. 123, where he writes: 'For Laruelle, a philosophical decision is a dyad of immanence and transcendence, but one wherein immanence features twice, its internal structure subdivided between an empirical and a transcendental function. It is

at once internal to the dyad as the empirical immanence of the datum coupled to the transcendence of the a priori factum, but also external as that supplement of transcendental immanence required for gluing empirical immanence and a priori transcendence together. Every decision divides immanence between an empirical datum which it supposes as given through the a priori factum, and a transcendental immanence which it has to invoke as already given in order to guarantee the unity of a presupposed factum and a posited datum'.

35. 'The problem with a new treatment of Marxism is isolating this kernel of a purely symptomatic universality, but whose isolation is also its determination in the last instance; its "radicalisation"' (Laruelle, *Introduction au non-marxisme*, p. 21).

36. Ibid., p. 61.

37. 'In-Man is the radical past which in-the-last-identity determines the Christian and the Gnostic, and every man-of-this-World, as Future Christ' (Laruelle, *Future Christ*, p. 29).

38. François Laruelle, *Dictionary of Non-Philosophy*, p. 71. Available at <http://speculativeheresy.wordpress.com/2009/03/25/dictionary-of-non-philosophy> (accessed 12 February 2012).

39. Laruelle, *Future Christ*, p. 76.

40. Ibid., p. 2.

41. Ibid.

42. Ibid., p. 18.

43. Although it surges from an event which sets 'time out of joint', from a position which is that of what Laruelle would call 'past-outside-time', it is still defined by a moment which has historic value and determination in the last instance which should cause reversal in the way the World is constituted, such as 'tuer le Père ou Dieu'. See Gilles Deleuze when he writes: 'The caesura, of whatever kind, must be determined in the image of a unique and tremendous event, an act which is adequate to time as a whole ... Such a symbol adequate to the totality of time may be expressed in many ways: to throw time out of joint, to make the sun explode, to throw oneself into the volcano, to kill God or the father. This symbolic image constitutes the totality of time to the extent that it draws together the caesura, the before and the after' (Gilles Deleuze, *Difference and Repetition*, translated by Paul Patton [New York: Columbia University Press, 1994], p. 89). Laruelle's 'time-outside-time' and 'radical past' on the contrary, does not envisage a historic change – it is an immanent struggle which is there before it receives any name.

44. 'But Life is not above all productive or auto-generative and so it is

first transcendental. The old problems of beginning and generation are for it not posed and we prefer to designate it by the paradoxical use of the term Living and even, according to our writing, *Lived-without-life*' (Laruelle, *Future Christ*, p. 22).

45. Ibid., p. 23.
46. Ibid., p. 64.
47. Ibid., p. 11.
48. Laruelle, *Théorie des Etrangers*, p. 133ff.

II

Is Thinking Democratic? Or, How to Introduce Theory into Democracy

François Laruelle

Translated by Anthony Paul Smith[1]

This somewhat provocative paradox hides a fundamental problem: to speak of politics and democracy as a philosopher is not to practise them. Neither by its object nor by its own act is philosophy democratic, but rather sets itself up as a state of exception and legislative pronouncement [*enonciation*] for common sense. Since to say it is to make it, in order to introduce an intrinsic equality within thought, something like a democratic ideal, it is necessary to find a new plane of reality that is no longer the philosophical or totality (democracy as abstract equality of everything) but that is generic, that is a duality of the individual [*individu*] and a universal without totality that they are foreclosed to, but that it determines in an ultimate and indirect way. The equality of 'all' is a contradictory concept, equality is not Real or human except in-the-last-instance and grounds a 'non-politics', which brings us back to the axiom: *there is something of equality, but equality is not (Real)*.

Under this paradox hides a threefold problem:

1. Is philosophising necessarily a democratic act?
2. Can political philosophy propose a theory of democracy that is itself democratic? Does democracy have any use for a category of the political?
3. Is there any thought other than a philosophical one?

It would be necessary to respond to these three questions with a measured or partial negative, more exactly by way of what I would call a unilateral negative. The comprehensive solution consists in finding a form or style of thought which is not itself reducible to philosophy in general any more than to its 'political' form, but which is necessarily driven there by making a certain, very controlled, usage. The principle of this solution consists in inverting, rather than reversing [*renverser*], the internal order of the initial question. If the known and present [*actuelles*] forms of thought are not democratic, then it is useful to posit this axiom in order to resolve the problem or render it decidable; democracy as Real is the presupposition for a new thought that includes, as one of its dimensions, the traditional (that is, from political philosophy) democratic practice. This is a response to the question, consequently justified: can we introduce, without 'playing politics', democracy within thought under the form of theory, or introduce theory into democracy? 'Without playing politics' does not exclude the political in general, but rather transforms its status and its place within or when it pertains to democracy. Might an unexpected combination of philosophy and other forms of knowledge (science, art, religion, politics, etc.) be possible under the form of a non-epistemology, non-aesthetics, non-religion, or non-politics? We are not saying that democracy does not already have the thought it deserves – democracy has it or thought gives it as much as is deserved but no more – but rather we say that it has not yet at all created the thought that it can, we do not yet know what democracy can do. These questions are hardly perceptible within philosophy, political or not, and what is the cause? 'Ignorance of the cause'.

It is through classical privilege that philosophy comes first. The first solution consists in its external politicisation; in, as we say, making a political reading or interpretation, and so in postulating democracy inscribed within the political sphere; subsumed under it.

The second solution is rather to localise politics within the same act of thinking or within the philosophising structure rather than in its external determinations.

The third solution consists not in setting politics and democracy's possibility either within conditions alone or within the act alone, but within the proper and specific objects of philosophy as if they formed the link or relationship of one to the other. This seems like a balanced solution between the premature, incomprehensible solution of the imposed and forced politicisation and the solipsistic, idealistic and, at bottom, apolitical solution of the single subjective interiority of the act. This is to confuse democracy and idealism.

External politicisation takes two forms. Firstly, that of its theoretical reading or its interpretation in political terms, with the help of politico-sociological schemas, and which will quickly reveal, following Plato and Nietzsche, how often philosophy is anti-democratic, or really from an aristocratic origin. Better still, that of the political practice of philosophy, for example, taking a stand [*prise de parti*] or a position in favour of the proletariat. But these are two versions of the problem, themselves philosophical, of decisions which postulate a certain form of the conditions of thought for the exterior forces which certainly can be called 'democratic' forces. The response made here to our question already assumes the philosophy in question (*what is* a political practice of philosophy; *how* is it *possible?* Democracy as *manner or style?*) and thus forms a vicious circle that is not a good response. The problem is thus thrown back into the interior form of the philosophising act independent of the reference to its objects received exteriorly and independent of its conditions of existence, bringing a response that is not certain, unique or stable. If the position of the question under the form of a political philosophy, for example a philosophy of democracy, is not satisfying, then can we perhaps reverse the question and instead ask: is there an interior politics and perhaps a universal democracy even within the act of philosophising? On this basis we can ask: is thinking in itself democratic? Since it seems that this is commonly admitted pretty much by the whole world, this question begins to take on a certain plausibility at the same that it seems superfluous. Hence the second solution.

What is an act of philosophical thinking? Of course, I respond to that question with my own resources, so-called 'continental' and not 'analytic' ones. Merely asking whether the content of philosophising is democratic or not is enough to see that we must respond in the negative. Primarily, we regularly confuse the business surrounding democracy, like a political object, with an attitude or a position or a democratic practice. Even from this point of view, that of the structural interiority of philosophising (which is not necessarily that of consciousness), nothing assures us of its democratic character – on the contrary. To philosophise on X is to withdraw from X; to take an essential distance from the term for which we will posit other terms, for example predicates of X, but the operation does not stop there. This relation cannot remain external but must be interiorised by the means of a supplementary term, a superior unity the circularly of which closes the system. Interiority signifies here that the concept skims over its object or over itself, contemplates and completes itself. And yet there is nothing democratic in this structure, which is hierarchical or dominating (as Nietzsche says) or is one of primacy (as certain Marxists say). Some anti-democratic consequences arise here, observed by Hegel and Husserl (the philosopher is a superior and disinterested self who sees and captures the meaning produced by a working or worker self), by Nietzsche (to philosophise is to dominate, the human sovereign as a master of himself), by Heidegger (the Western will as ontological mastery of self), etc. Or moreover the distinction between the pronouncement that the philosopher intends for ordinary and everyday consciousness and the proclamation that he puts forward as if it were the 'Big Other' (to parody Lacan). From this, I draw the conclusion that the philosopher, even when he says, like Nietzsche, that it is the rule and not the exception that interests him, can still only say this in the state of exception. The philosopher, legislating for reason, the life of the mind [*vie de la pensée*] or social life, makes an exception even of the fact that he does not do what he says or does not say what he does, but, speaking the law, he makes an exception and enjoys the privilege of speaking about it and imposing it with his authority. I speak the truth, says the liar; I speak democracy, says the anti-democrat: this is the paradox of the philosopher as thinker of the Whole who is never short of expedients for presenting the paradox as if it were acceptable.

Finally the third solution synthesises in one Whole the first two and combines their insufficiencies. It combines external politicisation and internal politics. And yet that combination is philosophy in person, its most complete concept or the totality of its possibilities as a structure that links external relations and internal relations, transcendence and immanence, and which does not return to the object = X except under this synthetic condition of complexity. It supports, within politics, a relationship of interiorisation submitting humans to the global sphere of the political, and at the same time of exteriorisation by which it rejects politics as an inessential and contingent simple object. Thus, it divides the identity proper, and those of individuals, and that of the political; it reflects the one and the other or redoubles them. At best, these relations give place to a chiasmus, as Merleau-Ponty would call it, a certain blending of the philosophical and the political such as is currently exploited by the Collège International de Philosophie.

Altogether, either democracy is foreign [*étrangère*] to philosophising, or democracy remains exterior to it and completely contingent at random in history, but not belonging intrinsically to the nature of thought.

So, one cannot respond philosophically to this question on philosophy; it is uncertain and gives place to aporias, in particular to those of the philosopher who positions himself to describe the ideal democracy, ideal for the others but not quite for him. Describing or reviving the democratic narrative is not practising it. And so our problem is that of finding the rigorous condition of thought's democratic destination and usage of philosophy. Not what philosophy does about democracy, which would be to conceive it as an exception or even an accident, but how to introduce the philosophical act itself into democracy.

Does this mean that I postulate that democracy must be said and done by *all*, that democracy must be complete in its subjects, formulations and effects? Precisely not; democracy cannot be complete because the Whole is composed and said by way of some exception. Philosophically, democracy is undecidable. Does the problem also imply that democracy perhaps has no need for a legislator or guardian (the model for which being, of course, the philosopher)? Still more profoundly, can democracy be an object of political philosophy? Perhaps the philosopher will no longer interrogate existing political thought to demand its credentials, treating it like a subject of whom we ask whether it is or has a democratic comportment, nor will he treat democracy like an attribute and a question of 'papers'.

The aporias of philosophy arise from this: the individual determining that the Whole is at the same time an element of the Whole, a classical formula for ancient and contemporary philosophers. Following this, there is a reciprocal determination in which the individual and the whole of the individuals are reflected, one within the other, reciprocally affected and remaining undecidable; it becomes impossible to choose or decide on a solution; it is an undecidable, though by way of indetermination.

In order to resolve this philosophical aporia of an undecidable democracy, hazardous and uncertain, I will dispense with the philosophical style and borrow from the axiomatic approach instead, putting forth axioms on democracy and politics, precisely resolving [*décidant*] with the view to rendering them decidable. I understand democracy as a certain decision of thought; as a form of decidability imposed upon political thought so as to render itself just and to remove its self-contradiction regarding democracy. The democratic path appears straighter and more just than the twisting paths of political philosophy in general, even if it still has business with the philosophical ones. Due to this necessary mutation, we must first change the very concept of thought, in its relations to philosophy and to other forms of knowledge. This is an inversion that concerns a reversal of old hierarchies, but through a formulation of a new type of primacy without relationships of domination; without relations in general. Thus, I put forward some axioms: when this inversion comes under the form of an equation, i.e. *democracy = Real*, then it is an overly simple indication which is too easily led astray; we must instead write *Real = (determination-in-the-last-instance of) democracy*. Democracy witnesses the Real, but the Real initially stands outside of political philosophy. It is not an underlying ontology or substructure, the real root assumed to be within and from political philosophy. The Real is not political but it is, from the start, cause of every democracy for which the political is required. We distinguish three spheres: the Real; politics and the all-political, which claim to be autonomous and sufficient; and democracy or, if we can put it this way, its political side (in as much as the Real subtracts it from the political).

Now let these axioms explain that general thesis and the Real as far it is definable through an axiomatic:

1. Democracy is not an attribute or a predicate for a subject, an attribute of political order or a sub-category of the political, as if politics and even the All-political were the Real and that democracy contents itself with denoting a regime or political functioning.
2. It is impossible to describe a democracy – democracy does not exist or is not a fact in history (which provides only models in the sense of axiomatic interpretations); only appearances or the desire for equality exist, an ideal democracy which is a form of oppression.
3. If democracy does not describe itself, it axiomatically decides itself as real rather than being posited or establishing itself by theses, or dogmas, but no longer by mathematic axioms.
4. The primacy of democracy as Real over politics implies that the latter is an illusory Real, a mode of the philosophical Whole.

5. If the Real is the phenomenal content of democracy rather than a function or a political regime, then it is inferred from this conflict that there is, between them, a universal sphere of the political, but not a global one. We will call it the 'politicisable', a category of political objectivity which is at once distinct from the All-political and from the Real itself.

There are three instances: firstly, the Real as democratic cause for politics itself, rather than submitted to this category. Secondly, politics or the All-political with its aporias. Finally, the sphere of the politicisable, reduced by real or democratic individuals, and which has lost the hegemonic ambitions of the All-political.

All decisions are undoubtedly too heavy; too remote from historical reality, but do we make political history? This concerns resolutely contesting the primacy of the political and of political philosophy. But there are few alternatives if we want to be delivered from the aporias of totality and to find for thought another place or another element. I call this plane generic and I propose finding the possibility of a democracy and a generic thought rather than a philosophical one, though with the help of these forms of thought.

I will call generic, in opposition to the philosophical, a structure of thought that posits that the individual is of course intrinsically determined, but indeterminable by the Whole which we will say is foreclosed. But being foreclosed or closed to the Whole allows the individual to determine that Whole, or to subtract it from himself, prohibiting him from self-reflection. To put this otherwise and to simplify it: on the one hand, there are radical individuals who are the Real itself, who do not form a part of a totality, but who are, on the other hand, brought together in a space of universal politicisability which is no longer the self-encompassing totality of philosophy but a hypo-totality, an under-totality, which is not even a 'weak' totality, and which is the universal generic. This theory utilises philosophy, but in a way that annuls the aporias linking the totality of individuals. The philosophisable is not the philosophical, but is derived through the determination of the Whole by the individual. Relatively speaking, it plays an identical role to that of the theory of types but applied to philosophy, to its vicious circles or paradoxes. Here I break from the definition of the generic and rather close in on the consequences for our problem.

1. Individuals are not philosophisable nor liable to an All-political treatment; they are no longer subjects; they have no

predicate and are thus politically indefinable and undecidable. We 'define' them indirectly through axioms which decide for individuals since political philosophy is incapable of doing so. With respect to philosophy, emancipation begins with a thought free of every predicate; with those individuals who are nothing other than real, and not formal, axioms. These are subjects-without-predicates, individuals without qualities or properties, which we call 'Men-in-person'.

2. But they are decided with the help of or by the means of philosophy, its concepts, which are however replaced in another place and with another function, with the generic universal of the politicisable. Undoubtedly, the politicisable comes from philosophy, but is simplified by the individuals that determine it; it acquires a function of a purely theoretical political position precisely because it is deprived of its reflection on itself and for itself. The politicisable is a theoretical function, no longer All-political; it is the dimension of objectivity by which the democratic interventions, or those determined in-the-last-instance under the form of axioms, finally enter into the political dimension. But this is a political that is no longer a category submitting humans and claiming to determine them. Of course, the political is first a natural-philosophical meta-language for forming and positing axioms, but reduced to something politicisable, its meta-language function changes and becomes a politically objective existence for democracy (objective but not empirical). There is no meta-politics which is not still politics, still a philosophy; however, a reduced politics or reduced political is a meta-language for democracy.

3. We call determination in-the-last-instance not the analytic or synthetic relation between a subject and its predicates, which we have eliminated, but rather the non-relation of indivisible individuals (or those without-predicates) and the politicisable as 'post-dicate'. The vicious circle of philosophy and its definitions is thus eliminated. The essence of the individual understood generically is that of being without-relation, but it is combined with the politicisable on the basis of this 'without-relation'. Does this support a relation between individuals in the Real? No, we will say that the politicisable is not 'in relation' with individuals or democratic decisions, but, 'in-taking-up' [en-apport], it is provided by individuals and un-taken-up [dé-porté] by philosophy. In short, political thought no longer determines democracy because it is undecidable; the generic individuals determine it in an axiomatic liberty. These

are not formal or mathematic axioms; they are without subject and objects, which leads to rendering them possible, but they trail behind them and with them a neutral and reduced politicisability. This, therefore, is a practice which emerges out of philosophy, in this case political philosophy, but on the basis of these axioms.

4. What then is this generic or democratic individual, who is not a sub-group belonging to the totality – simply a weakened philosophical subject? Who can determine the All-political without belonging to it? Who is this individual who is a real axiom, an axiom woven into the Real? Neither an internal, transcendental experience, which would reconstitute philosophy, nor a decision of formal writing. I call 'radical immanence' (and I oppose the radical to the absolute) the un-dividual [*indivi-du*], the One who is only One and who *is* not, who coincides with a void of political predicates or diverse affiliations. Not the One in a metaphysical or transcendental sense, but the One-in-One who radically escapes philosophy and subtracts it from itself or from its self-reflection. So I must put forward individuals as axiomatic or constituent decisions of democracy. And yet this is not the delirious, idealist project of an auto-foundation of the axiomatic. The individual-axiom is an already-being performed as I speak, and I only speak it as a subject through the radical advance that it possesses over me (who nonetheless is this individual in-the-last-instance). Of course, I barely resist the temptation to call this democratic substance 'people' or 'transcendental multitude'. I also call 'Man-in-Man' or 'Man-in-person' the axiom that comes ahead of the subject like an always future void of ultimate being, or even an ultimatum. Democracy is the ultimatum whose refusal, by the observer who characterises the philosopher, stirs the war of politics.

5. And now what is thinking democratically? Paradoxically, it is renouncing the sufficiency of philosophy, political or not, which recites the democratic ideal's conditions and falls into the aporias of All-equality like desire or an imaginary telos. It is to posit the primacy of the Man-in-person over the political which is not the Real; to decide for individuals-without-totality and for the thought which follows. This thought uses (transcendental) politicisability in a somewhat pragmatic manner; and it is very special in that it is non-reflected right up to the concepts that it requisitions, without a hierarchy (internal or otherwise). It neither dominates nor controls itself precisely because it is decided as a being without predicates. At the outset, Man is an apparatus [*dispositif*]; he is

philosophy's cause even while philosophy casts him out to its periphery, divides indivisible Man and democracy in reality and in the ideal in order to better dominate them. At the very least, only the subject who has a right to democracy is the one who struggles for it or exercises his axiomatic liberty. He who, in virtue of being-performed or of his humanity-in-the-last-instance, also does what he says and says what he does, or supports the axiom – *there is philosophisable equality but this equality is not Real, or must be determined in-the-last-resort by individuals.*

I now accept that we can say that it is a thought for the poor in philosophy, for the We-the-without-philosophy, for the 'simple ones', and I am close to siding with the Gospels or Rousseau and maybe some others of whom I am ignorant. But I will add that this call is not careless [*irréfléchi*] but axiomatically non-considered [*non-réfléchi*], having *an affinity with a scientific process*, and that to think this democratically is to unify from the interior, that is, by the decision in-Real or Man-in-person, science and philosophy: the two major sources of thought. The generic does not represent a weak version of philosophy but a thinking from the middle from where we can look to philosophy without succumbing to its prestige, and toward those disciplines which are practices of knowledge, and which are wrongly classified merely as 'regional' forms of knowledge. The middle is not the blended average called 'political philosophy'; rather, it is the association without synthesis of two components of thought, or two heterogeneous acts. *To think in a democratic way in-the-last instance is to make use of two approaches within the indivision of a single one.*

What does it mean to say two approaches within the indivision of a single one? Let us go back for a moment to the form of the democratic said to be the politicisable. This comprises two aspects: on the one side, a real decision which escapes from philosophy because it 'grounds' or performs itself void of predicates or reflection, this being its essential side and productive of properly scientific understandings: on this model of practical democratic interventions, it is an equivalency of understandings. On the other side, its philosophisable appearance or political existence which recovers or encompasses essence. Generic thought creates a new form of complexity which suspends the philosophical blendings with science, for example various epistemologies or political philosophies.

What explains the axiomatic style as well as its performed and futural nature is that the middle or mid-place [*mi-lieu*] that joins essence and existence is not itself a continuum or a fold (the *fold of the Logos* that denies democracy). Rather, it is a radical Logos(-) void; a hiatus or collapse, truly a non-place or utopia, which expresses the axiomatic form.[2] Democratic essence and political existence remain within the state of a duality without combination, by definition open; there is no complete unity that could claim to reassemble them in a Whole, each of which would assume the State and political philosophy within their order. Philosophy and politics can continue to work separately or in synergy, to capture the one for the other. Yet this is not important; it is no longer our problem since we have abandoned the philosophy of democracy in order finally to introduce philosophy to democracy. Ordinarily, philosophy and politics share Heaven and Earth, encroaching or overflowing one over the other. But now they have a common non-place, because it is no longer the place which is common but the human non-place of the axiom which is from neither Heaven nor Earth.

Far from the thought of the Whole and its aporias, there is a place, that of the non-place, for a thought which is neither global nor local, but uni-lateral with two complementary aspects. It is not even the combat of these two cultures, for that would be to render crucial the unification of these two irreconcilables. Rather, it is a struggle for that non-culture that is not the absence of every culture or its hatred; on the contrary, it is its best use and the true outsider, that which, instead of gunning it down, introduces justice to the sciences and democracy to theory. This is the last possible democracy, its eschaton or ultimatum that peace be made; a peace without a contract, between philosophy and the rest of knowledge. Democracy will not have taken place, if it is not the without-place of Man-in-Man.

Notes

1. I would like to thank Nicola Rubczak for checking the translation and suggesting a number of vital changes. [Translator's note]
2. The meaning of the original Greek *ou-topos*, from which both our English 'utopia' and the French 'utopie' come, of course literally means 'no place'. [Translator's note]

Non-Philosophy, Weapon of Last Defence: An Interview with François Laruelle

Translated by Anthony Paul Smith

The following interview was conducted on 30 May 2011 when John Mullarkey, Marjorie Gracieuse, and Anthony Paul Smith were hosted by François Laruelle and Anne-Françoise Schmid at their Paris home. The five of us spent the afternoon and early evening discussing the luminaries of French philosophy, the state of the French academy, the practice of vegetarianism and its foreignness in France, and, of course, non-philosophy. That discussion has been written up in an abridged form here. A number of questions were formulated ahead of time by the three of us and Laruelle was given them in advance so that he had time to think over his responses. However, the discussion itself lasted a number of hours, and moved freely in such a manner that many of these questions were not asked in the living moment and so what is produced here is not a full transcript of the conversation. Gracieuse acted as interpreter and also, as her name implies, graciously edited and transcribed by hand the audio recording of the interview. Anthony Paul Smith has consulted the recording as well as the hand-written transcript in order to produce this translation, though for the sake of readability he has followed Gracieuse in excluding the kinds of 'filler' common to verbal speech. Translation is just as contingent as Laruelle's construction of non-philosophy – as he claims in the interview – and so, where a word may take on further resonances lost in English, it has been inserted in brackets (though this practice has been kept to a minimum). As always, Nicola Rubczak has kindly checked over the translation, for which we thank her yet again.

Marjorie Gracieuse: How would you describe the earliest appearance of non-philosophical principles in your work? Is there, at least in your biography, a conceptual genealogy connecting your previous philosophical learning to that emergence?

François Laruelle: Not a conceptual genealogy, but in spite of everything there is a genesis of non-philosophy *in* philosophy or from philosophy. It is not a continuous genesis, which is a matter it must concede. Rather, there are two apparently contradictory phases, but the second takes over from the first.

Both of these phases play on the grounds of a practice, almost combinatorial, of two philosophies at once. In other words, I have always used two philosophies at the same time. Heidegger and Nietzsche, then Derrida and Deleuze. So it is always a matter of how to eventually combine several philosophies. The first phase is very negative, which is to say that I had the feeling, at the same time as practising philosophy, that there was a conceptual lack, as if a fundamental concept was lacking in philosophy itself.

At the same time, that absence made philosophy possible or effective. I did a lot of work on Deleuze, on Levinas, on Derrida, in order to try and find this missing concept which I ended by identifying as that of the One; as a certain One. The beginning of the solution is sketched out through my connection to the thought of Michel Henry, and through a reflection on Deleuze in particular, which is to say that this lack of the One nevertheless appears, but without a real thematisation.

I had the feeling that in order to completely change the concept of philosophy, two philosophies were always necessary, as if each of the philosophers represented half of philosophy, basically, which I felt to be the non-completeness of a particular philosophy; this problem would have to be resolved each time by the combination of two philosophers. I have followed this way of doing things, a little bit in spite of myself, always combining two philosophies as if each of them was lacking what the other had. You could think that this is a dialectical relation. But in fact that was not that at all, because it was, each time, two philosophies and not one philosophy and the entire history of philosophy in addition. Thus, I am part of a *conjugation*, I like this term a lot, of philosophies which replaced the missing concept. What was missing was the One, the One-in-One.

The second phase is a positive phase. Coming to the edge of the One, in particular with the *Principe de Minorité* which is a frontier book; a book on the threshold, I have crossed a threshold; I have made a leap concerning the One. This is first a conversion of the process of thought. Instead of beginning with a reflection on philosophy in order to sketch something in the margin that is the One, I have *inverted* the process. I am part of the One and I went to philosophy as a *margin* of the One. But, at the same time, in order to deal with the One I need philosophy, whence, of course, the idea of a complicated circle, which I am still fighting against. The solution consists in setting philosophy *under* the condition of the One, or what I later called the One-in-One or the Last-Instance. This reversal, because it is more than an inversion, represents the opening of a new field which appears with *Une Biographie de l'homme ordinaire*, which, of course, follows *Principe de Minorité* and which lacks the leap.

There, I completely inverted the problem. And all my later work reproduces this schema in a certain way, meaning that I always begin by philosophising on a classically philosophical context of a notion in order to raise myself toward the One. But in reality it's not about raising toward the One, because I *presuppose* it and the One is what allows me to deal with philosophy. I'm unable to deal with philosophy only from philosophy, but from something which represents, in a way, an extra-territoriality. I say 'in a way' because it is not a complete extra-territoriality.

So all my work now consists in fighting in this circle; in unceasingly rectifying my first attempts [*approches*], because I always start out as a philosopher of course, though increasingly less and less, one could say, but I am always compelled to rectify the perspective. So it's more than an inversion, more than a reversal, because I haven't reversed philosophy toward the One or the One toward philosophy, since that reversal is at the same time a displacement, as Althusser said about Marx, it's a displacement because the displacement is more fundamental than the inversion. It is now for me an effort of protecting the good sense of determination. Determination goes from the One to philosophy, so it's not simply a philosophical determination. It's about using philosophy without attributing its credibility or its faith to philosophy.

John Mullarkey: You endorse the possibility of multiple mutations of non-philosophy (by you and others), and, of course, in your own work non-philosophy has gone through five 'waves' to date. So, how 'plastic' is non-philosophy?

FL: There is a lot to say about this problem of plasticity; I take a lot from it. First, it's a concept that we can find in Kant and Fichte. 'The doctrine of science', it's essentially a plastic instrument which must not be weighed down too much with the technical aspects of this or that concept. Something of this plasticity evidently remains in Hegel, but in Hegel it is a much heavier system that closes down, in a way, plasticity, even for the non-philosophical instrument. Philosophy is now going to have that status of an instrument, or of a supple means, as its disposition. It can be manipulated by non-philosophy. We must avoid fixing non-philosophy on inert objects, so on Christ, Art, etc. It's not because of Christ that I am a non-philosopher. But being a non-philosopher, Christ becomes very interesting.

So, non-philosophy is a partitive apparatus, which we carry around; obviously it is dangerous as a formula, because we could believe in a reduction of non-philosophy to the state of being an instrument. It is an instrument, yes, but a very particular one, which forms a body with philosophy, while being separated or distinct from the objects that it deals with thanks to this apparatus. In order to constitute this apparatus or device that I use, I am compelled to use philosophical objects. So the relations between non-philosophy and philosophy are complicated. It's a question of constituting oneself, as sometimes we must think in a 'pop-philosophical' manner of a survival kit of thought in a philosophical environment (philosophy being a survival kit in a hostile environment, I interpret it like that).

The point of this instrument is not to interpret the world, because it's really a problem of transformation in order to recover a type of distinction which I like very much, which is of course from Marx. Non-philosophy, I would say, is a weapon of last defence [*défense ultime*] because I think that philosophy, left to its spontaneous presuppositions, is not very favourable to man. For me, it's about focusing a thought on the generic plane; on the human plane; it's about defending Man and so is an arm of ultimate, last defence. The entire problem for me is about finding the limit, the wall that we turn our backs against. We have our backs against the wall! We can no longer get back to somewhere else.

We defend ourselves and it is thanks to this ultimate detachment over the final bases of the defence of man that we can hope to return the situation. This defensive manipulation is very difficult, above all for me it concerns dispelling what is generically stifling in philosophy. That is the all-encompassing and determining character of philosophy, what I call the principle of sufficient philosophy, and that is what must be dispelled. I'm not concerned with dispelling philosophical materiality itself, and so I distinguish philosophical materiality and the principle of sufficient philosophy which must be suspended by the generic last instance.

In *Philosophie non-standard* I have highlighted a principle of sufficient mathematics, which is parallel to the principle of sufficient philosophy. So the two great opponents of non-philosophy are these two principles. Of course I'm thinking of Badiou, because in Badiou's work there is the conjugation of these two principles. We will need to use mathematics, and an algebraic property: the imaginary or complex number. This is a mathematical ingredient in philosophy, but this ingredient does not encompass all philosophical discourse. We are freed of mathematicism. The imaginary number is non-real, in the sense that some numbers, even in their arithmetic usage, are called in a particular sense 'real numbers'. I try hard to identify the adversary thanks to philosophy and mathematics. Philosophy and its language are always waiting in ambush, so my problem is smoking out these opponents. So there is truly a function of struggle, and for me it is inseparable from philosophy, which is nothing but a benediction.

But you are going to say to me, at bottom are you not succumbing to that illusion Lacan unmasked: the 'non-duped err'. 'You think you're smart, but you are done in by the unconscious or language.' It's true. But non-philosophy anticipates that it is always made and made again, that it is always deceived. I always postulate the possibility of an ambiguity within non-philosophy which can, in a certain way, return within philosophy, but that it turns around within philosophy – now that is a phenomenon we can somewhat understand. We are always the victims of transcendental illusion, but we can always understand it, demonstrate it.

And that understanding is what is between philosophy – assumed in itself to be sufficient – and the deduction or genealogy of philosophy from non-philosophy, there is an equivocation which survives. What survives of the philosophical within non-philosophy is an objective appearance, but it is no longer transcendental because we are within the immanental sphere. There is an immanental illusion; this is philosophy as in itself, as autonomous, as sufficient. Staying faithful to Kant, I think that we can limit illusion or appearance, even if maintaining the transcendental appearance no longer concerns a part of philosophy as in Kant, but concerns the whole of philosophy. This set is traversed by an immanental appearance in relation to man as last instance.

There are invariants and rules in non-philosophy. There are rules formulated for a school, a research collective, meaning in each of my books there is an exposition of rules that sum up what it would be necessary to do to be a non-philosopher. But it wouldn't be that I am the victim of delusions of grandeur. I know very well that these rules are made *not* to be followed. Leibniz himself said that the rules expounded by Descartes were very well and good but that it wouldn't do to leave the rules of thought to the genius of a single man! It's necessary to be able to make them accessible to all, so I try and make them accessible to all but I must say that it doesn't work very well. In each case, we can formulate the rules and this has been a constant concern for me.

It is true that this is not a methodological formalism, even if I often hold on to the notion of formalism, of method and style – for me philosophy is before all three of these aspects. A method is hardly formalisable outside of material; without being Hegelian we have to admit this relationship to experience, to material, particularly since this is the material that we will utilise in order to formulate the rules. In that the process is transcendental and immanental the central notion lies between empirical description and a pure logical formalism, as we can find in Badiou, where there was a place for formalism. Not concrete material [*materiel*] in the empirical sense of the term, but materials. Which is to say rules formulated a priori, but which are also formulated in the material and with the material. It's what I call a style and I think that non-philosophy is essentially a question of style. Not a writing style, but a style of thought. There is some theory, but it's not a theory. There is a bit of a system, but it's not a system, rather it's a style of thought. There is something of the living [*vécu*], but it's not life. If someone is unable to accept this kind of formula, they can't be a non-philosopher. Non-philosophy uses this kind of statement, which the mystics also used when they utilised the 'without'.

Anthony Paul Smith: Does non-philosophy have any necessary (and sufficient) principles that can be recognised across all its phases? Or, is it simply whatever Laruelle writes? Is non-philosophy simply whatever Laruelle says it is?

FL: Laruelle does not exist. There is a 'Laruelle' base [*support*] for non-philosophy. There is a subject-agent, a contributor, a manufacturer, but that's all. A proletarian because the structures need to be sustained by a concrete individual. Non-philosophy too. Non-philosophy is not what I've written even though that is a style. It's still what *I* have written in so far as I identify myself with humankind. While philosophy identifies itself with the philosophical tradition, myself, I back away from that identification: it's simply humankind.

MG: Maybe it is important to correct the misunderstanding found in the expression, 'Laruelle, the Pope of non-philosophy'.

FL: Pope! To think it was the cardinals of the Sorbonne who have reproached me like that! The cardinals of the Sorbonne!

JM: Non-philosophy is described as a practice, and even a performance. Does this make redundant the distinction between an *applied* non-philosophy and a *theoretical* non-philosophy? For example, a distinction between the non-philosophy of photography, or rather *as* non-photography, and the non-philosophy of philosophy? Would the latter hold any special position or not as regards any founding principles of non-philosophy?

FL: A style of thought. It's necessary to add that this is a practice and a performance. This practice and performance can't be immediately understood starting from a linguistic model, or an artistic model, or a practical one, because these practices are 'in-the-last-instance'. And this is the big obstacle for philosophy, this thing I call 'in-the-last-instance'.

Why is it a practice? It is unceasingly a question of theory, but theoretical problems are not only resolved by new theoretical concepts. They are resolved by a practice within theory, which means that there is a process of transformation for the most theoretical concepts. Left to itself, theory is something, in my view, like Platonism, a contemplative philosophy that contemplates itself in completing its objects, its ideas. But then with non-philosophy one must transform the context of concepts. Thus problems are resolved practically – and here I am a Marxist – and not theoretically so either.

The subject who operates and tests out non-philosophy is

always engaged as an object which is treated by non-philosophy itself. He is himself a transformed subject, but here the performance does not return to a singular act. He is subjective but only subjective in-the-last-instance: a generic subjectivity. There will be an individual subject, but we will talk about that in a while.

Performance and practice do not exhaust themselves in the hermeneutic, homogeneous circle, which would constitute the circle between material, the object produced, and the productive subject. They don't form a circle because the generic subject comes to be cut and separated from these objects completely, in being in itself also formable by the means of objects. This is what I call unilateral duality. It's the fact that the generic subject is implicated within its own work. Which is to say that one produces oneself within one's own work, but at the same time, one contains invariants within oneself. These structures, which do not budge – this represents algebraic idempotence: A + A = A. That is how I understand the subject. This can be amended: one can add A to it, but it will remain A. The subject can confront new objects like philosophy, art, etc., but he doesn't change himself as a subject, fundamentally.

The structures of the generic subject are invariant: you can't modify algebra like that, whereas philosophically, the structure of the subject is relatively objective. The structure is not exhausted in the hermeneutic circle through which this subject formulates itself by fabricating its objects.

This is the idea of the-last-instance: in Marx the last instance is more a predicate, an adjective, than a subject. Productive forces determine 'in the last instance', which means that determination is understood as a being in the last instance. But for me the last-instance is not a predicate; it is the subject itself. It is generic humanity, humankind. Only humankind can be in-the-last-instance. Neither the philosopher nor the ideas of the philosopher can. So it is a subject and not a predicate: it must invert and modify the relation unilaterally. This has recently been radicalised in *Philosophie non-standard*: in so far as this apparatus [*dispositif*], this instrument, is what I call the generic matrix, this generic subject is humanity which transforms philosophy but which is not exhausted in that transformative act. There is something irreducible within man, within human beings, which is not reduced to object, predicates, circumstances, etc. So I would not say, like Deleuze has, that essence must somehow get bogged down in accidents, but that there is a subject that resists the occasional or accidental becomings of philosophy.

The generic matrix is a collider because it bangs together philosophy and science; quantum physics. This banging together causes a lot of problems because these are incommensurable expositions which must be made commensurable and that is not possible unless we leave the empirical, positive register of science and the spontaneous register of philosophy. These two registers must necessarily be left. We must jump to a plane, but this is not a plane of immanence, but rather a plane that is at once material and formal; a generic plane. A priori, but a material a priori, like Max Scheler said. So we think a notion of material a priori against that of a formal a priori. But Max Scheler made that difference within an ultra-Catholic and largely Mediaeval context. Even so! It concerns the establishing of a hierarchy of essence grounded nevertheless, we'll say, ontologically.

MG: Non-philosophy resists philosophy but there is also an authoritarian resistance to non-philosophy by philosophy. How do you explain this difference or hierarchy of planes? How do you bring about the shift from one to the other?

FL: Philosophy for me is doubly hierarchised. In non-philosophy the notion of style implies a certain identity between the principles and the material. The materials serve to formulate the principles and the principles serve to elucidate the materials, and yet this is not a vicious circle because the principles cannot be elucidated with the philosophy that it is in the first instance. In the generic matrix we make the most of the ambiguity of sufficient philosophy and philosophy as an appearance deduced from non-philosophy. We make the most of this ambiguity in order to use philosophy with good reason in order to speak of non-philosophy.

Philosophical resistance remains within the interior of philosophy but perhaps it has not found, by virtue of its functioning, the means of thinking alterity as radical alterity. So, for what we will use of philosophy, we will need to explain why there is a language appropriate to immanence. We must find the means of formulating this new language without contradiction. What we have to leave in the vicious circle is this final ambiguity between philosophy in itself and the objective appearance that is this philosophy in itself.

JM: Why is non-philosophy 'difficult' or at least perceived as such? Is this only due to the resistance of philosophers to the ideas of non-philosophy? Or is it due to the level of abstraction at which it operates? Or are these two, resistance and abstraction, connected somehow? How do you understand this abstraction, if not in terms of a metalanguage of some sort? Is resistance due to unexamined presuppositions on the part of the philosopher? If so, are these presuppositions themselves *irresistible* so long as the philosopher remains a philosopher? And is this irresistibility *only* conceptual?

FL: There is an abstraction to non-philosophy, but that abstraction is sometimes much more difficult for the 'trained' (or 'formatted' – meaning that they've been wiped to prepare them for philosophy) philosophers than it is for analysts or artists. Often artists are more sensitive to non-philosophy than philosophers themselves are. I would say that my principal opponents are those philosophers who are the best trained in the tradition. Incidentally, Deleuze already remarked on this when he said that lay people understood *Anti-Oedipus* better than philosophers did. The affects pass them by and so on.

And it's true that in non-philosophy there is sometimes a certain kind of affect that also passes them by. Philosophy is very abstract, by definition, but it is an abstraction closer to the concrete; this is the first degree of abstraction. As non-philosophy is a theory of philosophy, we have an abstraction in the second degree. Non-philosophy is not a philosophy of philosophy or a metaphilosophy, but a non-philosophy, which is to say that it is not based on the transcendence of a 'meta'.

The One does not redouble Being. The One simplifies Being; the One simplifies the play of the concept. More importantly than a resistance, there is an abstraction to non-philosophy that is not artificial, I believe, even though they have often reproached me for its artificial character since it assumes that we play with philosophy. All of this results in a kind of analysis of philosophy that the philosophers, it seems, have not done, and one that they do not want to do. This analysis of philosophy takes philosophy as a system of doublets. It is an empirico-transcendental transcendental-real doublet. This is seen very well in Kant: there is a system of two doublets and they are found in all the philosophers. With this nuance it seems simple that it is the second doublet, the 'transcendental-real' double, that has a tendency to overcome itself somehow; to be no longer a duality as the empirical and transcendental are marked.

I would even go so far as to say that, if I have invented nothing else, there is this other analysis of philosophy. The idea had been suggested to me, amongst others, by Nietzsche, who broke the doublets within thought and utilised them. All those things, at bottom, which wear themselves down, one within the other. If we want to consider philosophy as a system of doublets then non-philosophy consists in reducing the artificial depth of philosophy. It's almost the application of Occam's razor to philosophy itself and not just to entities. We must reduce philosophy to its minimum.

You might say to me, why reduce it to that? To that which proliferates, which multiplies the layers. For me, the last great multiplier of layers is the great planner Badiou, a mathematico-transcendental philosopher. He's a real Platonist because Plato is a master of planning. He had planned out all knowledge that was received by the tradition and he is still admired for that. And Badiou, well, he is the great planner of human knowledge. Philosophy is there, at the top of the hierarchy. I believe that philosophy is not unidimensional, since forgetting the doublets, that comes with the practice, if a little simple, of philosophy. Philosophy is a soft element out of which we carve objects, parts; we carve up the body of philosophy. Philosophy is like a Parmenidean ball, but we must not make superposed layers but rather put back into question the circle of the ball. We have to find the means of carving up the Whole itself.

So, Deleuze . . . Deleuze . . . yes, with the idea of the molecular, is always nearby. But in Deleuze there are two principles which are a little bit mirrored, the one in the other; that is the molecular and the body without organs. *And for me there is no body without organs.* There is only the molecular, and more than the molecular there is the particulate.

APS: Non-philosophy has recently been connected to various new movements in philosophy (Meillassoux, Harman, Brassier, Grant) that dub themselves 'realist' or 'naturalist' in as much as they perceive themselves as tackling the world, reality, things, etc., with a directness hitherto deemed impossible by philosophers (due to the inevitable mediations of history, language, power, gender, and so on). How do you see non-philosophy's relationship with these new realisms? Does its approach to the Real overlap with theirs in any way?

FL: Like all the philosophers and non-philosophers I am looking for the Real. Even the idealist fathers looked for the Real; even Hegel looked for the Real. I look for the Real without being a realist, for materiality without being a materialist, the physical nature of generic man without naturalism. All of these philosophical positions want to obliterate the Real through reality; materiality through materialism; physical nature by naturalism. Here, as ever, there are returns, doublets, repentances of philosophy. Philosophy cannot see that the true presupposition of philosophy is a much more formal presupposition, which concerns double transcendence, as a presupposition concerning the very structure of philosophy. Philosophy does not look for this presupposition within the being of philosophy, which is a bilateral duality and not a unilateral one.

So, when I look at these movements (of Meillassoux, and so on), I do so with interest, with curiosity, but nothing more. With the pleasure that we have in seeing a showman who makes philosophy swing.

I would respond with Marx's maxim: man is a natural being but he must make nature human. This is the redoubling of the man who is not a philosophical doublet. Man makes up part of nature, but it is by praxis that he makes nature human. This redoubling is also in another great formula of Marx: the fusion of productive forces and relations of production *under* the relations of production. This intensification is not the same kind as the philosophical doublet which is a redoubling of transcendence over itself, while, with Marx, it is a step toward an immanence; a simplification of transcendence. Meillassoux and the rest are very interesting but locked up within the philosophical decision.

APS: Does non-philosophy's approach to *science* overlap with theirs then?

FL: I have always invoked science, except for perhaps in Philosophy I; in those texts which are purely philosophical. In Philosophy II there was an explicit relationship to science = X, without really explaining what I meant by science. But there was an axiom in *En tant qu'Un* that stipulates an affinity between the scientific affect and the vision-in-One.

So, I have constantly invoked science: there was fractality, the non-Euclidean style. There was the theme of non-Gödelian style.

Gödel limited the philosophical movement of mathematics but maintained something of the philosophical within that limitation. So I thought a limitation of philosophy necessary within the founding act of arithmetic. It is Gödel, but non-Gödel. It is a kind of limitation.

In my latest work, there is the application of a schema drawn from quantum mechanics. Out of the quantum nucleus I shaped a style of rationality or scientific thought against philosophy, but not scientifically positive. It remains a style. I use science as a style. The matrix is quantum and non-quantum. The problem is then of understanding what there is of the fundamental in non-philosophy. Is it the conjugation of a more or less hard science with philosophy, or even the ability to conjugate any ingredient, like Christ, with philosophy? Here and there I have had the tendency to say that everything must pass by science. Take theology for example: it is a science of Christ.

So non-philosophy is always a practice of conjugating philosophy without transcendence and a science without positivity: so in *Philosophie non-standard*, it conjugates a philosophy without transcendence and a quantum physics without calculation.

JM: In as much as non-philosophy might be *successfully* explained to philosophers, is the philosopher still a philosopher or has he or she already become (at least temporarily) a non-philosopher? How might non-philosophy be simplified and universalised even more?

FL: With philosophy it's necessary to proceed in two stages. Primarily, you have to make a formal theory of philosophy which is going to try to tell us what philosophy is by way of philosophy. This will always be an authoritarian conception of philosophy, each philosophy has its type of gathering together, of the unification of *the* philosophy. But this is a contingent fact [*donné*]. It's the multiple responses to the question 'quid facti?' And then what? You have to ask the question 'quid juris?' Which means trying to find a way of explaining 'scientifically' what there is in the question 'quid facti?' Concerning the fact of philosophy, can we explain it, legitimate it, in making it the object of a theory? This will be a deduction from the generic matrix, from this game of quantum mechanics and philosophy. Here, there is the whole play of contingency and necessity. There is a contingency to philosophy seen from itself and, at the same time, we can try to find a necessity, not transcendental but general, to the transcendental contingency of philosophy. So to explain non-philosophy to philosophers is impossible without a cure for the principle of sufficient philosophy. So we must be two, but this is not an explication.

People may ask me, but how then did you in fact arrive at non-philosophy? Then I must say that I have made my 'auto' non-philosophy. It is contingent, arbitrary, it depends on lots of things which are mine – maybe we could universalise non-philosophy even more. It would require making a body of knowledge accessible not only to humankind but to all individuals. So is that possible 'for all individuals'? I don't know. I don't believe that it would be possible. It has to pass through this mediation, this distorted mediation that is humankind.

Notes on Contributors

Ray Brassier is Associate Professor of Philosophy at the American University of Beirut, Lebanon. He is the author of *Nihil Unbound: Enlightenment and Extinction* (2007). He has written several articles about Laruelle's work and has translated a number of his shorter texts.

Alexander R. Galloway is a writer and computer programmer working on issues in philosophy, technology and theories of mediation. An associate professor at New York University, he is author or co-author of three books on media and cultural theory. Most recently, the Public School New York published *French Theory Today: An Introduction to Possible Futures*, a set of five pamphlets documenting Galloway's seminar conducted there in the fall of 2010. His future work will continue to focus on French philosophy and the Continental tradition.

Rocco Gangle is Assistant Professor of Philosophy at Endicott College and holds a PhD in Philosophical and Theological Studies from the Department of Religious Studies at the University of Virginia. His work has appeared in *Political Theology*, *Philosophy Today*, *SubStance*, and the *Journal for Cultural and Religious Theory* as well as other academic journals and edited collections. He is the translator of Francois Laruelle's *Philosophies of Difference: A Critical Introduction to Non-Philosophy* (2011).

Marjorie Gracieuse, after having studied at the University of Paris I-Panthéon-Sorbonne, went on to complete a PhD in Philosophy at the University of Warwick in 2011. She is currently working on the problem of hierarchy and desire in Gilles Deleuze's thought in relation to Spinoza and Nietzsche. Her research interests revolve around the possibility of rethinking the distinction and classification of differences in the context of a philosophy of immanence by elaborating the sense of a non-relativistic perspectivism in processual ontologies. She is the network facilitator for the European Network in Contemporary French Philosophy and a member of the editorial board of *Pli: The Warwick Journal of Philosophy*.

Katerina Kolozova is Professor of Philosophy, Sociological Theory and Gender Studies at the University American College in Skopje. She holds a PhD in philosophy and, besides teaching in her home institution, is visiting professor at several other universities in Former Yugoslavia and Bulgaria (the State University of Skopje, University of Sarajevo, University of Belgrade and University of Sofia as well as at the Faculty of Media and Communications of Belgrade). During 2008–9, Kolozova was a visiting scholar in the Department of Rhetoric (Program of Critical Theory) at the University of California-Berkeley. She is the author of *The Lived Revolution: Solidarity with the Body in Pain as the New Political Universal* (2010), *The Real and 'I': On the Limit and the Self* (2006), *The Crisis of the Subject* with Judith Butler and Zarko Trajanoski (2002), *The Death and the Greeks: On Tragic Concepts of Death from Antiquity to Modernity* (2000), as well as editor of a number of books from the fields of gender studies and feminist theory including *Gender and Identity: Theories from/ on Southeastern Europe* with Svetlana Slapshak and Jelisaveta Blagojevic. She is also Chief Editor of *Identities: Journal in Politics, Gender and Culture* (www.identities.org.mk), and belongs to the Editorial Board of Punctum Books, Organisation Non-Philosophique, and AtGender: The European Network for Feminist and Gender Studies.

François Laruelle formerly taught at the Collège international de philosophie and is Emeritus Professor at the University of Paris X-Ouest La Défense. Over the course of 40 years he has developed a science of philosophy that he calls 'non-philosophy' or 'non-standard philosophy'. He has published over 20 books including, including *Les Philosophies de la différence* (1986), *Philosophie et non-philosophie* (1989), *Principes de la non-philosophie* (1996), *Philosophie non-standard* (2010), and most recently *Anti-Badiou* (2011).

John Mullarkey is Professor of Film at Kingston University, London. He has also taught philosophy and film theory at the University of Sunderland, England (1994–2004) and the University of Dundee, Scotland (2004–2010). He has published *Bergson and Philosophy* (1999), *Post-Continental Philosophy: An Outline* (2006), *Philosophy and the Moving Image: Refractions of Reality* (2010), and edited, with Beth Lord, *The Continuum Companion to Continental Philosophy* (2009). He is an editor of the journal *Film-Philosophy*, and chair of the Society for European Philosophy. His research explores variations of 'non-standard-philosophy', wherein he argues that philosophy is a subject that continually shifts its identity through engaging with supposedly non-philosophical fields such as film or animal studies (the two realms of 'outsider thought' with which he is most acquainted). He is currently working on a book entitled, *Reverse Mutations: Laruelle and Non-Human Philosophy*.

Michael J. Olson is completing his PhD in philosophy at Villanova University. His research concerns the relation between transcendental and metaphysical idealism in Kant's theoretical philosophy with a focus on the possibility of constructing a transcendental materialism that does not lapse into the problems of transcendental realism.

Joshua Ramey is Visiting Assistant Professor of Philosophy at Haverford College. His work on critical issues in philosophy, art and spirituality has appeared in journals such as *SubStance*, *Angelaki, Discourse* and *Political Theology*. He is the author of *The Hermetic Deleuze: Philosophy and Spiritual Ordeal* (2012).

Nicola Rubczak recently completed an MLitt in Continental Philosophy at the University of Dundee. Her main research areas are the feminist critique and mutation of philosophy, as found primarily in Luce Irigaray, and philosophy as a performative practice. Along with numerous articles in French philosophy, she translated Anne-Françoise Schmid's essay for this volume and is the co-translator with Anthony Paul Smith of François Laruelle's *Principles of Non-Philosophy* (forthcoming 2013).

Anne-Françoise Schmid is Associate Professor of Philosophy and Epistemology at Institut National des Sciences Appliquées de

Lyon, member of ITUS-STOICA (UMR 5600 of CNRS), and associate member of the Poincaré Archives (UMR 7117 du CNRS). Her main interest is the conception and transformation of philosophy within scientific fields and through interdisciplinarity. She is currently collaborating with the Chair of Théorie et Méthodes de la Conception Innovante at École des Mines de Paris on the relations between 'fiction' (in the sense used within both philosophy of mathematics and non-philosophy) and C-K design theory, in order to develop a generic epistemology and new technological ethics. She is the author of five books, including *L'Age de l'épistémologie. Science, Ingénierie, Ethique* (1998), *Henri Poincaré, les sciences et la philosophie* (2001), and *Que peut la philosophie des sciences?* (2001), and editor of the French language edition of Bertrand Russell and Louis Couturat's correspondence and the forthcoming *Academos. Epistémologie des frontières*.

Anthony Paul Smith is the English translator of *Future Christ: A Lesson in Heresy* (2010) and co-translator with Nicola Rubczak of *Principles of Non-Philosophy* (forthcoming 2013), both by François Laruelle, and co-editor of the volume *After the Postsecular and the Postmodern: New Essays in Continental Philosophy of Religion* (2010). He is Assistant Professor in Religion at La Salle University and a Fellow at the Institute for Nature and Culture, DePaul University. He has authored numerous articles on non-philosophy in relation to environmental philosophy and philosophy of religion. At present, he is completing a monograph entitled *A Stranger Thought: An Introduction to the Non-Philosophy of François Laruelle*.

Select Bibliography

Books by François Laruelle

○ PHILOSOPHIE I
- *Phénomène et différence. Essai sur Ravaisson*, Paris: Klincksieck, 1971
- *Machines textuelles. Déconstruction et libido-d'écriture*, Paris: Le Seuil, 1976
- *Nietzsche contre Heidegger*, Paris: Payot, 1977
- *Le déclin de l'écriture*, Paris: Aubier-Flammarion, 1977
- *Au-delà du principe de pouvoir*, Paris: Payot, 1978

○ PHILOSOPHIE II
- *Le principe de minorité*, Paris: Aubier, 1981
- *Une biographie de l'homme ordinaire. Des autorités et des minorités*, Paris: Aubier, 1985
- *Les philosophies de la différence. Introduction critique*, Paris: PUF, 1987
- *Philosophie et non-philosophie*, Liège-Bruxelles: Mardaga, 1989
- *En tant qu'Un*, Paris: Aubier, 1991
- *Théorie des identités*, Paris: PUF, 1992

○ PHILOSOPHIE III
- *Théorie des Etrangers*, Paris: Kimé, 1995
- *Principes de la non-philosophie*, Paris: PUF, 1996
- *Ethique de l'Etranger*, Paris: Kimé, 2000
- *Introduction au non-marxisme*, Paris: PUF, 2000

○ PHILOSOPHIE IV
- *Le Christ futur. Une leçon d'hérèsie*, Paris: Exils, 2002
- *L'ultime honneur des intellectuels*, Paris: Textuel, 2003

- *La Lutte et l'Utopie à la fin des temps philosophiques*, Paris: Kimé, 2004
Mystique non-philosophique à l'usage des contemporains, Paris: L'Harmattan, 2007

○ PHILOSOPHIE V
- *Introduction aux sciences génériques*, Paris: Petra, 2008
- *Philosophie non-standard*, Paris: Kimé, 2010
- *Le concept de non-photographie/The Concept of Non-Photography* (Bilingual Edition), translated by Robin Mackay, Falmouth, NY: Urbanomic-Sequence, 2011
- *Anti-Badiou*, Paris: Kimé, 2011
- *Théorie générale des victimes*, Paris: Mille et Une Nuits, 2012

English Translations

- *Future Christ: A Lesson in Heresy*, translated by Anthony Paul Smith, London and New York: Continuum, 2010
- *Philosophies of Difference: A Critical Introduction to Non-Philosophy*, translated by Rocco Gangle, London and New York: Continuum, 2010
- *Principles of Non-Philosophy*, translated by Anthony Paul Smith and Nicola Rubczak, London and New York: Continuum, 2013 (forthcoming)
- *Struggle and Utopia at the End Times of Philosophy*, translated by Drew S. Burk and Anthony Paul Smith, Minneapolis: Univocal Publishing, 2012
- *Introduction to Non-Marxism*, translated by Anthony Paul Smith, Minneapolis: Univocal Publishing, 2013
- *Dictionary of Non-Philosophy*, translated by Taylor Adkins et al. and compiled by Nick Srnicek and Ben Woodard, 2009, <http://speculativeheresy.wordpress.com> (accessed February 2012)

Articles by Laruelle Collected in English

- *From Decision to Heresy: Introduction to Non-Philosophy*, edited by Tobias Huber and Robin Mackay, translated by Taylor Adkins, Ray Brassier, Christopher Eby, Robin Mackay, Nicola Rubczak and Anthony Paul Smith, Falmouth: Urbanomic, 2012
- *The Non-Philosophy Project: Essays by François Laruelle*, edited by Gabriel Alkon and Boris Gunjevic, New York: Telos Press Publishing, 2012

Secondary Literature

- Bertocchi, Alessandro, *Philosophie et non-philosophie du poétique*, Paris: Michel Houdiard Editeur, 2006
- Blanco, Juan Diego, *Initiation à la Pensée de François Laruelle*, Paris: L'Harmattan, 1997
- Brassier, Ray, *Nihil Unbound: Enlightenment and Extinction*, Basingstoke: Palgrave Macmillan, 2007
- Choplin, Hugues, *De la Phénoménologie à la Non-Philosophie. Levinas et Laruelle*, Paris: Kimé, 1997
- Choplin, Hugues, *La Non-Philosophie de François Laruelle*, Paris: Kimé, 2000
- Choplin, Hugues, *L'espace de la pensée française contemporaine*, Paris: L'Harmattan: 2007
- Del Bufalo, Erik, *Deleuze et Laruelle. De la schizo-analyse à la non-philosophie*, Paris: Kimé, 2003
- Di Manno de Almeida, Danilo, *Pour une imagination non-européenne*, Paris: Kimé, 2002
- Fontaine, Patrick, *L'amour de la non-philosphie*, Paris: Kimé, 2001
- Kieffer, Gilbert, *Esthétiques Non-Philosophiques*, Paris: Kimé, 1996
- Kolozova, Katerina, *The Lived Revolution: Solidarity With the Body in Pain as the New Political Universal*, Skopje: Euro-Balkan Press, 2010
- Mollet, Eric, *Bourdieu et Laruelle. Sociologie réflexive et non-philosophie*, Paris: Éditions PETRA, 2003
- Moulinier, Didier, *De La Psychanalyse à la Non-Philosophie. Lacan et Laruelle*, Paris: Kimé, 1998
- Moulinier, Didier, *Dictionnaire de la jouissance*, Paris: L'Harmattan, 1999
- Mullarkey, John, *Post-Continental Philosophy: An Outline*, London: Continuum, 2006
- Mullarkey, John, *Philosophy and the Moving-Image: Refractions of Reality*, Palgrave Macmillan, 2010
- Nicolet, D., *Lire Wittgenstein. Études pour une reconstruction fictive*, Paris: Aubier, 1989
- Non-Philosophie, Le Collectif, *La Non-Philosophie des Contemporains. Althusser, Badiou, Deleuze, Derrida, Fichte, Husserl, Kojève, Russell, Sartre, Wittgenstein*, Paris: Kimé, 1995
- Non-Philosophie, Le Collectif, *Discipline Hérétique. Esthétique, psychanalyse, religion*, Paris: Kimé, 1998
- Rannou, Jean-Luc, *François Laruelle et la Gnose non-philosophique*, Paris: L'Harmattan, 2003

- Schmid, Anne-Françoise, *L'Age de l'Epistémologie. Science, ingénierie, éthique*, Paris: Kimé, 1998
- Tousseul Sylvain, *Les principes de la pensée. La philosophie immanentale*, Paris: L'Harmattan, 2010
- Valdinoci, Serge, *Introduction Dans L'europanalyse*, Paris: Aubier, 1990
- Valdinoci, Serge, *Vers Une Méthode D'europanalyse*, Paris: L'Harmattan, 1995
- Valdinoci, Serge, *La Traversée de l'Immanence. L'europanalyse ou la méthode de la phénoménologie*, Paris: Kimé, 1996
- Valdinoci, Serge, *La Science Première. Une pensée pour le present et l'avenir*, Paris: L'Harmattan, 1997

Journals

- *La Décision Philosophique*, Vols 1–9 (1987–89), Paris: Osiris
- *Philo-Fictions: La Revue de non-philosophie* www.philo-fictions.com
  No. 1: *Clandestinité, une ouverture* (2009)
  No. 2: *Fiction, une nouvelle rigueur* (2009)
  No. 3: *Traduction, une dernière fidélité* (2010)

- A large number of primary and secondary French-language texts can be found at www.onphi.net

Index